Exotic Parodies

Exotic Parodies

Subjectivity in Adorno, Said, and Spivak

Asha Varadharajan

University of Minnesota Press

Minneapolis

London

Published by the University of Minnesota Press
111 Third Avenue South, Suite 290, Minneapolis, MN 55401-2520
Printed in the United States of America on acid-free paper

Library of Congress Cataloging-in-Publication Data

Varadharajan, Asha.
    Exotic parodies: subjectivity in Adorno, Said, and Spivak / Asha Varadharajan.
      p.   cm.
    Includes bibliographical references and index.
    ISBN 0-8166-2528-X
    ISBN 0-8166-2529-8 (pbk.)
    1. Subjectivity in literature.   2. Adorno, Theodor W., 1903–1969
—Criticism and interpretation.   3. Spivak, Gayatri Chakravorty—Criticism
and interpretation.   4. Said, Edward W.—Criticism and interpretation.
5. Literature, Modern—20th century—History and criticism.   6. Imperialism
in literature. I. Title.
PN56.S46V37   1995   94-23640
809'.93353—dc20

[Aziz] remembered that he had, or ought to have, a motherland. Then he shouted: "India shall be a nation! No foreigners of any sort! Hindu and Moslem and Sikh and all shall be one! Hurrah! Hurrah for India! Hurrah! Hurrah!"

India a nation! What an apotheosis! Last comer to the drab nineteenth-century sisterhood! Waddling in at this hour of the world to take her seat! She, whose only peer was the Holy Roman Empire, she shall rank with Guatemala and Belgium perhaps. Fielding mocked again. And Aziz in an awful rage danced this way and that, not knowing what to do, and cried: "Down with the English anyhow. That's certain. Clear out, you fellows, double quick, I say. We may hate one another, but we hate you most. If I don't make you go, Ahmed will, Karim will, if it's fifty or five hundred years we shall get rid of you, yes, we shall drive every blasted Englishman into the sea, and then"—he rode again furiously—"and then," he concluded, half kissing him, "you and I shall be friends."

"Why can't we be friends now?" said the other, holding him affectionately. "It's what I want. It's what you want."

But the horses didn't want it—they swerved apart; the earth didn't want it, sending up rocks through which riders must pass single-file; the temples, the tank, the jail, the palace, the birds, the carrion, the Guest House, that came into view as they issued from the gap and saw Mau beneath: they didn't want it, they said in their hundred voices, "No, not yet," and the sky said, "No, not there."

— E. M. Forster, *A Passage to India*

Contents

Acknowledgments

This project owes much to the critical acumen and generosity of friends, colleagues, mentors, and institutions. I can't, of course, cite them all, for which sin of omission I hope I will be forgiven. Let me begin with the progenitors, as it were, of this book.

To Janaki Bakhle (Mrs. Fury is my preferred appellation!), my deepest gratitude for impromptu lessons on the incommensurability of the object (augmented by the number of times her last name is consigned to various food groups, including bagels and broccoli), for ruthless and entirely appropriate excisions of examples of verbosity and density in my prose, for unremitting faith in the value of my work, and for what I hope will continue to be a deep and abiding friendship.

To Robert Mosimann, Laura Westlund, the staff of the University of Minnesota Press, and my student Emily Todd, my appreciation of their energy and efficiency.

To the anonymous readers of my manuscript, my gratitude for their generous and thought-provoking comments.

To the University of Minnesota's English department, my thanks for a nonteaching quarter at the beginning of my tenure. It helped me to make quick progress on my book.

This book continues to bear traces of its inception as a doctoral dissertation at the University of Saskatchewan in Canada. Len Findlay's theoretical rigor and political commitment inspired me to write this work, while my professors and colleagues at Saskatchewan, Newfoundland, and Kingston remained sources of constant encouragement through this book's numerous transmutations.

This book is dedicated to my family (for enabling and understanding my reluctant exile) and to Rhonda and April Anderson (for making me feel at home in it).

Introduction

This book attempts to reformulate the agenda of postcolonialism and to establish much-needed ground for the evaluation of specific critical positions and practices occasioned by its discourse. Complaints are, of course, routinely made regarding the depoliticization and domestication of this discourse within the Anglo-American academy; by the same token, the epistemological stakes and consequences of a materially grounded politics are rarely elucidated in a sustained fashion. The two purposes of this work are to discover the possibility of critique beyond a certain kind of paralyzed reflexivity and to locate this critique in a staged confrontation between dialectics and *différance*.

The ensuing account delineates the circumstances or set of questions that produced and inform this work, rather than announcing intentions as such. In attempting, pace the "death of the subject," to foster a different series of rapprochements between feminism, postcolonialism, Marxism, and deconstruction, I find myself struggling with the following seemingly obdurate problems:

1. If the discourses of postmodernism and poststructuralism have been responsible for decentering the patriarchal and imperialist subject by demonstrating that the unity and self-sufficiency of this subject is possible only at the expense of the racial, ethnic, and feminine object, why has this perception not produced the emancipation and self-acceptance of the object? The object, in other words, continues to function as a dark continent of sorts, a species of otherness whose point of reference remains the Eurocentric and masculine self. The relationship between self and other, therefore, needs rethinking to articulate the resistance of the object, not as the elided difference *within* the imperialist self, but as the defaced inhabitant of cultures, histories, and materialities, subject *to* and other *than* this self.

2. In order to begin this reconceptualization of the dynamic between selves and others, I turned to the currently preeminent theorists of the orientalizing imagination of the West, Edward W. Said and Gayatri Chakravorty Spivak, only to discover that the problem of representing empirical and his-

torical others remained unresolved in their work too. Clearly, then, there is need for a theory that is sensitive both to the complicity between knowledge and power and to the possibility of resistance on the part of the objects of the power-knowledge nexus. Although poststructuralist discourse (Foucault in Said, Derrida in Spivak) informs these authors' respective trenchant critiques of imperialist representation and enables them to demonstrate the manner in which knowledge is produced in the service of colonialist appropriation, that discourse simultaneously refuses to contemplate the opposite or perhaps complementary possibility: that the production of knowledge can also serve the cause of emancipatory critique and of resistance.

Theodor W. Adorno's *Negative Dialectics,* in my view, seems to offer this double opportunity. His notion of the dialectical relation that obtains between subject and object simultaneously insists on the carapace of identity that encloses the subject and on the resistance of the object to the subject's identifications. This project began with these inseparable objectives—to shift the focus from the decentered subject to the resistant object and to disentangle the practice of epistemology from the violence of appropriation.

I imagine that my desire to deploy Adorno's philosophy in the postcolonial scene as a diagnostic tool of sorts has already aroused (dare I say predictable?) ire. I hope to challenge the bulk of the critical work on Adorno, which focuses on the dialectical and historical failures of his thinking rather than on the possibilities to be found there. Simultaneously, I contend that the corpus of Said and Spivak functions as an urgent reconstitution of the power of dialectical thinking in the service of difference. The point is not to deny the independent importance of Said and Spivak in favor of a belated redemption of a modernist mandarin; rather, my aim is to transfer Adorno's abstractions to material or concrete grounds in ways that would illustrate the import, timeliness, and promise of his critique of identity and of his resuscitation of the dialectic.

The converse holds true, too. The projects of Said and Spivak gain more political purchase, I think, when their writings are viewed as dialectical or determinate negations rather than as genealogies or deconstructions. Said himself, in his numerous strategic and provocative but unelaborated (except, appropriately, in *Musical Elaborations*) references to Adorno, seems to suggest as much. Because Said's writings demonstrate how the absence and monstrosity to which the other has been consigned can be transformed into negation as the repudiation of Western values, Adorno's insistence on critical negation seems particularly apt. The historical context of Nazism, which provided the locale for Adorno's philosophy, seems singularly telling, because it bears witness to the material consequences of identity thinking and provides a poignant opportunity for reflection on Said's claims for Palestine—ironically subject to the identitarian politics of Jews.

When I began work on this idea, Spivak's writings bore virtually no obvious trace of Adorno. Her *Outside in the Teaching Machine,* however, confirms my suspicion that, read as an Adornian problematic, her corpus is more or differently political than she intends, though her allusions to him remain determinedly casual. I argue here that her tortuous attempts to bring Marxism into relation with deconstruction (as critiques of consciousness in the name of materiality) might be more usefully accomplished via Adorno. In other words, given the inescapable contradiction between metropolitan theories and subaltern realities, I want to explore aspects of this contradiction that would be productive rather than merely debilitating for postcolonial intellectuals. In this limited sense, I do believe that both the subaltern object and the native informant are better served by Adorno than by Derrida.

The sustained attempt in this book to pit dialectical against differential thinking is a consequence of my insistence on the failure of poststructuralism to appeal to the dispossessed. This failure inheres in poststructuralism's desire to deconstruct the very notion of the political; to destroy the very possibility of a conjunction between interest, insight, and agency; to collapse what Seyla Benhabib has called the distinction between consensus and conquest; or to interrupt the very relation between epistemology and ethics or politics except insofar as knowledge serves to bolster (an often undifferentiated) power. My espousal of Adorno, therefore, is to be understood as a break with a certain version of the practice and profession of epistemology. The break rests quite simply on a desire to make the critique of epistemology inseparable from political commitment. I think that the deposed subject within poststructuralist discourse exemplifies rather than examines the problem of the interrupted relation between politics, ethics, and epistemology. Rather than close the gap between insight and agency with the very discourse whose political inconsequentiality I will be at some pains to demonstrate, I want to harness, once again, the power of dialectical thinking (particularly its valorization of negation as opposition and as contradiction) in the interests of the alterity that Hegel, for one, notoriously repressed in the name of identity.

I am not, of course, effecting an easy transition between epistemological and ethicopolitical revolution—the fate of theory has made it all too clear that the vocabulary of risk, scandal, and rupture is no substitute for "real" change. It seems important, nevertheless, to insist that one cannot proceed without the other. The sensitivity to the nexus of knowledge and power, or to the fallibility of knowledge, is no excuse for a modest abstinence from the desire to know and to act on that knowledge. The propensity to error and to self-interest does not destroy the potential for change; rather, it exists in tension with that potential and, indeed, produces the hope of a better world. If one is to make reason a poor ally of reaction, one must allow reason to become the instrument of its own eclipse or recognize that a philosophy incapable of error is also incapable of truth.

I introduce these familiar tenets of the writings of the Frankfurt school, particularly those of Max Horkheimer and Theodor Adorno, in order to produce the conjunction I suggested earlier between an attention to the feminine and ethnic object's suffering and an epistemological practice in the service of emancipation rather than appropriation. Contrary to deconstructive practice, which often confines itself to exposing the structure of contradictions that informs any hypothesis or historical situation, that of Adorno and Horkheimer deploys the perceived contradictions *of* historical reality to fashion a contradiction *against* reality. In this sense, the very agent that produces power also thwarts it. Such a notion of philosophical or theoretical responsibility ensures that the subject, whose power poststructuralist discourse tirelessly excoriates, makes good (Rainer Nägele's phrase) for what it has done to the object.

Neil Lazarus, to the best of my knowledge, is the only scholar within postcolonial studies to offer a similar appreciation of Adorno. I depart from his reading on two scores. First, Lazarus deploys Adorno's thinking to comprehend white intellectual production in South Africa, whereas I transfer Adorno's import to the predicament of the (whitewashed) postcolonial intellectual and to a rethinking of the objects of the said intellectual discourse, to those who Lazarus suggests are the "real" subjects of (South African) history. Second, I take issue with Lazarus's claim that the moment of denial gets short shrift in Adorno's work. For me, *Negative Dialectics* is the antitext of the vanquished of history. Armed with this hope, I open some crucial polemical areas for discussion.

A personal note may elicit the traces of memory, desire, and invention that animate this conjunction of self, writing, and historical moment. Perhaps it would be more accurate, in the spirit of Walter Benjamin, to petrify the self in a "Medusan glance," and thus turn it into "the stage on which an objective process unfolds" (Adorno 1967, 235). I have the rudiments of a dialectic at my disposal as well as the notion of a subjective dimension as a *staging* of the articulable violence and silent depredations of history.

The history in question is precisely that of decolonization. The object, product, and survivor of this necessarily incomplete process is the postcolonial subject. Her "otherness" in the discourse of Western empire serves to consolidate the identity of her colonizers even as it reifies her own, and her perceived tendency to elude the categories of Western rationality renders her dear to mosaics, melting pots, and postmoderns.

My interest in this traffic of selves and others, colonizers and colonized, men and women, color and whiteness, is that of a member of the familiar, if still anomalous, breed of intellectual émigrés, or, as they are now called, "native informants." My contribution to the vexed enterprise of inscribing the margins, of representing the colonized, and of letting, so to speak, Caliban curse freely, must therefore be accomplished with both difficulty and delicacy. Let me suggest some of the familiar institutional compromises that beset, without necessarily eroding, my intellectual situation, integrity, and identity.

I have, after all, "thrown in my lot with salaried profundity" (to adapt a phrase from Adorno 1974b, 66), can do little about the persistence of neoimperialism, and am applauded for my perceived conformity to Macaulay's caricature of "a class of persons, Indian in blood and colour, but English in taste, in opinion, in morals and in intellect" (as quoted in Anderson 1983, 86). In the current theoretical climate, one could well substitute "Derridean" for "English" (see Radhakrishnan 1987, 212–13). Worse, I am often perceived as belonging to the cadre of "colourful personalities" (Adorno 1974b, 135) who have turned their experience of alienation into a profitable commodity.[1] I function then no longer as the "white man's burden" but as his scourge, able to "ingratiate [myself] with aggressive jibes masochistically enjoyed by [my] protectors" who then congratulate themselves on their liberality (136).

I acknowledge that this form of self-positioning can all too easily turn into one more version of "blaming the victims" (Said's phrase) for the historical violence of colonialism or of the culture of imperialism; however, I articulate my position as honestly as I can in order to avoid the opposite, but equally dangerous, problem of parading as the paradigmatic emblem of the victims of colonization. I embody, in short, one of many and differently brutal versions of the conflict between economic privilege (or lack thereof) and cultural deprivation within the discourse of colonialism.

Agency is a treacherous business in the realm of "mental miscegenation" (Anderson 1983, 87) that postcolonial intellectuals inhabit. The reproduction of the conquest of land in the colonization of the mind serves as a baleful yet crucial reminder of the impossibility of authenticity. That the postcolonial intellectual is "a stranger in his own native land" (Bipin Chandra Pal, as quoted in Anderson 1983, 88) is no longer surprising and is in fact the condition of her claim (one that she makes at her peril) that she "really knows what [s]he is talking about" (Said 1988, 47).

This inauthenticity also denotes her inability both to *be* the other of Western empire (the splendid but mute savage) and to *speak for* the "wholly other," whom Gayatri Spivak characterizes as "the curious guardian at the margin" (Spivak 1991, 172). The "native informant" both constitutes and adjudicates the limits of knowledge about the other and prepares the ground that awaits the other's presence and inscription.[2] The postcolonial intellectual represents the visible sign of a deferred postcoloniality even as she marks the limits of colonization. How then can she articulate the impossible possibility she seeks and prefigures?

Spivak is probably right to dismiss most attempts to call the place of the writing or investigating subject into question as instances of "meaningless piety" (Spivak 1988, 271); however, that such attempts can never suffice or that they dwindle into no more than knee-jerk responses to various forms of political correctness does not obviate the necessity for a reflection on "beginnings."[3] Besides, reflexivity can constitute the grounds for, or at the very least can supplement, critique, even if it cannot substitute for critique.

The reflection on subject positions has become unavoidable for the sympathetic Western critic who chooses to engage with the other without presumption or patronage. The danger of this timely recognition of a perhaps inescapable ethnocentrism is that it could be turned easily enough into an excuse for inaction. This conscientious refusal to speak for those whom the discourse of Empire designates as other would become a way of absolving oneself of the responsibility for the brutality of history. Since the Western critic is inevitably implicated in the history of colonization, any intervention on behalf of the other, it could be argued, will be contaminated by that history and therefore futile. The process of self-scrutiny would then translate itself into consolation for the wrongs of the past and into paralysis in the present.

Reflexivity may also be less innocent than the phrase "meaningless piety" suggests; that is, critical restraint could reconstitute itself as yet another colonizing gesture. It is not often noticed that the critic who refrains from speaking on behalf of those whom she can never "know" presumes that, having spoken, she would have said it all and that the other will be moved neither to challenge nor to supplement her. In other words, her humility has all the trappings of a gracious and patronizing self-effacement that still reserves the right to grant the other "permission to narrate" her (hi)story.[4]

The native informant is equally subject to these problems; indeed, they are compounded by the contradiction between her political allegiance to her "origins" and her facility with the discourses of the colonizer. It seems pertinent, given the paradoxes of decolonization, to distinguish between reflexivity as the willed paralysis of the purveyor of master narratives or even of the overscrupulous native informant, and reflexivity as commitment to a dialectical mode of critique

> in which the mind . . . reckons itself into the problem, understanding the dilemma not as a resistance of the object alone, but also as the result of a subject-pole deployed and disposed against it in a strategic fashion—in short, as the function of a determinate subject-object relationship. (Jameson 1971, 308)

The forms of reflexivity I have described deal with a "petrified otherness" (Adorno 1974b, 135) and conceive of the relation between subject and object as a logical rather than a dialectical contradiction. The paralysis of the self-reflexive critic stems from her designation of the other as a barrier that brings epistemological hubris up short. The other as object of analysis is thus pitted against the investigating subject in stark, antithetical terms—the hubris or hasty retreat of one confirming the blank impenetrability of the other.

The perception of otherness as radical and irreducible leaves one trapped within the confines of the colonial encounter in which the colonizer "perceive[d] as human only [his] own reflected image, instead of reflecting back the human as precisely what is different" (Adorno 1974b, 105). In other words, the respect for the integrity of the other functions as a complement to the colonizer's paranoid insistence that the other serve to consolidate his identity.

Dialectical thinking eschews antithesis except as "determinate negation."[5] As the passage just cited from Jameson's *Marxism and Form* indicates, the relation between subject and object must be construed as a dynamic interaction subject to historical conditions or, in the colonial situation, as an interplay between the power of the colonizer and the resistance of the colonized. The split between subject and object, therefore, is not inherent but historically produced and negated.

Jameson's insistence on the strategic deployment of the subject-pole of the dialectic avoids the willed paralysis of reflexivity, because the intellectual's power of negation resides not only in recognizing the pervasiveness of ideology or of systems of power/knowledge, but also in constructing a mode of critique that does more than confirm what it attacks.[6] The task for the postcolonial intellectual, to borrow Adorno's words, "is to let neither the power of others, nor [her] own powerlessness, stupefy" her (Adorno 1974b, 57).

Reflexivity (as I have been discussing it) thus reveals itself as an inadequate comprehension of the functioning of ideology: it assumes that there are no chinks in the armor of the system and fails to recognize that the processes of both colonization and decolonization were and will remain incomplete. Adorno remarks that "the world is systematized horror, but therefore it is to do the world too much honour to think of it entirely as a system" (Adorno 1974b, 113).

Interestingly, Edward Said's pertinent critique of "orientalism" allows itself to do the system too much honor. In his pathbreaking work, Said's focus remains on the misdeeds of the oppressor rather than on the resistance of the oppressed. Such an emphasis is perhaps unavoidable in a polemic; however, his subsequent writings continue to call for the production of "new objects for a new kind of knowledge" (Said 1985c, 91) without specifying the contours of such a novel discourse. He shows salutary caution regarding hasty projections of a decolonized future in which orientalism will cease to influence representation; nevertheless, his insistence on empirical others who are historically constituted rather than ontologically given (Said 1989, 225) implies that the "other" is invocable if not definable.

I should emphasize here that the *fact* of Said's engagement with the self-contained (at least in his view) "system" is not at issue; after all, I am advocating a rereading of Adorno, a figure who has traditionally been received as the champion of European (and imperialist) "high" culture and as a "radical" with paradoxically little faith in the aspirations of the powerless (these are, needless to say, views I hope to challenge). My concern is with the *nature* of that engagement, particularly in Said's early analyses of colonialist discourse. In chapter 5, I discuss whether Said's newest work, *Culture and Imperialism*, addresses this lopsided focus.

The fashionable gesture of decentering the subject resembles, much too closely for comfort, the classic gesture of self-deprecation common to colonials who believed that "by careful mimicry [they] might become men [*sic*]"

(Walcott 1979, 12). If we collaborated with their power once, we might just as easily be co-opted by their overtures of humility. In this sense, the belief that the "mirror, where a generation yearned / for whiteness" (Walcott 1981, 43) is now willing to return that gaze with candor is no more than wish fulfillment. Abdul JanMohamed and David Lloyd aptly observe that the "non-identity which the critical Western intellectual seeks to (re)produce discursively is for minorities a given of their social existence" (JanMohamed and Lloyd 1987, 16).

The problem remains, however, that the consequence of negating the negation that constitutes the (minority) self as other appears to be stable identity of a sort that produces exclusionary politics as well as "pontification about what makes 'us' worth protecting and 'them' worth attacking" (Said 1988, 60). The trick, then—to use Adorno's trenchant comment on Nazism (and not inappropriately in this instance)—is "not to choose between black and white but to abjure such prescribed choices" (Adorno 1974b, 132). I shall consider in a moment Said's and Spivak's rewriting of such prescribed choices as the dialectic of friend and foe in the context of my claims for an epistemology that is not dismissible as colonization or appropriation.

My stake in the defensible claims of otherness is as much personal as political, and the trajectory of my engagement with the discourse of Empire has its roots in the (literal) subalternity of my ancestry. My introduction to the power and possibilities of historical dialectic occurred in my experience of the irreducible contradiction of the lives of my grandparents. I share their legacy of (enabling) schizophrenia, of lives conducted in the consciousness of their status as victims and agents of the British Empire.

My maternal grandfather turned his master's degree in English (with irony and alacrity, no doubt) into a career in the Indian Police; my paternal grandfather let his own skills as a lawyer slide when he languished in jail for joining, and to some degree spearheading, the freedom movement in southern India. One chose to honor the claims of family; the other, following Mahatma Gandhi's example, pursued what were then, perhaps, more pressing concerns. The latter's person, however, was subject to violence from nationalists too, who stoned him when he chose to conduct one of the first widow remarriages in the Brahmin, Tamil-speaking community. To this day, he runs a school for "untouchables" or "Harijans" (God's people or children), as Gandhi courageously labeled the others within.[7]

My maternal grandfather chose to rebel on the level of language. His children received education in the vernacular despite his passion for English literature, and he wrote his own unpublished poetry in his native tongue, Malayalam, refusing the option to publish in English. The social reformer in my paternal grandfather did not penetrate the opacity of Brahmin ritual in his home and produced its own subaltern (I am aware that I'm making a somewhat loose use of this term for the moment) in his wife. Here, it seemed, his authority remained (in)effective in that his radicalism could not, and did not, command submission from her in the way his conservatism did from them both.

This exercise in self-situation may help to illustrate the problematic status of nationality and of "nativism" in the discourse of postcolonialism. The awakening of India to self-consciousness had less to do with an essence that achieved fruition than with unity in the face of a common enemy—a point that the epigraph to this book makes with the poignant reminder that dissension was essential to British dominion. As Benedict Anderson points out, "'India' only became 'British' after the 1857 Mutiny" (Anderson 1983, 86). Anderson's nice ambiguity is salutary—the "mutiny" confirmed "India" as both a nation and a British possession—even if one balks at his leaving the word "mutiny" unchallenged. India had thus to invent itself as an entity, to dream "an imagined political community" in order to come into being (Anderson 1983, 15ff.).

My own desire for national allegiance, then, emerges as an irrevocable contradiction and involves the dialectical mediation of Brahmin orthodoxy and colonial education. That sexism was not coterminous with colonialism was ammunition enough for me to begin the difficult task of representing a self that could not claim to be *representative*. The "intellectual in emigration" (Adorno 1974b, 33) inhabits a "twilight" world, to use Derek Walcott's evocative metaphor (1975, 5), but the wound that history has inflicted creates the urge to begin again.[8]

Adorno claims that every such individual is "mutilated" because "his [*sic*] language has been expropriated, and the historical dimension that nourished his [*sic*] knowledge, sapped" (Adorno 1974b, 33). Adorno's situation as a "permanent exile" (Martin Jay's phrase; see Jay 1986) serves to clarify and distinguish my own. I cannot experience my situation as an uprooting in the way that he implies because, as the respective locations of my grandparents indicate, I inhabited an authentic linguistic and cultural dimension in India only at the cost of ignoring my unexamined investment (even then) in colonial education.

I was subject, in other words, to all the familiar confusions: English became synonymous with education, my training in teaching English as a second language involved indoctrinating my unwilling students in received pronunciation, and my incipient feminism rested firmly on the conviction that female emancipation was inconceivable outside the discourse of Western modernity. Unpleasant reminders of this investment continue to taunt me in Anglophilic America, where I am routinely complimented on my "English" accent.

This process of cultural and linguistic displacement was also enacted in the constitution of my "Indianness." I was a Tamil-speaking inhabitant of a state whose official language was Kannada, and my university education in Delhi made me the butt of ridicule because I spoke Hindi with all the proverbial bravado and infelicity of a south Indian novice. The contradictory categories of caste, class, and gender only served to confound my sense of self. The dialectic of friend and foe, therefore, plays itself out on the interlocking levels of (native and colonizing) language, history, and identity. In short, the dimensions that "nourish my knowledge" are precisely those that "sap" it: there is no Archimedean point outside the history of the colonial encounter and its consequent national and communal divisions. Perhaps my relatively sanguine reaction to the horrors of schizophrenia as well as my unwillingness to romanticize its creative potential (I have in mind here Gilles Deleuze and Félix Guattari's claim for a minority discourse that thrives on the revolutionary potential of schizophrenia as a radical disintegration of the socius, not a clinical disorder of the mind) has something to do with the complex set of determinants I have just delineated.

Adorno's cultural alienation was itself subject to the corrosive irony of his position as a witness to the Nazi extermination of Jews, as well as to the guilt of a survivor of that extermination. His searing awareness that authenticity is bought at the price of the decimation of others animates his sustained critique of identity thinking.

I want to endorse Adorno's willingness to "affirm" this mutilation as the ever-present capacity to negate an administered world. If, as he says, "wrong life cannot be lived rightly" (Adorno 1974b, 37), the "neurosis" that defines the "native informant" must be transformed into the source of "the healing force, that of knowledge" (Adorno 1967, 252).[9] Lest I be accused of being in danger of forgetting myself and of uncritically embracing the material suffering of "mutilation," I want to say that I carry with me the image of my maternal grandfather's last days, when his "senility" manifested itself as an in-fallible memory of Shakespeare and Tennyson and an inability to recognize the anxious faces that hovered over him. The resistance to the ill-gotten gains of colonial education begins, perhaps, in the memory of such loss.[10]

I have thus far treated Adorno, Said, and Spivak as "presences" rather than as objects of sustained critique in the course of developing a paradigm of knowledge that is no longer in danger of treating epistemology *as* viola-tion, representation *as* colonization, or theory as the shortest distance be-tween "the stalled origin and the stalled end" (Spivak 1991, 158). Such an enterprise entails a "negative dialectic" between subject and object in which "otherness" functions as resistance to, rather than retreat from, identity and stable definition. This resistance includes the notion of otherness as a strate-gic assumption of identity; indeed, I will argue that identity cannot be other than strategic. The point is to resist imposed identities and stable definitions that serve occidental, colonialist, orientalist, or merely metropolitan inter-ests. In this sense, retreat from identity might be equally strategic.

In the Hegelian dialectic, the subject engages with the object only inso-far as the latter's powers of contradiction and of predication are subsumed in the process of *Aufhebung,* which produces a subject whose presence has been preserved or reinforced at the expense of the object. This model of subject-object relations has characterized both the discourse of colonialism and its self-reflexive critiques. Adorno, on the contrary, argues for a dialectic be-tween subject and object whose motive force is the resistance and negation of the object.

This strategic shift in emphasis produces a dynamic between subject and object that is contingent on dialectical negation rather than on dialectical reciprocity. The subject can no longer seek its reflection in the object or absorb negation as a transient moment of vulnerability in the inexorable production of subjective identity. This identity is itself a form of negation, one that denies the object the possibility of location, materiality, and history. Moreover, this hierarchical reversal of subject and object positions has a con-comitant effect on the subject's will to know (I have already pointed out its effect on the subject's will to power). Dialectical negation, in asserting the recalcitrance of the object, also explodes the (epistemological) categories of the subject.

To explain how all this happens, I turn once again to Spivak's "Theory in the Margin." My discussion challenges Spivak's contention that the ob-ject's capacity to elude the instrumental rationality of the knowing subject is to be construed as the "native's" tantalizing mockery of epistemological desire. This certainly seems to be Spivak's implication when she remarks that, as agent and victim, the native "simply withdraws [the native's] graphematic space" (Spivak 1991, 175).

Spivak does not entertain the possibility that the recognition that the "desire to help [or "know"] racially differentiated others [has] a threshold and a limit" (Spivak 1991, 177) may be the prelude to a mode of critique that becomes "a matter, indeed, of the reversal of limits" (Jameson 1971, 309). The error (I realize that the opposition between truth and error is itself something she would wish to "undo") in Spivak's conception of this process of discovering the "native" as "the unemphatic agent of withholding" lies in the conclusion she draws from her analysis (Spivak 1991, 172).

"Theory," she writes, "is always withdrawn from that which it seeks to theorize, *however insubstantial that object might be*" (Spivak 1991, 175; my emphasis). Spivak's analysis often assumes that the interaction between subject and object poles in the dialectic is analogous to the failure of a force to move a simply resistant object. She collapses the poles of the dialectic because theory's capacity to be "off the mark" is matched by the insubstantiality of the object it seeks to theorize. It is difficult to escape the tautological conclusion that theory is its own (insubstantial) object. In other words, "the explanation . . . is inherent in the initial description of the event" (Jameson 1971, 344).[11]

This problem reappears in Spivak's representation of the desire of the "native" to retain "a space of withholding, marked by a secret that may not be a secret but cannot be unlocked" (Spivak 1991, 172). This cautionary measure leaves knowledge with no choice but to demand (insensitively and unsubtly, of course) the key. She puts the "native" in the odd position of coyly refusing the lumbering advances of the knowing subject and puts knowledge in the impossible position of a violator of mysteries or, worse still, turns knowledge into a species of mysticism. As far as the tautological character of this kind of argument is concerned, I merely want to point out that the representation of one pole of the dialectic (Friday with his withholding slate) has repercussions on the other (knowledge becomes colonization—a command for the native "to yield his 'voice' "; see Spivak 1991, 172). The reverse, of course, holds true too.

The tautology occurs in a different guise when Spivak attempts to refute Benita Parry's charge that she never permits the subaltern to speak. Spivak points out that Parry has forgotten that Spivak is a native too (Spivak 1991,

172). Her response continues to beg the question of the subaltern, because she dissolves the distinction between knower and known. This dissolution makes Spivak guilty of appropriating the subaltern woman's powerlessness to unlearn her own privilege, or catches her in the act of making the damaging admission that the subaltern (the object of her critique) is Spivak (the subject of her critique). This is a different point from the one that acknowledges that the subject must reckon herself into the problem she addresses or the object she describes.

Moreover, the space she grants the "wholly other" becomes the hazardous groundlessness of theory itself, which must seek, fruitlessly, its ground. This contention unwittingly clarifies theory's insubstantial object. In the name of a respect for thresholds and limits, the subaltern is once again silenced. By the end of her essay, "theory" contains the dialectic of friend and foe, as it does the web of desire and power. The "native" represents the ineffable, ontological residue of the failure of representation; the impossibility of theory; the sign of the inadequacy of self-reflection; and the occasion for, one imagines, further musings on that inadequacy. I shall have more to say on Spivak's reliance on emblematic constructions that do the work of analysis. At this stage, it seems enough to suggest that a Marcusian "great refusal" will simply not do.

Adorno's claim for a negative dialectic that acknowledges "the preponderance of the object" suggests a different possibility. The dialectical method allows for the reciprocal modification of facts and categories so that the recognition of limits becomes the occasion for a "politics of the possible" (see Sangari 1987), grounded in the particular, that escapes the conceptual net of the category.

The "locus of hope," not the a priori limits of theory, lies in the nonidentity of the particular, in the "perishing present" in the process of transforming itself into a new order, and in the "refuse of reality," wherein lies the defiance of the present and the promise of a different future.[12] Spivak makes room only for a Friday who withdraws his graphematic space rather than for one who demands that she "express the 'logic of the matter' in a new modality" (Buck-Morss 1977, 87).[13] She is right to drive thought to its limit, but she must also let it turn back on itself in a dialectical reversal committed to serving "that which would be different" (Buck-Morss 1977, 189).[14]

The postcolonial intellectual, then, is like Benjamin's Angel of History, who would "like to make whole what has been smashed" but is irresistibly propelled into a future to which "his back remains turned" (Benjamin 1968,

259–60). The postcolonial intellectual is in danger of reducing her language to "phonetic pain" and her experience to "the suffering of the victim" (Walcott 1978, 40), but compelled both to resist that pain and to envisage the task of decolonization and the condition of postcoloniality.

It is possible now to return to the epigraph from E. M. Forster's *A Passage to India* to suggest the ways in which the opposition of friend and foe can be undone to produce a process of knowing not only as "enabling" violation (Spivak 1991, 175) but also as healing and resistance. The passage (to continue my evocation of Benjamin) is a "dialectical image" that functions as an "objective [crystallization] of the historical dynamic" (Adorno 1967, 238). This notion can be explained initially in terms of the use of perspective in Forster's paragraphs. The landscape dwarfs human pretensions to understanding just as the history of colonialism destroys the possibilities of friendship between Englishman and Indian. In short, the novel's finale encapsulates the dynamic of self and historical process because the dream of a nation is inextricable from the invention of self.

Theories of postcolonial discourse seem trapped in a version of Forster's conclusion to his novel, coyly averting the inevitable political encounter because they persist in slippages that reproduce the "native" as unrepresentable and the dialogue between ex–colonizer and colonized as impossible. Said argues, for example, that the last sentence is an instance of "aestheticized powerlessness" that "can neither recommend decolonization, nor continued colonization" and that it is "all Forster can muster by way of resolution" (Said 1989, 223).[15]

To charge Forster with a failure of nerve is to miss the unnerving point his novel makes—the relations of desire that bind Fielding and Aziz are, precisely and disconcertingly, the relations of power. The choice between colonization and decolonization proves self-contradictory because it reflects a contradictory reality. Aziz and Fielding find, respectively, that desire and power turn into each other; simultaneously, as Said's predilection for Foucauldian analyses should have indicated, power produces both colonizer and colonized as it does their respective configurations of desire. In this sense the concluding scene functions as a dialectical image: it pits opposites against each other only to reveal what connects them or contains the dialectic of friend and foe. I shall develop this idea in the context of both Spivak's and Said's tendency to freeze the dialectic and to overlook the symbiotic relation of master and slave except insofar as it confirms one's power and the other's powerlessness.

Moreover, while it is true that the context includes Fielding's, not Forster's, mockery of India's pretensions to nationhood (the narrative voice, as the wealth of critical material on this novel attests, is much too complicated and elusive to be collapsed summarily with Fielding's; Said, in short, has to ignore Aziz's reaction in order to make Forster and Fielding one), the immediate context of the last line of the novel is Fielding's question, "Why can't we be friends now?"—a subtle but significant distinction, or at least a question that invites engagement with a set of issues other than those directly concerned with (de)colonization. In his essay "Dante" from 1908, Forster comments that to claim love's possibility for those we do not know is sentiment. Instead, what is involved is a different process of acknowledging the claim people we do not or cannot know have on us (Forster 1971, 146).[16]

Fielding's desire contains within it what Adorno would describe as the intolerable tolerance of democracy. As Adorno explains,

> to assure the black that he is exactly like the white man, while he obviously is not, is secretly to wrong him still further. He is benevolently humiliated by the application of a standard by which, under the pressure of the system, he must necessarily be found wanting, and to satisfy which would in any case be a doubtful achievement. (Adorno 1974b, 103)

But Said does not notice that the answer to Fielding's question and, in a sense, to his own, is in Aziz's preceding exclamation that such friendship will be the outcome of driving "every blasted Englishman into the sea." The doubleness that animates this dialectic of friend and foe is encapsulated in Aziz's actions, which begin with his riding furiously against Fielding and conclude with his half-kissing him (here too, Forster does not allow for completeness—one more instance, Said would argue, of a lack of muscular resolve?).

Spivak would probably read the refusal of Fielding's desire (after all, even the earth proves implacable in this regard) as another instance of her contention that "when one *wants* to be a friend to the wholly other, it withdraws its graphematic space" (Spivak 1991, 175; emphasis in original). The language of thresholds, deferral, and abysses is not foreign, of course, to a passage that widens the gap between (English) self and (Indian) other. I think, however, that Forster demands, as the dialectical method does, that we formulate the riddle another way.

Instead of congratulating oneself on the pitilessness of one's realism, one begins to wonder whether, to use Fredric Jameson's words, "the fact of our judgement stood as a judgement on us rather than on the utopian speculation that we are unable to take seriously" (Jameson 1971, 90). Forster does not merely ask (in ontological terms) whether the friendship between Aziz and Fielding is real or possible, but also what sort of world it would have to be in which such a friendship would be realistic.[17]

More interestingly for my purposes, the conjunction between desire and knowledge (that Fielding cannot love what he does not know and that he fails to acknowledge the brutalization that Aziz has suffered at the hands of the Empire) suggests a radical dimension to cognition. Adorno claims that "the need to lend a voice to suffering is a condition of all truth" (Adorno 1973c, 17–18). This ethical and political imperative distinguishes the critique of epistemic violence practiced by Adorno, Said, and Spivak, the figures who form the privileged foci of my project. The future of postcolonial discourse, at least from this diasporic intellectual's point of view, resides in the transformation (to borrow and reverse the implications of Samuel Weber's pun) of conditions of imposability into those of (im)possibility. This transformation, I believe, can occur only if the tensions and contradictions of a historically produced antagonism between self and other are reintroduced into the reigning atmosphere of fluid identities and infinitely transgressible boundaries. In order to infuse universal categories with the richness and density of individual and historical experience, more than a rhetoric or aesthetic of opposition might be in order.

Even as I share a general impatience with intellectuals who devote themselves to the endless refinement of analytical categories, I think a degree of caution is valuable on at least two scores: (1) discourses of resistance, even as they assert the desire of the vanquished to (in Walter Benjamin's terms) explode the continuum of history, must avoid implying that the experience of victimization necessarily provides one with the wherewithal to make the transition from experience to awareness to action; and (2) these discourses must not indicate the incommensurability of Western categories and "other" realities without consistently pointing out the determinate rather than the ontological nature of their irreconcilability.

I am all too aware that the dangers of complicity and co-optation are daunting enough even when those engaged in confrontational politics are not taken to task for indulging in concretization of a most limiting sort. I simply want to reiterate that in order to align oneself with a political constituency of any kind, one too often becomes subject to prescribed choices that preclude the possibility of a form of opposition that caricatures neither the self nor the other. In wishing to participate in my particular present's struggle for self-definition, in critically challenging the course of imperialist history, I hesitate to argue for a necessary connection between otherness and revolution, just as I abjure any such connection between self-reflexive discourse and correct politics.

For the postcolonial intellectual, whose relation to occidental thought is not one of alienation but of agonizing proximity, the moment of dissidence occurs when her immersion in the destructive element enables her, as Adorno might say, to hate it properly. The "societal calluses" (Adorno's phrase) or limits of all that presumes to know, exceed, and transcend the world must be discerned, not with a knowing self-deprecation but with a genuine stake or investment in what a critical knowledge of limits makes possible. In Pierre Bourdieu's succinct formulation, without the investment (as opposed to self-interest) in thinking "the possibility of *freedom* in relation to [social and institutional] conditions," one can do no more than play "institutionally directed games with the institution" (Bourdieu 1983, 4–5; emphasis in the original).

1 / The End(s) of (Wo)Man; or,
The Limits of Difference

Hope cannot aim at making the mutilated social character of women identical to the mutilated social character of men; rather its goal must be a state . . . in which all that survives the disgrace of the difference between the sexes is the happiness that difference makes possible.

Theodor Adorno, *Prisms: Cultural Criticism and Society*

Contemporary feminist debates over the meanings of gender lead time and again to a certain sense of trouble, as if the indeterminacy of gender might eventually culminate in the failure of feminism.

Judith Butler, *Gender Trouble: Feminism and the Subversion of Identity*

To us, the man who adores the Negro is as "sick" as the man who abominates him. Conversely, the black man who wants to turn his race white is as miserable as he who preaches hatred for the whites. These truths do not have to be hurled in men's faces. They are not intended to ignite fervor. I do not trust fervor.
Every time it has burst out somewhere, it has brought fire, famine, misery. . . . And contempt for man.

Frantz Fanon, *Black Skin, White Masks*

All discourses . . . would then develop in the anonymity of a murmur. We would no longer hear the questions . . . Who really spoke? Is it really he and not someone else? . . . Instead, there would be other questions, like these: What are the modes of existence of this discourse? Where has it been used, how can it circulate, and who can appropriate it for himself? What are the places in it where there is room for possible subjects? Who can assume these various subject functions? And

1

behind all these questions, we would hardly hear anything but the stirring of an
indifference: What difference does it make who is speaking?
                        Michel Foucault, "What Is an Author?"

Not long ago, the cover of *Time* magazine bore the words, "God is dead,
Marx is dead, and I'm not feeling too well myself." The magazine's wry en-
capsulation of polite unease was both appropriate and prophetic, at least if
the sentiments expressed in the current discourse of the Western world's
well-bred and, one imagines, well-read academics are to be believed. The
essays devoted in recent years to the imminent demise of the Cartesian cogito is witness to the dis-ease or, if you will, lingering malaise, of an ethos that
dates back to the eighteenth century when the likes of Immanuel Kant re-
sponded to the query "Was ist Aufklärung?"

The dis-ease in question afflicts the claims of occidental rationality as
well as its supreme exemplar, Western Man, as both herald and heir of the
motto of the Enlightenment: "aude sapere," or "dare to know." The secular
hubris implicit in this motto inaugurated what has come to signify "modernity." The agonistic progeny of this historical moment, then, battle the consequences of modernity in the effort to produce an aftermath of sorts, postmodernity.

The break, the postmoderns claim, is as much historical and epistemological as it is lexical or typographical, and they assume the mantle of the past
reluctantly at best, guiltily aware of the continuing predication of the legitimacy of knowledge upon the instrumentality of power. I have, of course,
been precipitate on at least two scores: in characterizing postmodernism as an
only recent or emergent phenomenon and, more hazardously, in asserting its
phenomenality.

Postmodernism rests its claim to difference on precisely its rejection of
teleological representations of temporality, of history as the unfolding of an
idea or as a version of manifest destiny. In this sense, postmodernism might
be said to have always already begun, to signify, so to speak, an infinite regress. One immediate way of indicating that postmodernism is not so much
a historical problem as a problem *for* history, or a problem posed *to* history,
suggests itself.

If I might return to the catchy idiom in which *Time* captured the accents
of postmodernism, the slogan alludes to Friedrich Nietzsche, Karl Marx, and
Sigmund Freud. In their separate but related ways, this unholy trinity can be
held responsible for the initial onslaught on the hubris of reason and on the

mastery of self-consciousness that postmodernism now makes its distinctive prerogative. Postmodernism's Oedipal angst can thus be viewed as a doubled movement—one that refuses the heritage of instrumental rationality bequeathed to it by the patriarchs of the Enlightenment, while simultaneously celebrating the decentering of the transcendental subject of knowledge practiced by its other fathers, themselves enacting the "anxiety of influence" (Harold Bloom's familiar and appropriately f[am]ilial phrase).

The doubled movement I have just delineated not only affects the content of the historical struggle within postmodernism but also shatters the confines of conventional historical understanding. The trajectory of (post)-modernity cannot be described in evolutionary terms, as the unfolding of historical necessity. Because the agonistic progeny I have described simultaneously inherit and dismantle the legacy of modernity, the history they inscribe or inhabit acquires the character of a genealogy, thereby producing instability and discontinuity in the seamless teleology of historical becoming.

This disdain for the continuity of before and after with which I began reveals both the vulnerability of truth (as historical necessity) and the inevitability of its masquerade. The constituted character of historical necessity renders its narrative suspect and exclusive and draws attention to the marginal elements enslaved by its ruthless course.[1] This desire to turn historical necessity against itself accords postmodernism the political dimension in which its deconstructive character finds expression.

Because I have conjured the specter of deconstruction, I should perhaps indicate that Jacques Derrida, as is well known, also undertakes a critique of the search for origins or final causes, and names the process Nietzsche identifies as the "will to power" as the itinerary of a "metaphysics of presence from which the multiplicity of existence can be deduced and through which it can be accounted for and given meaning" (Ryan 1982, 9). Deconstruction, too, can be described as a genealogy that recovers the repressed and effaced other of the concepts that claim self-sufficiency or that, in Derrida's terms, deny the *différance* that constitutes and undermines their identity. In other words, nothing indisputably *is;* it "is only as it differs from or defers something else" (Ryan 1982, 11).

In this sense, Derrida's concern is of a piece with Nietzsche's: both expose truth as the masquerade of error, as the willed mastery of concepts that must conceal their dependence on the alterity they suppress. If, according to Nietzsche, truth is merely a congealed form of error, Derrida displaces the opposition between truth and error to reveal, so to speak, error as the soft underbelly of hardened or congealed truth. Simply put, Derrida transfers to a linguistic and spatial dimension the struggle of historical (temporal) forces. When Foucault identifies power as the appropriation of discourse, of a system of rules for constituting "reality," he is closer to Derrida's version of "things." Truth/error in Nietzsche becomes, in Derrida, a historically constituted system of reference that is both relational and exclusive by definition. In this way, Derrida too questions the developmental model of history by treating concepts/words/forces as items in a series that are *laterally* determined.[2]

For Derrida, the marking out of *différance* "is a strategy without finality" (Derrida 1973, 135), and, accordingly, the political dimension I teased out from the very instability of truth might itself be "at risk" for acquiring the character of a telos. Derrida and Nietzsche share the view that consciousness is the effect rather than the cause of the system of determinations (linguistic or discursive in Derrida and the randomness of events in Nietzsche) in which it is inscribed.

In the context of this challenge to the power of consciousness to determine events, to the interpretation of events as the unfolding of Reason or the manifestation of Spirit, the corpus of Marx and Freud assumes its deserved importance. Because Nietzsche held that concepts functioned as forces, he paradoxically succeeded in defining history as the bloody *conceptual* struggle of an undifferentiated and curiously anonymous truth and error. Even his famous characterization of history as the battle of Apollonian and Dionysiac forces has all the charm and veracity of metaphor in the service of allegory.

In short, Nietzsche did little more than assert the determined rather than the determining nature of truth and identity. It would take the concerted efforts of Marx and Freud to locate those determinations in a precise historical configuration (capitalism) and in the ravages of desire, sexuality, and the unconscious. Nietzsche's rage against philosophers as "the lustful eunuchs of history" chained to "an ascetic ideal" (quoted in Foucault 1977b, 92), his demand for "life," finds its logical culmination in the work of Freud.

Freud's discovery of the unconscious makes it possible to situate the randomness of events in the unpredictability of desire. One must, of course, note the crucial shift in emphasis from truth/consciousness as the oppression of alterity to consciousness as the repression of desire. The utilitarian dimension (reality pressed into service) implicit in Nietzsche's version of consciousness gains a juridical form in Freud—consciousness as the prohibition of desire. The inscription of consciousness in systems of power or discourse finds an analogous interpretation/representation in Freud's notion of the "mystic writing pad" (Harvey 1986, 178). Just as the imprint remains on the wax slab even after the celluloid sheet has been removed, and cannot become visible except in certain lights, the "foundational process of the psyche" (Harvey 1986, 178) is transformed into a gnarled landscape of latent and manifest content, and of the exigencies of condensation and displacement. Freud's reading of the nonerasable but obscured imprint of the unconscious lends substance to Nietzsche's provocative refusal of teleology and its penchant for mechanical sequences of cause and effect derived from human intention.

Harvey describes this process of imprinting as an incomplete exchange. She writes that "the 'imprinting' so well explicated in terms of the world to consciousness does not return full circle or ellipse such that the subject also inscribes itself upon the world, which in turn inscribes itself upon the subject" (Harvey 1986, 179). This inability to account for the moments when ideology fails and agency becomes possible is a problem common to the various depictions of the human subject as a function of discursive practices.

Although Nietzsche's emphasis on the exteriority of accidents might be analogous to Marx's perception that history occurs behind the backs of its ostensible protagonists, the latter discovers that there is a method to the madness of events. Marx might be said to emphasize the *singular* randomness of events; that is, the dialectical relation between chance and necessity finds its locus in the material conditions of production to which the (de)formation of the subject can be traced.

Marx's conception of history

> has not, like the idealistic view of history, in every period to look
> for a category, but remains constantly on the real ground of history.
> It does not explain practice from the idea but explains the formation
> of ideas from material practice. (Marx [1846] in Tucker 1978, 164)

Marx effects a twofold displacement: the critique of history takes place from within history and relates the efficacy of concepts to their material effects. Instead of a totalizing vision of the will to power, Marx restricts his vision to a specific exercise of power—the history of capitalism. If the contradictions of material/discursive practices can demystify the truth of concepts, the human subject can be shown to be an effect of ideology (of which it remains unconscious or which it [mis]recognizes as reality) rather than the author of its destiny or, as Hegel would have it, the embodiment of the World Spirit.

Marx shows, for example, that the subject's experience of alienation does not move inexorably to self-recognition in its objectifications, as Hegel argued. Alienation is not a necessary moment in the dialectic of subject and object that ends in their identity. Instead, alienation is a mark of the dialectic between forces and relations of production. The rule of the principle of exchange and the power of the commodity reduce the relations of production to transactions between things—labor and capital. The Hegelian dialectic is itself an unconscious reflection of the "real" relations of production even as it serves to transform the accidents of history into immutable necessities. In short, Marx's remarkable analysis serves not only to read history as a kind of ontological or inherent violence of the concept, but also to specify the kinds of domination that particular concepts serve to mask.

Moreover, Marx emphasizes the "radical" dimension of his work; his "genealogy" serves not only as diagnosis but as a handbook for revolution. In these terms, the recognition that "the tradition of all the dead generations weighs like a nightmare on the brain of the living" and that history is the product of "circumstances directly found, given and transmitted from the past" does not invalidate the contention that people "make their own history" (Marx [1852] n.d., 13). Marx does not succumb either to the determinism of the Absolute Subject or to that of the displaced subject. Nietzsche, Marx, and Freud "illuminate" the tangled web of knowledge (discourses of rationality), desire (sexuality and the unconscious), and power (ideology and the relations of [re]production) in which the postmodern subject must find its (dis)place(ment).

This charting of postmodernism's debt to its "other" fathers serves to reinforce the point that the fall of reason is in infinite regress. It might therefore be best to remember with Andreas Huyssen that "modernism as that from which postmodernism is breaking away remains inscribed into the very word with which we describe our distance from modernism" (Huyssen 1984, 10), or with Derrida that "breaks are always, and fatally, reinscribed in an old cloth that must continually, interminably, be undone" (quoted in Fraser 1984, 131).

But what is the "modernity" at stake in the conflict of interpretations to which the "meaning" of postmodernism has been subject? In her essay "Epistemologies of Postmodernism: A Rejoinder to Jean-François Lyotard," Seyla Benhabib defines modern philosophy as "caught in the prison-house of its own consciousness" (Benhabib 1984, 107)—both empiricism and rationalism rely on a notion of representation as adequation and on a dualism between appearance and essence, mind and body, idea/word and thing. This dualism is a function of the mastery of the concept that imposes identity on heterogeneous matter.

Postmodernism's antirepresentational stance is an attempt to refuse the appeal to the subject as the source of meaning. In the process, however, postmodernism jettisons the value of reflection as the source of "emancipation from self-incurred bondage" (Benhabib 1984, 109) as well as the means to distinguish between consensus and conquest, truth and deception, because the oppositions are themselves caught in a play of differences (Benhabib 1984, 115). Benhabib accepts postmodernism's break with the episteme of modernity, but rejects what she perceives to be the unpalatable consequences of that break.

Foucault's reading of the postmodern dilemma in "What Is Enlightenment?" articulates a similar approach. The Enlightenment has bestowed "the outline of what one might call the attitude of modernity" (Foucault 1984b, 38). This "attitude . . . marks a relation of belonging and presents itself as a task" (39). Postmodernism must continually address the problem of the Enlightenment because this problem has determined the postmodern mode of knowing and being. The critique of modernity inheres in the very ethos of modernity.

Foucault is uninterested in whether one is for or against the Enlightenment. If the Enlightenment has made the Western world what it is, the prophets of postmodernity must exploit this historical contingency to envisage the "possibility of no longer being" what it is (Foucault 1984b, 46). In other words, that "we are always in the position of beginning again" (47) does not put us at the mercy of the in-difference of the play of language. Instead, questions of truth become implicated in questions of justice when the limits of critique take "the form of a possible transgression" (45).

This summary of the complex course of postmodernism serves as a prelude to my focus on its attempt to put the self at stake in order that the latter's "other" might speak. It should be clear that postmodernism marks the limits of modernism and is itself the other hitherto suppressed by the brutal trajectory of reason in the service of power. Postmodernism, then, is repetition not only with a difference, but with a vengeance.[3] I shall turn now to discourses of subjectivity that (dis)articulate the self to determine their usefulness for a strategy of negation.

Whether the discourse of postmodernity envisages its patrimony as an unfinished task that must be undertaken in the "spirit" of the Enlightenment, or as a weed that must not only be uprooted but beheaded as well, no one on either side of the issue seems willing or able to shake off the burden of a style or an attitude that is quintessentially "modern." Descartes's "crowning" achievement, after all, is the posture of doubt that grounds the certainty of reason. Foucault, who has perhaps done more than anyone else to trace the "archaeology" of modern (Western) "man's" "being," remarks that the Enlightenment produced "man" as

> a finitude without infinity [that] no doubt [is] a finitude that has never finished, that is always in recession with relation to itself, that always has something still to think at the very moment when it thinks, that always has time to think again what it has thought. (Foucault 1973b, 372)

In this "analytic" (Foucault's term), "man appears as a truth both reduced and promised" (Foucault 1973b, 320) because the contents of his knowledge and the products of his labor appear as both alien and determining (Marx and Hegel would no doubt concur) and yet he is their source. This strange "empirico-transcendental doublet" (Foucault 1973b, 322) is a creature who is perhaps no more "than a kind of rift in the order of things" (xxiii), but who must nevertheless trust his fallible reason to determine the conditions of (his) being. The discourse of postmodernity explores this inescapable dilemma, not only in order to explain how "man" came into being, but also, in the course of undermining his authority as the transcendental ground of knowledge, to translate the reduction of being as the promise of difference.

The "death of the subject" has, of course, been both announced and denounced with appropriate zeal. I undertake this journey through familiar landscapes, and negotiate, once more, treacherous ground, in the hope that an-other story waits to be told. Like Lily Tomlin's character Trudy, who finds reality acceptable in small doses but much too confining as a lifestyle, I hope to transform the experience of displacement, as she does, from the sign of a "breakdown" to the evidence and imminence of a "breakthrough."

The notion of the subject has come to replace that of the individual because critical discourse has become increasingly aware of "the necessity of understanding consciousness as something produced rather than as the source of ideas and the social world—as constituted and not constitutive" (Henriques et al. 1984, 7–8). This necessity is itself a consequence of a "global" attempt to understand the workings of ideology and of the machinery of power without falling into the familiar dualism of self and world.

If either self or world constitutes the "privileged beginning" of analysis (Henriques et al. 1984, 9), one is in danger of casting the individual in the role of the rational author of his or her destiny, while simultaneously treating social processes as the workings of immutable necessity. Such an analysis leaves no room for an understanding of the complex interactions between self and world and does not explain the often contradictory and constraining nature of those interactions. The aim, then, of contemporary critical analysis has been to treat "interior and exterior as problematic [indeed fluid] categories" (Henriques et al. 1984, 9), and to suggest an approach that both situates the subject and determines the conditions of its possibility (see Mowitt's foreword in Smith 1988, xi).

Louis Althusser's essay "Ideology and Ideological State Apparatuses (Notes towards an Investigation)" has been crucial in the formulation of a method sensitive to the (de)formative powers of ideology. Althusser argues that capitalism maintains itself as a mode of production not only through the reproduction of labor power but also through the reproduction of the mechanisms that ensure that labor power's submission to the established mode of production. This reproduction affects both the agents and the victims of exploitation, so that capitalism becomes a self-fulfilling prophecy.

Althusser offers a more complicated reading of the relation between base and superstructure within orthodox Marxism. Ideology is not merely a camera obscura of the real relations of existence that socialism will one day transform into a camera lucida of relations free of ideology; instead, "the peculiarity of ideology is that it is endowed with a structure and a functioning such as to make it a non–historical reality" (Althusser 1971, 161). Althusser breaks with the traditional Marxist notion that ideology is a function of a specific mode of production. His notion of ideology is not ahistorical but transhistorical, and it recognizes that "revolution" might leave the apparatus of power unchanged.

By contending that, even if one acknowledges that the economic base is determinant in the last instance, one must account for the relative independence of the superstructure as well as for its reciprocity with the base, Althusser avoids the familiar pitfalls of "vulgar" Marxism. His insistence on theorizing the relation between base and superstructure rather than assuming an unexamined correspondence between them forms the basis of his refashioning of "false consciousness." If ideology is not simply a passive reflection of the real relations of existence (albeit in an inverted form), it is not mere illusion either. Its existence is material because it is embodied in the apparatuses of state, church, and family. Capitalism reproduces itself through the interplay of repression and ideology, a policing, so to speak, from within and without.

Althusser introduces the category of the subject as the instance of the functioning of ideology. If ideology is the imaginary relation of individuals to the real relations in which they live, they must nevertheless recognize themselves in that representation. This commonsensical notion of reality, that the real is the obvious, makes the individual the source of "his" representations (I will return to the en-gendering of interpellation). However, the individual identifies his experience with its representation in ideological apparatuses, suggesting thereby that his recognition is also a *méconnaissance*, and that it becomes constitutive of what he believed to be his "own" experience.

Althusser owes this structure of ideology in which the individual is rewritten as the "specifically subjected *object* of social and historical forces and determinations" (Smith 1988, xxvii; emphasis in original) to Jacques Lacan's notion of the imaginary. As Paul Smith argues, Althusser misreads Lacan in order to ensure that interpellation always produces a compliant subject.[4] Although Althusser is right to see ideology as constitutive of reality rather than the latter's distortion, he fails to take note of Lacan's cautionary emphasis on the subject as merely the place of the operations of the symbolic and imaginary orders, as the process and product of their division rather than the unified effect of ideology (Smith 1988, 14ff.). Interpellation, then, is less the arbitrary imposition of ideology and more the "locus of negativity and conflict" (Mowitt in Smith 1988, xv). To put it bluntly, ideology produces both repression and resistance.

Althusser cannot account for such negativity because the individual, in his scheme of things, recognizes himself only through the imaginary relation in which the ideological apparatuses ritually "hail" him. But "what is the nature of the entity that must already exist . . . in order to recognize her/himself in the interpellation?" (Henriques et al. 1984, 97). It appears then that Althusser has not transcended the confines of the dualism I described earlier—he cannot discard a rudimentary notion of an entity that preexists its determinations.

If Althusser's attempt to complicate the function of ideology has been salutary, his notion of the real remains contradictory. As Andrew Parker has shown, Althusser seems trapped between a desire to accord the economic base a delegatory function and an awareness that the system comes into existence all at once and the relation between base and superstructure should be thought along the lines of reciprocity rather than of structural causality. What happens, however, is that "the category of subjectivity is . . . displaced . . . onto an economy *personified* by" its representatives, because delegation implies a subject who initiates representation (Parker 1985, 60; emphasis in original).

Further, Althusser's antihumanist stance, his interest in processes without subjects, makes it impossible for him to theorize agency except as "the outline [of] a discourse which tries to break with ideology, in order to dare to be the beginning of a scientific (i.e., subjectless) discourse on ideology" (Althusser 1969, 173). This advocacy of "science" continues to beg the question of the agent of this "break with ideology." The problem, then, is to develop a notion of power that does not transform ideology into a monolith that the subject swallows whole (the whale in the belly of Jonah that pitches Jonah into the belly of the whale) and a notion of ideological representation that breaks with tropes of resemblance, correspondence, adequation, or delegation in favor of the materiality of discursive practice.

What is at stake is a different exploration of Althusser's own "seminal" perception that "the order of knowledge does not recapitulate the order of reality" (Lewis 1985, 37). Wherein does this noncorrespondence lie? How might this disjunction serve the interests of critical negation? If discourses can be said to produce rather than to describe objects, is one in danger of transforming the "brute fact" of oppression into the mere conflict of interpretations? In short, is there life after ideology?

The juridical model of power in Althusser's essay needs to be complicated by one that allows for specific and contextual determinations of the efficacy of power and that, *pace* Foucault, creates sites of contestation rather than only those of imposition. Even Althusser's useful concept of overdetermination paradoxically serves to confirm the impenetrability of ideological apparatuses rather than to produce the disordering of asymmetrical power relations. Because Foucault shifts the emphasis from the materiality of (discursive) conditions and practices to the materiality of their effects, he produces an attractive notion of power relations as a series of transformable matrices or, at the very least, a notion more credible than Althusser's, which assumes rather than explains the omnipotence of ideological state apparatuses.

The importance of Foucault's corrective notwithstanding, the relation of subjectivity to the drama of power remains curiously vague, because Foucault's interest in the productive rather than only prohibitive dimension of power makes it difficult to determine who regulates whom or how (in

Althusser's terms) the differential interpellation of the sexes would refigure the nature and mode of power *and* resistance. In other words, the arbitrary, alienating, and inaccessible model of power in Althusser lapses too readily into what Judith Butler has described as "the religious idealization of 'failure'" before the Law (Butler 1990, 56), whereas the protean configurations of Foucault's version of power make resistance indistinguishable from complicity.

This fuzziness is a consequence of Foucault's complementary model of power and resistance. If power and resistance produce each other or are effects of each other, the critique of power can occur only within the discursive parameters that power makes possible. This is an odd claim for Foucault to make, given his investment in the diagnosis of and challenge to the disciplinary gaze of power. Foucault, therefore, makes the act of negation either impossible or deluded. Even if one wishes to avoid static contradictions or reversals of power, is there not room for a model of negation that would challenge the very terms of the opposition between power and resistance and that, by the same token, would function in contra-diction to the machinations of power?

The gendered dimensions of Foucault's analysis have not, of course, escaped the notice of feminist scholars. My interest here is to suggest that the circulation of power and pleasure that Foucault describes has different and dangerous consequences for women who know, only too well and to their cost, the dangers of seduction. I do not wish to privilege a heterosexual model here given, among other things, Foucault's own different sympathies. Nevertheless, Foucault treads dangerously close to the pleasures of complicity and he certainly wields the metaphor of seduction at will. As for Althusser's own obliviousness to gender, the problem lies in his failure to acknowledge that the transformation of (masculine) subjects into objects of historical and social determination precludes the possibility of feminine subjects who exist at a further remove; that is, the mark of gender transforms women into objects of objects—masculine subjectivity is often bought at the price of feminine objectification.

It has been the task of feminism to take its cue from the strengths of these interrogations to present a view from elsewhere (to use Teresa de Lauretis's phrase). Theories of subjectivity, in short, must account for "woman" as the docile and (re)productive *object* par excellence of the web of desire/power/knowledge. The "sudden intrusion, the unanticipated agency, of a female 'object' who inexplicably returns the glance, reverses the gaze, and contests the place and authority of the masculine position" (Butler 1990, ix) does not duplicate the (masculine) attempt to predicate identity upon anatomy; instead, what is at stake is precisely the discourse of identity that produces "woman" as uninscribed body and that oppresses women in their bodies. If both sex and gender are viewed as "regulatory fictions" (Butler 1990, 32), identity becomes a "kind of persistent impersonation" (Butler 1990, x) "open to intervention and resignification" (32).

One version of the subject in process, of "woman" as the sign of becoming rather than the guarantor of being, has been the writing associated with feminist reappropriations of Lacanian psychoanalysis. Lacan's stress on the "division and precariousness of human subjectivity" (Rose 1982, 29) has seemed potentially liberating for women uncertain of the value of essentialism, strategic or otherwise, and unwilling to cast opposition to penis envy in the terms of womb envy. If, as Lacan argues, sexual identity operates as a law, women seek to disobey the law that renders being as the struggle between the haves and the have-nots (the nice conjunction of the phallus and the commodity as fetish should not go unnoticed). The phallus, as Lacan was aware, is a fraud, the signifier to which the value of the transcendental signified accrues (Rose 1982, 43).

The construction of femininity is predicated on this fraud, and the job of feminists has been, in the course of "the description of feminine sexuality," to conduct "an exposure of the terms of its definition" (Rose 1982, 44). This job practices negation in the interests of women; that is, it challenges the phallic economy that produces woman as the negative term in the definition of what constitutes the human and that forbids her desire to negate the terms of her definition. The strategy of exposure and critical negation has been accompanied by the quest for a female libidinal economy and the simultaneous affirmation of a mode of being that disdains any form of containment.

The joyous, celebratory mode of *écriture feminine* suggests that dissimulation is the very mark of the feminine and, like the strategic and adventurous movement of *différance*, cannot be forced to *mean* anything in relation to a specific political and historical juncture. The affirmation here would be more appealing if it were tied either to the critical negativity of feminine resistance to a phallic economy, or to the assertion of autonomy. Instead, Hélène Cixous, for example, offers the consolation of "innocence," of a relation to the body that is autoerotic but not necessarily conducive to a homosexual libidinal economy. The volatile "jargon" is often unnecessarily cute. To "BLOW UP words," or to prefer "DADA to data" (Marks 1984, 110; capitals in original), is all very well; unfortunately, it sounds increasingly apologetic, like a cover for a discursive femininity in which no more than words are at risk. As Cixous says, "the political is something cruel and hard and so rigorously real, that sometimes I feel like consoling myself by crying and shedding poetic tears" (Cixous 1984, 58).

Cixous's strategy bears an uncanny resemblance to Derrida's own claims for a graphics of the hymen, for an expenditure without reserve (*dépense* is Cixous's word), and for a logic of supplementarity beyond the binary opposition that encodes sexual difference. He describes his project as a relationship to the other that "would not be a-sexual, far from it, but would be sexual otherwise" (Derrida 1972a, 66). Both *Dissemination* and *Spurs* rewrite femininity as radically undecidable—indeed, as the name for what rails against identity and propriety. Yet, as many of Derrida's female readers point out, the very sincerity with which he flaunts his transition from "the cavalier in spurs to the dreamer of multiplicities" (Conley 1984b, 75) might give one reason to doubt him. Derrida's interest in "a rebellious force of affirmation" (Derrida 1984, 83) that resists the reduction of the "'anatomical' thing in question . . . to its most summary phenomenality" (89) might not be sufficient proof that the masculine subject who affirms the feminine has escaped the "discriminating . . . code of sexual marks" (Derrida 1972a, 66).

The sexual politics as well as the rhetorical violence (or "scission," in Derrida's terms) of Derrida's disseminative textual (and bodily) surgery are worth noting because the displacement of the sexual and historical specificity of the feminine body transforms "woman" into the figure of the malaise of phallogocentricism and precludes discussion of either her oppression within or her resistance to that system. Teresa de Lauretis's fine essay, "The Technology of Gender," seeks a subject of feminism who is no longer confined to the terms of patriarchy, which keep her chattering about her difference *from* man, or, worse, condemn her, as the "mere" effect of signification, to be the instance of difference *in* man (de Lauretis 1987, 1).

The aim of de Lauretis, instead, is to make it possible to talk about differences among women and even within women. The straitjacket of identity does not draw attention to what, in women as in the real, escapes categories of representation. This is not to suggest that women occupy the dimension of the unknowable with which the likes of Lacan identify the "real"; rather, it demands that difference be articulated as "the tension of contradiction, multiplicity, and heteronomy" (de Lauretis 1987, 26).

With characteristic caution, de Lauretis gestures to "the space not visible in the frame but inferable from what the frame makes visible" (26) from which, presumably, the new subject of feminism will voice her dissidence. De Lauretis's call to create spaces in "the chinks and cracks of the power-knowledge apparati" (25) curiously reproduces the very deconstructive strategy of subversion, of excess and rupture, that her essay so effectively dismisses.

I want to suggest the possibility of a strategy that does not acquiesce to being beyond the pale of masculine and cultural intelligibility (see also Benhabib 1984). If I might recall my Introduction, respect for the integrity of limits might preclude the active desire to "expand [not merely exceed] the boundaries of what is, in fact, culturally intelligible" (Butler 1990, 29). Or, as Sherry B. Ortner says laconically in response to the question whether one can ever really know the other, "try" (Ortner 1984, 143).

I have been concerned thus far with phallogocentrism's other insofar as she is sexually determined. I must turn now to discourses of ethnicity that seek to understand otherness specifically as the product of the colonial situation in which racial difference was equally determining. This other is the object of the discourse of Empire as well as the means to the colonizer's self-definition.

The process and product of the representation of the colonized reflect the "primary Manicheism [*sic*]" (Fanon 1968, 50) that governs the colonial situation in which white and black function as the metaphysical opposition between good and evil. The relationship between colonizer and colonized develops in a representational economy in which blackness is produced not only as the negative term of the dialectic between self and other, but as negation itself. The presence of the colonized is simply effaced—they are people caught in "historylessness" (Hegel's word) just as their land is uninscribed territory on which imperialists build their home away from home.

This is a familiar scenario in which epistemic violence reflects the march of Empire—the actual extermination of the brutes has its complement in a paranoiac mode of representation that constitutes the other as the descent into chaos, the horror of absence, and the terror of silence. The postmodern delight in the simulacrum has a certain irony in this context. For the colonized, who have never experienced the luxury of being, figurality denotes not the play of the signifier but the trap of a specular economy that confirms, precisely, their "inessentiality" (Fanon 1968, 36).

The writings of Fanon, Albert Memmi, and Wole Soyinka, to name but a few, can be seen as sustained attempts to decolonize the "native," as well as to demystify the rhetoric of humanism. Fanon calls on Algeria to "leave this Europe where they are never done talking of Man, yet murder men everywhere they find them" (Fanon 1968, 311). The task of decolonization is also one of self-representation, a way out of the peculiar dilemma in which "not only must the black man be black; he must be black in relation to the white man" (Fanon 1967a, 110). In a deceptively simple formulation, Fanon indicates that "alterity for the black man is not the black but the white man" (Fanon 1967a, 97), setting the tone for a modality of exchange in which the "native" both returns the glance of the colonizer and contests the process of splitting in which she or he "can only conceptualize [herself or himself] when . . . mirrored back to [herself or himself] from the position of another's desire" (Juliet Mitchell 1982, 5).

Fanon's texts are a remarkable testimony to the material consequences of the production of discursive effects. He is all too aware that the "negro" in the colonial situation is a creation of the white man. The interest of Fanon's reading of the affective dimension of colonial power resides in his searing conclusion that self-representation is not merely a matter of hatching oneself out of alien discursive containment. The struggle against the ideological valency of white fictions must nevertheless acknowledge that they constitute the reality of the "negro" just as much as they obscure it. The black man's body, therefore, is decipherable; it is, to use Francis Barker's words, "the site of an operation of power, of an exercise of meaning" (Barker 1984, 13). Fanon stages a colonial history of the body in which the "negro" body serves "as the locus of the desire, the revenge, the power and the misery of [the white man's] world" (Barker 1984, 22). Because the "negro's" subjection is epidermally determined, Fanon deploys the visibility of this body to startling effect.

Over and over again in *Black Skin, White Masks,* Fanon represents his body trapped in the gaze of the (white) other, arrested by the word "Look!" and unable to resist the fear and desire that animate that gaze. The very gesture that immures his body in darkness paradoxically dismembers it. Fanon describes the effect of the gesture that both identifies and accuses him and induces him to brand himself guilty because black, black because guilty: "What else could it be for me but an amputation, an excision, a hemorrhage that spattered my whole body with black blood?" (112).

Homi Bhabha identifies fetishism as the distinguishing feature of colonial discourse because it is the classic mode in which difference is simultaneously recognized and disavowed. Bhabha describes these scenes of misrecognition as "primal" because the child who is frightened by the "negro" turns to her mother to confirm her sense that reality is white and whole (Bhabha 1983a, 202). "Primal" seems to me a difficult term because the cultural encoding of the scene is precisely the point.

Fanon of course defends the discourse of psychoanalysis, but always in a troubled, even contradictory fashion. He occasionally expresses satisfaction that none of his patients suffers from the Oedipus complex, a remark intended, I think, to suggest that the acquaintance with the colonizer's fantasy brings him no closer to an understanding of the colonized. Bhabha reads the fetish of the stereotyped other as revealing "something of the 'fantasy' (as desire, defense) of that position of mastery" (Bhabha 1983a, 208)—exactly! The fantasy is theirs, not ours.

Bhabha's analysis, in Derridean fashion, seeks to discover the weakness at the source, the division at the heart of being, the fantasy that vitiates mastery. Fanon traces the effect of that fantasy on the self-conception of the colonized. That the colonizer desires what he fears and abuses is no consolation for the sufferings of the colonized body or for the self-hatred that fear induces. Fanon's strategy, therefore, is not one of subversion or of parodic glee in beating the colonizer at his own game. His intelligent analysis of the process of subjection is also a species of mourning for the body *his* imaginary cannot restore.

The rhetoric of violence that informs the dialectic of self-affirmation in Fanon's writings has unsavory consequences, particularly when one considers the place of the white woman's body in Fanon's narrative of black neurosis. Although Fanon remains sensitive to the circulation of power and pleasure in the attempt to subjugate black corporeality, he fails to examine the implications of the black man's desire for whiteness, which centers on the body of the white woman. In this case, the fetishization of her body becomes the means by which the "negro" disavows his masters in the instant of possessing their "property."

In this drama of usurpation, Fanon seems unaware that his explaining away of the neurosis of the "negro" colludes in the brutalization of the white woman. In *Black Skin, White Masks,* Fanon piles assumption upon assumption about the psychosexuality of the white woman, openly claiming that her fear of rape itself cries out for rape (156) and, more tortuously, that "when a woman lives the fantasy of rape by a Negro, it . . . accomplish[es] the phenomenon of turning against self, it is the woman who rapes herself" (179). Fanon seems incapable of imagining desire for a white woman that is not a substitute for power over white masters, an incapacity revealing, in it-self, of the damage colonization has inflicted. Because his choices seem lim-ited to "big blondes" and "stupid little stenographers," he might perhaps be forgiven.

In a different context, Kimberly W. Benston reads Eldridge Cleaver's penchant for turning white women into scapegoats as "negative affirmation" (Benston 1990, 157). In a bizarre comparison (the difference between con-sensual sex, albeit in adultery, and rape seems to escape Benston) with Hester Prynne's attempt in Hawthorne's *Scarlet Letter* to endow stigma with author-ity, Benston argues that Cleaver purifies that stigma's destructive force. Nei-ther Benston nor Cleaver considers the implications of self-assertion bought at such a price. After all, they see things clearly enough when men are in-volved.

As for "the woman of color," Fanon says, baldly, "I know nothing about her" (Fanon 1967a, 179). This (disingenuous) silence is broken briefly in *Black Skin, White Masks* and at length in *Studies in a Dying Colonialism*. In *Black Skin, White Masks,* Fanon discusses the case of an Algerian whose wife has been raped by the colonizers and who now suffers from impotence. Fanon probably never met the wife, but it is curious that his attention re-mains focused on the consequences for the man and his sense of self. In *Studies in a Dying Colonialism,* Fanon undertakes a sharp analysis of the cul-tural sclerosis consequent upon decolonization, a process located in the body of the woman of color.

Here, too, a clever shift occurs. Fanon speaks of the way in which cul-tural mores become rigid in the face of the colonizer's threat to free the Al-gerian woman from the veil. The pleasure the colonizer experiences in be-holding at last what had been hidden from his omniscience is itself "veiled" in the guise of modernization. However, Fanon believes that the position of women would have remained an inert issue if it had not been exacerbated by the violence of the colonizer.

His approbation for the Algerian woman's difficult path to "freedom" is conditioned by its alignment with the interests of nationalism. Fanon resigns himself to the inevitability of the change in the status of women whose bod-ies are "unveiled." The agency of women continues to be obscured because they affirm their identity through the sacrifice of their bodies to the national cause. Through all this, one never hears the voice of the Algerian woman. Her emergence on the stage of history is turned into a defense of the Alge-rian man's refusal to "see" her. Therefore, she becomes a historical agent despite herself. Both empire and nation are forged at the expense of women's bodies, black and white.

Fanon nevertheless leaves us with salutary lessons: his refusal to cast his choices in the stark terms of Manichaeism, his repudiation of negritude, his emphasis on nationalism as the dynamism of a culture in the process of reinventing itself, and his precise attention to the materiality of colonial oppression and to the speculary structure of colonial ideology. Most important, Fanon rejects Jean-Paul Sartre's faith in historical necessity, in the "torch that was already there, waiting for that turn of history" (Fanon 1967a, 134). Instead, he calls on his "bad nigger's misery, bad nigger's teeth, bad nigger's hunger [to] shape a torch with which to burn down the world" (134). The dialectic, in his view, conforms not to the inexorable course of history but to the active resistance of its victims.

In praying to his *body* to "make of [him] always a man who questions" (Fanon 1967a, 232), Fanon suggests the dimensions of an otherness that relates the discursive to the material, and the somatic to the psychic and the cognitive. In the dialectical noncoincidence between the object of knowledge and the discursive "spirals" (Foucault's word) of power and pleasure might lie the scope of uncompromising critique as well as the lineaments of the object's resistance, self-representation, and desire.

2 / Rethinking the Object

The demise of the Cartesian subject seems at first to elicit the potential of its object, its self-effacement a necessary prelude to the emergence of a visible and voluble object. Within the discursive domain of postmodernism, which identifies and exacerbates the displacement of the subject, a problem immediately presents itself. The very process that exposes the illusory mastery of the subject forecloses upon the resistance of the object. If the subject is always already discontinuous with itself and its identity only a necessary illusion, is the power exerted in the name of that fiction of identity and mastery equally illusory? If the subject was never whole and undivided, was the object never powerless, traduced, and excluded? Whom shall the object hold accountable for its suffering?

The displacement of the subject can all too easily become a convenient ploy to withhold subjectivity from those for whom it has never been anything but an illusion. The critique of essence, identity, and authenticity does not account for the experience of being bereft of all three; indeed, such critique appropriates that experience and transforms it into a moment of self-discovery rather than a recognition of otherness. Critical attention remains focused on reconstituting the self, on coming to terms with its timely demise, rather than on making room for other voices clamoring, precisely, for self-recognition. The powerlessness of the subject, as its power did once, leaves the object out in the cold. One might very well ask how a potentially radical discourse took a conservative turn or, in current terminology, how subversion became recontainment.

The object in question is the feminine and ethnic other of the discourse of Western patriarchy and Empire. The postmodern subject, in representing itself as constituted rather than constitutive, has enabled the analysis of systemic relations that govern the constitution of subjects and that determine the possibilities for self-representation. This sensitivity to economies of power, desire, and knowledge that traverse and engender subjects has given postmodernism its undeniable edge. Nevertheless, precisely the political import of its strategy of displacement must be rethought when the critical gaze shifts to the other, who is no longer content that the erstwhile subject has walked off the job (Raulet 1984, 155) or abdicated its throne.

The problem remains that the feminine and ethnic other of the masterful Cartesian cogito, excluded as it were from its self-fashioning, reappears in the self-deprecatory postmodern ego as the difference *within*. Teresa de Lauretis describes one aspect of this problem, that is, the effort of contemporary French philosophers to deny the sexual specificity of real women in favor of "a radically 'other' subject, de-centered and de-sexualized" (de Lauretis 1987, 24). In this strategic ploy, Derrida, for example, identifies the "feminine" with the structure and movement of *différance* itself, which opposes meaning, sexual identity, and truth. This movement is precisely "objectless and non-referential" (McGraw 1984, 144): Derrida's delineation of the process of *devenir-femme* has "little to do with woman" (144). Derrida's deconstruction of "woman" is effected in the interests of a reconstruction of "man." My interest aims to do the opposite, to posit the feminine as an inhabitant of different cultural and material locations who reverses the limits of masculine and ethnocentric knowledge in her behalf rather than his. "Woman," in short, ceases to be the agent of, occasion for, or catalyst to masculine self-knowledge. Her project is, precisely, incommensurable with his.

A related aspect of the problem de Lauretis describes involves the critique of ethnocentrism implicit in Derrida's rereading of "white mythologies." Derrida's well-known articulation of the limits of logocentrism depends on a theory of the predestined frustration of the desire for presence. This constitutive lack needs a symbol, a marker of the limits of logocentric desire—a need, as Homi Bhabha argues, that cultural otherness fulfills (Bhabha 1983a, 194–97).

Derrida's appropriation of otherness here is of a piece with his appropriation of the feminine. In both cases, otherness functions as "the discovery of

[Western and masculine] assumptions" (Bhabha 1983a, 197) rather than the investigation of the history and materiality of other cultures (196). What might this other mode of representation be, in which the colonized function as more than the West's "limit-text, the Anti-West" (195), or in which the feminine subject's "critical negativity" does not preclude the "affirmative positivity of [feminism's] politics" (de Lauretis 1987, 26)?

To my mind, both Bhabha and McGraw offer unsatisfactory solutions to the problem they present so lucidly, solutions that entail a replication of the deconstructive strategies they reject so strenuously (de Lauretis shares this tendency). Both the "supplementary strategy" Bhabha defends and the structure of seduction McGraw offers suffer from the continued insistence on otherness as that which insinuates itself *within* the boundaries of hegemonic discourse, its deviation from the dominant economy of the same defined in terms of dominant categories.

McGraw suggests that in what she calls "seductive writing"

> the feminine is *not* outside the masculine, nor is it its canny opposite. It is, instead, *inside* the masculine, its *uncanny* difference from itself. The feminine inhabits the masculine as its otherness, as its own disruption. It is pure difference and can only be defined by the way in which it *differentially* relates to other differences. (McGraw 1984, 151; emphasis in original)

Surely this is Derrida's point, that the feminine constitutes the very structure and movement of *différance!* The difference between this strategy of seduction, and the simultaneous production and appropriation of otherness Foucault describes, also escapes me. This desire to render the terms of the opposition reversible or to posit a subject who is continuously coming undone also characterizes Bhabha's formulations, which privilege a strategy of displacement at the expense of a search for alternatives.

In a recent essay, Bhabha repudiates the dialectical power of negation in favor of what he calls a "supplementary strategy," designed to "disturb the calculation" in the process of suggesting that "adding 'to' need not 'add up'" (Bhabha 1990, 305). Bhabha draws here on the Derridean notion of the supplement as that which exceeds the structure of signification even as it marks the lack that compromises all claims to completeness. Instead of a different logic of articulating otherness in pursuit of which Bhabha claims to be writing, his essay endorses a disappointing "ambivalence" (319) that reveals "the instability of any division of meaning into an inside and outside" (314). Bhabha is correct in pointing out that incommensurability structures all narratives of identification (319); however, the task of minority discourses cannot be confined to taunting dominant discourses with their failure to achieve their objectives.

The recognition of incommensurability has not prevented the proliferation of Procrustean beds in which bodies are simultaneously identified and othered. Bhabha writes this incommensurability as the "native's" active withholding (306), but such a withholding seems to me impossible without a concept of dialectical negation. The reasons for this claim will soon become clear; suffice it for the moment to say that the continuous exposure of the lack that helps to constitute identity brings one no closer to modes of representation that reconstitute the relationship between self and other rather than confining themselves to the limits of the self or the mystery of the other.

Bhabha's rejection of the attempt to confront hegemonic discourses "with a contradictory or negating referent," or to "turn contradiction into a dialectical process" (306), has, of course, ample precedent. The appropriative strategies of deconstruction have their counterparts in Jean-Paul Sartre's reading of negritude "as the minor term of a dialectical progression" (as quoted in Fanon 1967a, 133) toward the raceless society. Sartre argues that negritude as an antithetical value is necessary but not sufficient and, as such, "is the root of its own destruction . . . a transition and not a conclusion, a means and not an ultimate end" (133). Fanon counters Sartre's claim with the ironic statement that white intellectuals could come up with no better response to black self-affirmation "than to point out the relativity of what they [the blacks] were doing" (133). Sartre retains the privilege of relating negritude to the "universal" value of racelessness, of completing the process of dialectical negation.

Fanon rejects Sartre's argument on two scores: it intellectualizes the experience of being black (134) and fails to acknowledge that black consciousness is "not a potentiality of something" (135) but wholly what it is. Fanon's position is itself in danger of countering one pernicious Manichaeism with another (to use Soyinka's phrase); nevertheless, as he says, one must not be too hasty in transcending the historical moment of negation or in rejecting the identity that is its product.

The black consciousness that emerges from the moment of negation has value precisely because the white man is not only the other but also the master (Fanon 1967a, 138n), because the meaning of negation is forged in the specific situation of decolonization and fashioned out of material suffering. The voice of the black man, therefore, is "torn through and through"

(Fanon 1967b, 49). In this powerful image, Fanon undermines his own lean-
ings toward identity; he insists, instead, on a complex voicing of self that reveals the negation at the center of identity. Identity in the colonial situation
is in fact the *refusal* of Man rather than his apotheosis.

Sartre's faith in the dialectic bears a curious affinity to deconstruction's
insistence on the constitutive lack imbricated in discourses of presence. In his
introduction to Albert Memmi's *The Colonizer and the Colonized,* Sartre endorses Memmi's contribution to the "infamous death-struggle of colonialism" (Memmi 1965, xxix). Sartre's awareness that "relentless reciprocity
binds the colonizer to the colonized," however, leads him to the problematic
conclusion that the colonialist apparatus "will manufacture its own destruction of itself" (xxviii).

Sartre is not unaware of the dangers in manipulating the revolt of the
oppressed to serve the cause of rejuvenating a decadent Western society or
of making his country live up to its own vaunted humanism (see, for example, his introduction to Fanon's *Wretched of the Earth*). Nevertheless, his
faith in historical necessity makes him shift the emphasis from the struggle of
the colonized to the rigidity of the colonialist apparatus at its inception that
will wreak havoc at its end. The colonized bear the secret of the death of colonialism; they are its nemesis, just as otherness functions as savior in current
deconstructive rhetoric. The colonized function as the occasion for the self-
realization of the colonizer—the latter's "product and his fate" (Sartre in
Memmi 1965, xxviii). Nationalism, within this state of affairs, is merely another name for a colonial apparatus programmed to self-destruct.

Both Sartre's version of the dialectic and the strategy of reversal and displacement characteristic of deconstruction are in danger of emptying negation of its political content. Sartre grants the resistance of the colonized
merely antithetical status in the movement of the dialectic toward a society
without races; deconstruction turns otherness into the secret at the heart of
identity rather than the latter's determinate (and therefore deeply political)
negation. Moreover, Derrida's plea for a discourse in which sexual codes
would no longer be discriminating bears the unmistakable stamp of Sartre's
vision of a raceless society.

Deconstruction conceives of negativity as a form of rot within history; it
can be read, therefore, as a version of the dialectical faith in necessity. The necessity at issue here is not the inexorable movement of the Hegelian dialectic
toward the identity of subject and object, but that which vitiates all teleologies, that which structures desire. This conjunction is particularly significant

because deconstruction styles itself as the critique of dialectical reason. For his championing of the colonized, Sartre draws, of course, on Marx's vision of the proletariat as the bearer of the secret that will destroy the bourgeoisie; however, as Walter Benjamin was aware, perhaps nothing is so destructive of revolutionary potential as the belief that history is on one's side.

Fanon's faith in a black self that is wholly what it is seems naive in the face of current skepticism regarding the possibility of an unmediated relation to reality. Memmi provocatively includes the period of revolt in the period of colonization precisely because he sees the pitfalls in opposing a black essence to a white one. Moreover, in accepting the definition of (black) self as a form of otherness one might be acquiescing to a symbolic violence that produces one as the negative term in the dialectic between male and female, colonizer and colonized. Fanon's own trenchant analysis of the psyche of the colonized reveals the difficulty of contending with the object without accounting for the fantasy of it that shapes its appearance to the subject. How, then, can one rethink the object without resorting to a prediscursive reality?

Although these difficulties that attend the representation of the object cannot be summarily dismissed, they deny agency to the vanquished of history because they inadvertently accede to the notion of history as a process without subjects or one with only those subjects who can afford the luxury of such a view. More to the point, the poststructuralist critique of authenticity leaves the colonized with the equally unpalatable choices of a reverse ethnocentrism or essentialism, and a resignation to absence and silence within "white mythologies."

Poststructuralist tenets of representation often lapse, despite themselves, into nostalgia for the purity, wholeness, and authenticity of being they resolutely deny or render categorically impossible. My claim for the self-representation of objects rests squarely on their location within and struggle against imperialist discourse and history. The production of an epistemology and a mode of representation that takes account of the object and that desires to redress past betrayal cannot occur without careful attention to the process of overdetermination to which any discursive object is subject. Such sensitivity, however, cannot afford to give in to the temptation to render a defaced and silenced object an absent and silent one. In this regard, the scrupulousness of radical thinkers who trace the progressive disappearance of the object must also be read as violence of a piece with that historical and epistemic violence against which they write.

Given the political context of patriarchy and of Empire, then, signifiers cannot be construed (if they ever could be) as innocent markers of provisional identity. They must be understood as words that "designate that which cannot be classified inside of a signifier except by force and violence and which goes beyond it in any case" (Cixous 1984, 51). Cixous argues that in order to institute "respectful modalities" (56) of exchange between self and other, the "enigmatic kernel of the other . . . must be absolutely preserved" (61). The nature of this "respect" is never developed except as a vague appeal to *jouissance,* a knowledge that cannot do without the experience of the body, a knowledge that asserts that in touching the other one alters the self. I like Cixous's attention to the dynamism of the exchange between self and other, as well as her sensitivity to the violence of identity that is intolerant of mystery. And yet . . .

Cixous's analysis continues to privilege the self; the dynamism of which she speaks seems to produce a mobile, fluid, receptive, and unstable self, but the other remains stubbornly enigmatic and therefore incapable of genuine participation in or resistance to the encounter initiated by the self. Adorno's project produces a crucial counter to this modest self-effacement on the part of writers like Cixous. The respect for enigmas is not merely the occasion for shivers of delight in transgressing (at least in desire) the boundaries of self-enclosed identities; it is the *condition* of the possibility of the different knowledge whose absence she bemoans. The focus shifts from the transgressive desire of the self to the strategic elusiveness of the other. In this sense, the other ceases to be the name for the self's endless becoming; instead, the other dispels the self's reason for being.

To indicate how Adorno's thinking would refashion epistemology as we know it, let me say that Cixous's respect for enigmas does not escape the charge that what "is demonstrated as the exotic charm of another system of thought" collapses into or becomes "the limitation of our own, the stark impossibility of thinking *that*" (Foucault 1973b, xv; emphasis in original). Cixous is right in suggesting that a different mode of cognition is required, but wrong in implying that knowledge itself is incapable of thinking otherwise or, in Foucault's words, that knowledge condemns itself "to never knowing anything but the same thing" (1973b, 30).

Foucault's own concern with the discursive constitution of subjects and objects seems, initially at least, a more promising approach to the status of the object, of the world of things that in some sense remains anterior to discourse and that exceeds its grasp. He asserts, after all, that discourse is a violence done to things. Foucault asks a different set of questions: instead of determining the nature of the object, he proceeds to ascertain the conditions that ascribe it that status, that make it "manifest, nameable, and describable" (Foucault 1972, 41).

Foucault's procedure concentrates on discursive practices "that systematically form the objects of which they speak" (Foucault 1972, 49). Foucault wishes to dispense with things because the order of knowledge or of discourse has, in his view, a "productive rather than reflective character"; that is, "the process of signification itself gives shape to the reality it implicates" (Henriques et al. 1984, 99).

Despite Foucault's emphasis on the materiality of discursive practices, he shares with Derrida the exclusive delineation of the conditions of possibility of the object and therefore of knowledge. In their castigation of the pretensions of reason, Foucault and Derrida succeed in emptying the space of the knowing subject rather than in relocating and reformulating its position. This move is a consequence of their (implicit) acknowledgment of the impossibility of escaping the language of reason in the attempt to comprehend or represent its other.

Equally, they ignore the possibility that the other (in whose name they speak) might have a stake in the apparently relentless course of reason and be moved to "speak." It is precisely this moment of nonknowledge, of the articulation of an unfamiliar language, that radically alters the contours of subjectivity. In other words, neither critic conceives of an-other knowledge that involves not the annihilation of the subject but its reformulation in confrontation with a resistant object. Surely the surrender of identity by the postmodern cogito should entail an explosion of the *categories* of the subject rather than of its substance.[1]

Their sleight of hand has of course reformulated the question of adequation so that it is no longer a matter of knowledge conforming to reality but of implicating reality in a regime of truth. Nevertheless, Foucault's and Derrida's analyses shift attention away from what is to be done and keep it trained on the impossibility of speaking about the object. This impossibility is defended on the grounds that the rules of discourse constrain what can be said. The subject can do no more than redefine the conditions that make the object intelligible. All the subject encounters, in other words, is the genealogy of the object. In this sense, the object can provoke no other response from the subject than one that explains how it came to be an object in the first place, the oppressed "other" of a discourse whose principles of intelligibility cannot help excluding it.

I have no wish to resurrect an object untrammeled by the traces of power/desire/knowledge or to pluck it from the tangle of discursive and material relations within which it finds its place. Foucault and Derrida have been indispensable to the discovery by critical discourse of the hubris that animates the order of knowledge. Because the rules of discourse delimit the sayable, the object cannot be re-presented in its own terms. But does that mean that the object cannot be encountered *on* its own terms (see Fabian 1983)? The genealogical enterprise, in short, is necessary but not sufficient. Its demand for continued vigilance, its assertion that resistance is implicated in its opposite, power, must be heeded. But it is time, once again, to rethink the relation between the order of knowledge and that of the "real."

The "radical intransitivity" of the discourse of poststructuralism seems an inevitable consequence of the contemporary consensus that "the order of knowledge does not recapitulate the order of reality" (Lewis 1985, 37). Certainly no theory of ideology or sensitivity to asymmetrical relations of power between subject and object can afford to ignore this disjunction. And yet the transition from the absence of epistemological guarantees to the impossibility of reference seems both hasty and presumptuous. It is precisely this transition that Thomas Lewis explores, bearing in mind Marx's warning that the question of objective truth isolated from practice can never be more than an empty scholastic question (Lewis 1985, 38).

Under what conditions might the noncorrespondence between metaphor and referent, knowledge and reality, representation and object, serve subversive ends? In order to avoid the pitfalls of poststructuralist contentions that contest the trope of resemblance that determines metaphorical and conceptual adequacy while retaining the analytic theory of reference in order to ground their critique, Lewis deploys the writings of Althusser in a provocative fashion. I shall emphasize two aspects of Lewis's complicated argument as a prelude to my discussion of Adorno as the figure who incorporates the insights of poststructuralism without succumbing to its weaknesses.

According to Lewis, Althusser dispenses with "a metaphysics of the referent" because he shifts the emphasis from resemblance—or, in the case of scientific knowledge, from verification—to the "discursive systematization and effectivity" of knowledge (Lewis 1985, 49). This shift not only subjects knowledge to continuous historical revision but also acknowledges that epistemology or representation does not involve an immediate encounter with a sensuous object.

Instead, the distinction between objects of knowledge and real objects is irreducible: both are tied to specific processes of production. Concepts are in no way identifiable with their objects; they are nonetheless "real" (recall Althusser's notion of ideology as the imaginary relation to the real relations of existence). Because knowledge of empirical existence is not "that empirical existence itself" (Lewis 1985, 48), this very incommensurability ensures that the consumption of knowledge might serve very different ends than its production does. This attention to the failure of ideological productions in the moment of their consumption prepares the ground for the profession of the object's political desire.

In order to make this ground possible, I want to investigate the respective potential in dialectical and differential thinking for theorizing the resistance of the object. The concept of *différance* with which Derrida has become identified represents deconstruction's attempt to part company with classical dialectics. *Différance*, however, remains indebted to the dialectic, at least insofar as it recognizes the "mediated nature of all supposedly proper entities" (Ryan 1982, 67) and endorses the power of negativity. Derrida takes issue with the movement of the dialectic toward an identity that suppresses alterity as well as with Hegel's desire to turn the moment of negation or of contradiction into a stage in the process of self-recognition when consciousness "appropriates the other as itself" (Ryan 1982, 67).

The heterogeneity that constitutes identity (the notion that every entity is only as it differs from and defers something else) is turned, within the confines of the dialectic, into "a system of simple binary oppositions or contradictory negations" (Ryan 1982, 67). The movement of the dialectic is specular, because difference or alterity functions not as the enemy of all claims to identity, property, and propriety, but as that which enables "the return of the other-relation into the self-identity of the entity, concept, or subject" (67).

The identity that emerges at the end of the dialectical process, in other words, is the product of sublation *(Aufhebung)* because the antithetical term is both negated and conserved in the self-presence of the subject or concept. Derrida describes this sublation as an "idealization and reappropriation" because the concept or the subject "comes back to [it]self, recognizes [it]self, reassembles. . . or resembles [it]self, outside [and] in [it]self" (Derrida 1981b, 253).

This rather complicated, if tongue-in-cheek, play on words *performs* or mimes the circular trajectory of the Hegelian Idea, in which the contradiction, negation, or "other-relation" is always "within (or in sight of) reappropriation" (253). Derrida questions the very notion of constitutive or originary concepts that are not themselves effects of a process of substitution and displacement or, in Hegelian terms, "derivative in relation to what they supposedly subordinate and exclude" (Ryan 1982, 67). In short, Derrida questions the power of the concept to consume its own negation (its object) and that of identity to neutralize alterity.

Derrida insists on a *graphics* of *différance* because the sign is "deferred presence" and, as such, "embodies" the structure of *différance,* which also "defers the moment in which we can encounter the thing itself, make it ours, consume or expend it, touch it, see it, intuit its presence" (Derrida 1981b, 9). For this reason *différance* is objectless and nonreferential; it is "a movement of mediation" (9) without origin or telos.

Similarly, the structure and movement of *différance* is subjectless, because "the subject (in its identity with itself, or eventually in its consciousness of its identity with itself, its self-consciousness) is inscribed in [the] language, is a 'function' of [the] language" (Derrida 1981b, 15), which, in turn, constitutes itself as the "systematic play of differences" (11).

Derrida shifts the focus from the relation between subject and object to the order of conceptuality, which produces the relation and which constitutes that relation as opposition. This is doubtless an important move, not least because—like Nietzsche, Marx, and Freud before him—Derrida puts the authority of consciousness in question. However, he becomes inscrutable precisely when the political implications of his attention to the "radical alterity" (Derrida 1981b, 21) that troubles the logic of contradiction cry out to be addressed.

One aspect of the unreadable nature of Derrida's politics may be discerned through a gloss on Derrida's fascinating rhetorical ploys in his delineation of the movement of *différance*. The circularity of Derrida's sentences attests to the way in which *différance* undermines its own possibility. Consider, for instance, the characterization of *différance:* "In the end it is a strategy without finality" (Derrida 1973, 135). This oxymoronic construction corroborates my claim that politics (a reasonable enough interpretation of "strategy," I think) becomes an end in itself in Derrida's terms. The sylleptic character of the word "hazard" is also worth noting. In French, *hasard* suggests at once the positive connotations of "chance" and "luck" (as in *jeux du hasard*) and the negative connotations of "risk" and "danger." The unity of chance and necessity therefore seems less paradoxical in French because the play of chance as risk necessitates strategy, that is, political commitment as a calculated risk in the service of a goal or telos. David B. Allison, the translator of *Speech and Phenomena,* translates "aventureux" (Derrida 1973, 135) as "risky" and as "hazardous," whereas Alan Bass translates it, literally enough, as "adventurous."

My interpretation may be seen as problematic. I think that Allison intuits the turn Derrida's passage takes when the concept of play is introduced as the unity of "hasard" and necessity. The notion of the "endless calculus" in which the unity of chance and necessity finds its expression seems drawn from Democritus, who provides the epigraph for Jacques Monod, *Le Hasard et la nécessité: essai sur la philosophie naturelle de la biologie moderne:* "Tout ce qui existe dans l'univers est le fruit du hasard et de la nécessité" (Everything that exists in the universe is the fruit of chance and necessity). The risk in question also indicates the economic character of *différance* because it suggests an investment without "the perception of gain" (Derrida 1973, 151). The "calculus" is endless because the play of *différance* involves a game in which "one wins and loses each time" (151). This duplicitous character of *différance,* which is, "logically" enough, neither word nor concept, explains why political commitment is hazardous as well as inevitable.

Derrida's attention to, so to speak, the letter of the law of *différance* keeps him confined to the radical intransitivity of the pure medium of fiction he affirms in *Dissemination,* to the act of writing in which language is its own object. Foucault, in his discussion of Mallarmé, describes this process as "a silent, cautious deposition of the word upon the whiteness of a piece of paper, where it can possess neither sound nor interlocutor, where it has nothing to say but itself, nothing to do but shine in the brightness of its being" (Foucault 1973b, 300). Foucault ascribes to Mallarmé the "discovery of the word in its impotent power" (300). The oxymoron is significant in that it identifies what I have been demonstrating—the curious complicity between the postmodern/poststructuralist death of the subject and the abnegation of responsibility for the continued implacability of power. Moreover, against his will and despite his good intentions, Derrida is in danger of ontologizing *différance* when he characterizes it "as the entirely other relationship that apparently interrupts every economy" (Derrida 1981b, 19), and aligns it with the death drive in Freudian discourse.

Derrida wishes to reject the desire that animates the economy of the Hegelian dialectic, that "implies that the deferred presence can always be found again, that we have here only an investment that provisionally and calculatedly delays the perception of its profit or the profit of its perception" (1981b, 20). If, however, this alterity is "exempt from every process of presentation by means of which we would call upon it to show itself in person," and *différance* maintains our relationship with the object as "that which we necessarily misconstrue and which exceeds the alternative of presence and absence" (20), what is to prevent the descent into a kind of metaphysical pathos in which knowledge, representation, and resistance become simultaneously impossible?

The emphasis on a playful affirmation of *différance,* which resists nostalgia for the logic of presence and absence (27), does not account for the *conflict* between self and other. Derrida transforms the logic of contradiction or of opposition into the doubled economy of *différance* "in which whoever loses wins, and in which one loses and wins on every turn" (20). Because the subject and object in question have been dismissed from the indifferent scene of *différance,* Derrida is not obliged to explain who loses and who wins and in what historical circumstances this game of chance and necessity is played. This strategy begins to read very much like equivocation and is perhaps guilty of a sleight of hand by which relations of power are transformed into relations of meaning (see Foucault 1984a, 56). Derrida would of course retort that relations of meaning are always implicated in relations of power; however, acquiescing to the inevitable deferral of its presence leaves the object no alternative but to defer to the subject's assertion of its absence.

Différance establishes itself as the alternative to dialectical negation, as the adventurous strategy that, contrary to the Hegelian economy, which reappropriates the alterity that troubles it, puts that alterity into play. I have already indicated the ways in which the reversal and displacement essential to the practice of *différance* themselves become forms of appropriation of the otherness they elicit; more important, *différance* offers no genuine engagement with the dialectical mode of reason.[2] *Différance* does not serve as a *critique* of the Hegelian dialectic; instead, Derrida posits *différance* as the dialectic's condition of possibility, as that which is necessary to discover "what indicates that each of the terms [of the dialectical opposition] must appear as the *différance* of the other" (Derrida 1981b, 17). How, then, does one think against Hegel without shifting the argument to another level (Derrida's own version of *Aufhebung,* perhaps?) and without dismissing the dialectic as merely a form of orthodoxy? If the choice between dialectics and semiotics is false, in that the one transforms the hazardous and random nature of events into the structure of necessity and the other belies the "lethal character" of conflict (Foucault 1984a, 56–57), how can one render such conflict intelligible? Can one deploy the power of dialectical negation in the *interests* of the alterity, the object, the other, that Hegel seeks to repress in the name of identity, the concept, and the subject?

Despite the hazards of the dialectic, I believe it necessary to reclaim the dialectical method in the very instant that I deny its "matter." Curiously enough, Foucault reveals how. In his tribute to Jean Hyppolite, Foucault speculates on the impossibility of being truly free from the Hegelian system. He wonders whether "our anti-Hegelianism is possibly one of his [Hegel's] tricks directed against us, at the end of which he stands, motionless, waiting for us" (Foucault 1972, 235).[3] Foucault suggests that the answer, for Hyppolite, lay in reconceptualizing the Hegelian system as one in which philosophy dissolved the concept in "the extreme irregularity of experience"; that is, the supple, uncertain, and mobile character of the philosophy Hyppolite envisaged was a function of his desire for an order of knowledge that begins "to formulate itself . . . amid the murmuring of things" (236).

This principle animates Adorno's negative dialectics. Apart from scattered, and for the most part dismissive, comments on Jürgen Habermas toward the end of his life, and a belated admission of affinities between his thought and theirs (see Foucault 1991), Foucault never engaged directly with the philosophy of the Frankfurt school (see Dews 1991, 1). His subtle homage to Hyppolite's enterprise, however, suggests that he might have endorsed Adorno's singular attention to the dialectic of Western history as the domination of the concept or, in Foucault's own terms, to discourse "as a violence that we do to things" (Foucault 1972, 229).

3 / Theodor W. Adorno

Theory and Praxis: The Case of the Frankfurt School

The only philosophy which can be responsibly practiced in face of despair is the attempt to contemplate all things as they would present themselves from the standpoint of redemption.

T. W. Adorno, *Minima Moralia: Reflections from Damaged Life*

The philosophy of Adorno was formulated in the context of a collective enterprise articulated by a group of disaffected German intellectuals known as the Frankfurt school, many of whom emigrated to the United States during and after the Second World War. Adorno and Max Horkheimer returned to Germany, Herbert Marcuse and Leo Lowenthal chose to remain in America, and the influential yet marginal Walter Benjamin committed suicide because he was unable to escape from the Nazis during the war.

The philosophical premises, political pessimism, mandarin and messianic pretensions, and disavowed Judaism of the Frankfurt school have been well documented. Rather than contribute to the heated debate surrounding these issues, I seek to elicit a "structure of feeling" (to call upon Raymond Williams's useful phrase) within which Adorno's thinking took shape.

In *The Dialectical Imagination,* Martin Jay describes the founding members of the Frankfurt school as "an extraordinary generation whose historical moment has now irrevocably passed" (Jay 1973, xvii). My contention is exactly the opposite: the utopian moment in their thinking seems particularly pertinent to emancipatory critique in ours. Indeed, the very rigor with which they resisted the instrumentalization of their theory by the forces they sought to oppose suggests the power of their philosophy of praxis, of their faith in revolution. Faith in utopia is transformed into responsibility for the ravages of history and, as such, is contingent, simultaneously, on the determinate negation of the existing order and on eliciting the historical potential of a new one.

I wish to address the implications of critical theory in the context of my stated interest in professing the object's political desire. This interest will occasionally entail working against the grain of the texts of critical theory, insofar as they claim that "all organized or organizable opposition [has] long since capitulated" (Arato and Gebhardt 1990, xiv). Nevertheless, I hope to demonstrate that readers' justified impatience with the complex, paradoxical, and aphoristic formulations of the Frankfurt school has blinded them to the possibilities in its philosophy, precisely in terms of its commitment to revolution.

Rather than reproduce the tendency of scholarship in the field to veer between the aesthetic and materialist pretensions of the Frankfurt school, I want to suggest the conjunction between the two. For the moment, I want to address the school's relation to Marxism. Their commitment, in principle, to the goals of Marxism becomes heavily qualified as time wears on, because conventional Marxism's "scientism, economism, mechanistic determinism, [and] dogmatic materialism" (Kellner 1975, 142) become anathema to the members of the school. Leszek Kolakowski's unsympathetic portrayal of the school, too, has its roots in what he perceives to be their failure to treat Marxism "as a norm to which fidelity must be maintained" (Kolakowski 1978, 341). He concludes that the school is "not so much a continuation of Marxism in any direction, as an example of its dissolution and paralysis" (395). I contend that the school's astute reformulation of Marxist shibboleths makes the philosophy of dialectical materialism more rather than less viable.

Critical theory's indebtedness to Marx and Georg Lukács (despite periodic quarrels with the latter) reveals itself in its willingness to adopt a metacritical stance toward its own methodological presuppositions while retaining its commitment to revolution. As critical theorists acknowledge, Marx's indispensable contribution is his complex sense of the inescapable relation between mental and manual labor. Consciousness, in Marx's terms, "can flatter itself as being independent of the social life process, though the forms of consciousness continue to belong to the complex of the division of labor and hence possess neither independent life nor history" (Arato and Gebhardt 1990, 186). Because the vaunted independence of consciousness is an illusion, its representation of the world is not to be trusted either and can be counted on to align itself with the forces of reaction.

Marx's philosophy of praxis (action that is informed by a dialectical relation to theory) is the outcome of a sustained intervention in the pretensions of Hegelian Reason. As Andrew Feenberg remarks, "Marx attempts to reconstruct the concept of reason so that capitalist alienation appears as reason's essential problem, a problem to be resolved through historical action" (Feenberg 1981, 14). Instead of the Hegelian emphasis on thought realizing itself, Marx argues for the equal importance of reality striving toward thought (Feenberg 1981, 42).

Marx opposes Hegel's attempt to construe "real" alienation as merely the phenomenal appearance of the fundamental alienation of thought, an alienation that thought conceals when it seeks to recognize itself in its objectifications. Hegel therefore makes reification "an eternal foundation of knowledge and experience" (Feenberg 1981, 83) rather than the historically contingent form in which reality constitutes itself as appearance. Also implicit here is a critique of Kant's tendency to posit the laws of formal rationality as a priori categories that "logically . . . precede and organize all experience" (Schroyer 1973, 106).

Lukács takes up where Marx leaves off, suggesting that thought is "a form of reality . . . a moment in the total process" (Lukács, as quoted in Feenberg 1981, 72). If, as Marx suggests, the economy is the determinant in the last instance, even of the antinomies into which reason "resolves" itself, rationality itself can be shown to obey the laws of capitalism and thus cannot presume to "serve as the paradigm of explanation" (Feenberg 1981, 74). Lukács's concept of totality includes, therefore, Antonio Gramsci's sense that political action and awareness of that action are aspects of a single phenomenon (see Kolakowski 1978, 233).

The problem is that Lukács's concept of revolution is predicated on the dialectical union of subject and object. Marx insists that the realm of philosophy is precisely the realm of need and labor in which the proletariat moves (Feenberg 1981, 55), and Lukács is able to realize the potential union between action and awareness in the figure of the collective subject, the proletariat. Lukács wishes to avoid turning the proletariat into the passive medium through which the cunning of reason in the guise of historical necessity realizes itself. He constitutes the proletariat, therefore, as the subject of revolution, which "comprehends reality in the very act of transforming it" (Kolakowski 1978, 271).

This conception of the proletariat is inseparable from a notion of the dialectical method as "an active constituent" (Kolakowski 1978, 269) of the reality it seeks to comprehend. The dialectic cannot be conceived outside its visceral connection to the struggle of the proletariat, or outside its desire to transcend the split between theory and practice. Dialectic, at least within the discourse of traditional Marxism, is "the self-knowledge of a social process by which the world is revolutionized" (Kolakowski 1978, 271).

In dialectical terms, this conjunction of awareness and action is a possibility contained in "the difference between concept and reality" (Horkheimer in Arato and Gebhardt 1990, 109). Horkheimer's notion of the basis of revolutionary praxis echoes the critical (as opposed to the descriptive) character of Marx's concepts. These concepts, as Paul Connerton explains, "bear in themselves a particular imprint: the tension of a condition which they need to surpass" (Connerton 1980, 47). When the proletariat comprehends its place in the structure of capitalist production, it has already begun to revolt. As Horkheimer would put it, "thought itself is already a sign of resistance, the effort to keep oneself from being deceived any longer" (Arato and Gebhardt 1990, 116).

Yet, how is this demand that the subject be "commensurate with the reality which it knows" (Feenberg 1981, 116) to be met without turning the proletariat into the unconscious agent of necessity or without transforming historical laws into "hidden deities using human beings to bring about their ends" (Gramsci, as quoted in Kolakowski 1978, 233)? Feenberg insists that Lukács wishes precisely to dispense with the notion of the proletariat as incarnated freedom antinomially opposed to necessity (129). Instead, as Feenberg goes on to claim, Lukács understands the freedom of the proletariat as a specific act of mediation (of determinate negation) of the given (129). In other words, the proletariat perform a dialectical maneuver whereby they recognize themselves as the subjects of the critique of political economy, and the practitioners of critique discover, in the historical possibility the proletariat embodies, the reality of their categories. This smooth reciprocity of theoretical and practical mediation, which produces the proletariat as privileged subject of revolutionary transformation, comes increasingly under the merciless scrutiny of the proponents of critical theory.

Critical theorists are, first of all, unconvinced by Lukács's protestations in favor of an imputed class consciousness that will balance the failings of the individual consciousnesses of empirical workers. Connerton points to the subjunctives that begin to litter Lukács's prose when he cannot account for "the ways in which the conditions and constraints of the capitalist process of production [become] *introjected* by those who are subject to its power" (Connerton 1980, 51; emphasis in original). The self, for critical theorists, becomes an increasingly threatened entity because of the complex network of relations into which it is integrated.

Given this state of affairs, critical theorists experience only aversion for "the emergence of a collective subject composed of the human fragments of [their] day" (Arato and Gebhardt 1990, 200). Adorno, particularly, comments that the proletariat "bear all the marks of the typical bourgeois character" except for "their interest in revolution" (Arato and Gebhardt 1990, 216). The fears of the Frankfurt school were of course borne out in the success of Nazism, but my interest here is in their skepticism regarding the common purpose of intellectual and worker. As Horkheimer comments ruefully in "Traditional and Critical Theory," "even the situation of the proletariat is, in this society, no guarantee of correct knowledge" (Horkheimer 1972, 213). Critical theory, in Horkheimer's terms, will not accept that critique can ever become identical with its object. As I suggested earlier, the dialectical noncoincidence between concept and object, or the incommensurability of knowledge and reality, functions as the basis for determinate negation or as incitement to revolutionary praxis.

This recalcitrant insistence on the open-endedness of the dialectic has complex implications for the relationship between theory and practice and for the role of the intellectual in the struggle for social justice. Horkheimer wants to argue simultaneously for the inseparability of theory and proletarian struggle and for the inevitability of tension between the two. This tension, however, is productive and necessary. For postcolonial intellectuals, informants, or subjects who wish to make commitment the hallmark of their theorizing, unlearning their privilege (as Spivak would have it) is inescapable. Concomitantly, the task of representation and decolonization in the name of the subaltern object must continue. In this sense, and despite, for example, Edward Said's conformity to Antonio Gramsci's vision of the organic intellectual, that vision amounts to ignoring the productive and dialectical tension between mental and manual labor.

The division between mental and manual labor, itself a product of capitalist ideology, needs to be confronted in the difficult transition from capitalism to "communism." Horkheimer emphasizes the importance of reducing this necessary tension between the critical theorist's "insight and oppressed humanity in whose service [the theorist] thinks" (Horkheimer 1972, 221), but he also envisions a role for critical theory that is not confined to the dimensions of the proletarian struggle. Horkheimer calls for "constructive thinking" that disdains the criteria of empirical verification in favor of the "obstinacy" (220) of fantasy. Although the "existential judgment" of theorists "is conditioned by its conscious relation to the historical practice of society" (234), they must realize that in a society that deflates all pretensions to oppose prevailing modes of perception, the "universality" of theorists' concerns is not recognized as such (218). Horkheimer's comment on the eve of World War II is particularly revealing of his weary sense of the necessity and futility of thought:

> The entire situation in Europe is quite sad. Even the fear of war itself forms but a moment within a social development in which, in any case, all cultural values of any significance are perishing with an uncanny necessity. Those few to whom the truth has fled appear as ridiculous, dogmatic persons speaking a bombastic language, as empty, completely without foundation. (Horkheimer, as quoted in Dubiel 1985, xi)

The messianic overtones of this passage should not be overlooked, yet it would be a mistake to read it merely as an assertion of theory's pedagogical relation to practice. In my view, it glosses a profound sentiment: if knowledge is to coincide "with the struggle for certain real ways of life" (Horkheimer 1972, 245), that possibility is contained in the theorist's continued willingness to remain "outlawed but imperturbable" (241).

Horkheimer overturns theory's implied splendid isolation from and martyrdom to the insensibility of the masses when he writes:

> One day we may learn that in the depths of their hearts, the masses, even in fascist countries, secretly knew the truth and disbelieved the lie, like catatonic patients who make known only at the end of their trance that nothing has escaped them. Therefore it may not be entirely senseless to continue speaking a language that is not easily understood. (Horkheimer 1972, 290)

The vindication of theory, therefore, lies not in itself but in the "masses," whose apparent gullibility will reveal itself as knowledge biding its time.

Rather than shift the onus to the emergence of the organic intellectual who will realize philosophy in the abolition of the proletariat, Horkheimer retains the tension between thought and action. This dialectical tension is productive, because theorists must alter their conceptions in relation to the historical practice of society. This continuous mediation does not permit a simple and accidental recognition by theory of the reality of its categories; instead, theory is committed to a hazardous exchange between concept and object in which "there can be no corresponding concrete perception" of the essential kind of change at which critical theory aims "until it actually comes about" (Horkheimer 1972, 220).

Critical theory rejects, therefore, "the foolish wisdom of resignation" as well as the lure of "petty satiety" (Adorno 1978c, 168). It chooses to retain "a firm grasp on possibility" without "objectifying itself as utopia" (168) or hoping to bind knowledge and reality in a "spurious harmony" (Adorno 1967, 32). It must be remembered that critical theory's commitment to what Adorno calls "open thinking" (Adorno 1978c, 168) is not a sop to the privilege of the concept but a tribute to the intractability and complex modalities of the object. I shall turn now to the problematic (yet promising) character of an interest in emancipation that is not tied to the apotheosis of privileged subjects. The utopian projections of the Frankfurt school draw on this commitment to historical possibility, to the contours of change that can be traced in the very opacity of an alienating and apparently immutable economic necessity.

The process of cognition, at least as the Frankfurt school understands it, is inseparable from the critique of ideology. Indeed, critique becomes "the medium of a possible confrontation between claim and reality" (Connerton 1980, 45). Marx and Hegel become simultaneously complementary and antagonistic figures—the "idealist" method grounds the "materialist" attempt to pierce the ideological veil of Hegelian Reason. The members of the school, along with Marx, introduce an awareness of the dynamism of concepts in that they exist in dialectical tension with the reality they describe. In this sense, the school can argue that "the demand to abandon the illusions about man's condition is the demand to abandon a condition which needs those illusions" (Connerton 1980, 43).

Connerton charts a history of the concept of critique, pointing to the derivation of "critique" from "crisis." The exercise of reason has always been in some sense an intervention, a form of troubleshooting, so to speak. Connerton notes that during the Enlightenment the notion of critique undergoes a curious shift, a "fundamental displacement of accent, from critique as *method* to critique as *principle*" (Connerton 1980, 18; emphasis in original). Critique is no longer merely a means that might serve discernible ends; instead, the interest shifts (in Kant, for example) to reflection on the conditions of knowing. Critique, in other words, becomes reflexive.

This turn has provocative consequences for the status of reason but also explains the Frankfurt school's faith in "open thinking." The power of critique is irreducibly contingent and contextual, and its commitment to "a truth which has yet to be established" (Connerton 1980, 19) avoids "the notion that truth and immutability [are] synonymous" (Jay 1986, 69).

Critique must be more than mere crisis management that reinforces conformity to the existing order of things. The rational reconstruction of reality involves a contrapuntal interaction between two modes of critique. As Arato and Gebhardt explain, the transcendent critique of culture inhabits an imaginary space outside of cultural constraints, whereas the immanent critique finds itself trapped within the terms of the very object of its critique (Arato and Gebhardt 1990, 188). Even though there is an unresolved contradiction between these modes of critique, they are equally necessary or, at any rate, unavoidable.

The school remains partial to the process of immanent criticism, in which "empirical reality [is] confronted with its own logic, not with moral commandments imported from a transphenomenal Beyond or deduced from the 'vanity' of the subjective consciousness, the ego" (Lichtheim 1971, 8–9). This repudiation of "false ultimates" stems from Horkheimer's conviction of the impossibility either of neutrality or of objectivity on the part of the theorist whose vision remains irreducibly partial.

The theorist negotiates the elusive terrain between a commitment to the concrete and an equal belief in redemption. This slippery ground of theoretical endeavor ensures that knowledge remains "a representation which is a product" of particular people in a particular society, context, and moment of time but makes room for it to "become a productive force in turn" (Horkheimer 1972, 35). Implicit in Horkheimer's different conception of the relation between the particular and the universal is a dismantling of the dualism of bourgeois philosophy.

Horkheimer writes in "Authority and the Family" that bourgeois philosophy is unable to bridge the gap between self and world because it conceives of the individual "as a purely intellectual essence, a being which must . . . acknowledge [the world] as an eternal principle and perhaps as the expression of [the individual's] own true being" (Horkheimer 1972, 79). Consequently, the world assumes the "blind power" of a "faceless economic necessity" (82) to which the individual submits. This submission, which reveals the powerlessness of the self, is justified "by supposed insight into eternal matters of fact" (87). The first task of critical theory, therefore, is to distinguish between "the knowledge of facts" and "the acceptance of facts" (124).

The resistance of theory consists in its ability "to look behind the facts," to "distinguish the superficial from the essential without minimizing the importance of either" (Horkheimer 1972, 181). Here, once again, Horkheimer reveals the dialectical character of his thinking; that is, the elements of the process (in this case, the superficial and the essential) "determine each other continuously, so that in the total development neither of them is to be presented as an effective factor without giving the other its role" (Horkheimer 1972, 28).

Horkheimer reinforces the importance of understanding the dialectic as antinomial here, in the course of making it possible to defend utopian thinking (the transcendence of facts) as the only form of critical apprehension that keeps its "eye unwaveringly on the facts" (Horkheimer 1972, 191). Adorno's work, too, bears witness to the insight that "appearances are dialectical; to reject all appearances is to fall completely under [their] sway, since truth is abandoned with the rubble without which it cannot appear" (Adorno 1967, 84).

But what, in Horkheimer's terms, is the status of "facts"? What might be at stake in understanding appearances as dialectical? How does knowledge of facts serve critical rather than "affirmative" ends? Horkheimer wants, at the outset, to bring to the fore the social construction of reality. The inescapability of brute fact is double edged. On the one hand, it enforces obedience to a world that appears as a self-contained reality in direct confrontation with the knowing subject (Horkheimer 1972, 78). On the other hand, the "penetration" of the workings of this seemingly self-regulating mechanism exposes the "fact" that the world is "dependent on man and changeable at his will" (78). Moreover, this dependence on "man" has crucial implications for the relation between knowledge and its object.

If "every datum depends not on nature alone but also on the power man has over it" (Horkheimer 1972, 244), theoretical activity is obliged to explain how its failure to grasp the object is bound up with the power it exercises over the object. Horkheimer's sensitivity to the nexus of knowledge and power here paves the way for Adorno's interest in the object's resistance. Crucially, Horkheimer, like Adorno, does not want to relinquish the power of the subject to transform its object; the sensitivity to the object must not preclude the object's desire to accommodate its concept. I say this because an exclusive focus on knowledge as violation rescinds any critical value or political purchase that might accrue to the process of discerning the limits of knowledge.

For a postcolonial intellectual of my stripe, critical theory's deployment of its complex sense of the contingency of knowledge to bolster the productive force of knowledge sutures the gap between insight and agency. If knowledge of facts cannot afford to be translated as acceptance of facts, postcolonial intellectuals must work to discover whether and how they can declare with impunity that the link between reason and reaction is neither necessary nor inevitable.

Horkheimer's *Eclipse of Reason* attempts to unpack the contradictory process by which the critique of instrumental rationality as the disease of reason and the defense of philosophy as the discourse of reason capable of self-transcendence and reflexive critique constitute the mainsprings of critical theory. Horkheimer's ruthless display of the limits of reason becomes the way to redeem its potential. His argument, as I have indicated, thrives on the irony that reason must become the instrument of its own eclipse. This position is different from related attempts (à la Jürgen Habermas) to salvage the use of reason from its abuse.

I offer a detailed exposition of *Eclipse of Reason* because of Horkheimer's comment on its opening pages that "it would be difficult to say which of the ideas originated in [Adorno's] mind and which in my own; our philosophy is one" (Horkheimer 1947, vii). Adorno's dedication of *Minima Moralia* to Horkheimer echoes this bond. Horkheimer's claim has, of course, been disputed on the grounds that his thinking is no match for Adorno's subtlety. I think, however, that the clarity and elegance of Horkheimer's prose do him a disservice in critical eyes accustomed to Adorno's recursive meditations. Although Horkheimer does not attempt revolution at the level of both style and content in the manner of Adorno, his disquisitions reward the reader willing to accord him the same care and critical scrutiny that have hitherto been Adorno's due.

Eclipse of Reason establishes that the rejection of objective reason as a principle inherent in reality recoils upon itself and, rather than reflecting the freedom of the subject, turns reason itself into an instrument, into a slave of an objective apparatus that is impervious to subjective scrutiny. The lectures in this volume demonstrate that thought must retain the right to determine, register, and contradict facts to avoid elevating a critical (scientific) method into a principle of truth. Several insights combine to reinforce Horkheimer's conviction that instrumental reason does not reconcile knowledge and reality; rather, it merely reinforces conformity to the existing order. Simultaneously, he does not advocate a return to objective reason because he is aware that the crisis of metaphysics was a consequence of its abstraction from the historical process that turned speculative reason into an apology for the harshness of social reality.

Let me elaborate, then, on the insights that produce his conviction and that address the question, once again, of the relation between the superficial and the essential, the transcendence of fact that keeps its eye unwaveringly on the facts, the rubble of appearance without which truth cannot appear, and the knowledge of facts that precludes acceptance of facts. In the course of his discussion of the status of fact, Horkheimer posits a version of theory that preserves the human content of cognition without turning the transcendence of reality into "metaphysical nonsense" (Horkheimer 1947, 83).

The attention to the surface of reality ensures that intelligence becomes "the servant of the apparatus of production, rather than its master" (Horkheimer 1947, 82). Horkheimer concurs here with Marx's sense that the categories of rationality must be analyzed in terms of their basis in the capitalist system of production. This undermining of the categories of rationality serves as a baleful reminder that intellectuals derive their leisure precisely from the capitalist system of domination that produces the split between mental and manual labor (103).

Even though "intelligence" must concede that concepts cannot be extricated from their process of production, and that philosophy is always in danger of abstracting from, misrepresenting, and degrading the concrete into "mere stuff to be dominated" (Horkheimer, 1947, 97), it has no alternative but to engage in the ceaseless diagnosis of the dis-ease of reason. Herein lies the vexed character of reason—it must put itself at stake in order "to recognize the extent to which it is still unreasonable, blind, the victim of unmastered forces" (Marcuse [1960] 1990, 450). Without, therefore, privileging critical consciousness or detachment, my endeavor restores theoretical practice to its rightful importance. More to the point, theory undertakes to do more than confess to its privilege; it participates in a negative dialectic with the institutional constraints that condition its existence.

To my mind, the crucial distinction between the critique of Enlightenment undertaken by the Frankfurt school and by postmodernists lies in their comprehension of the status of reason. The explosion involved here is of the categories of rationality and not of reason *tout court*. If the latter were the case, the limits of reason would be in danger of being misconstrued as a call to obscurantism. If the double-edged nature of reason is to assume its place in the exercise of critique, the promise of accountability must be taken seriously.

Critical theory is not content with noting the incommensurability of knowledge and reality or with exposing the vanity of epistemology. Horkheimer's concession to the finite and fallible nature of knowledge is a function of his interest in reading the text of the object's suffering, whether the object in question is nature or the martyrs of the concentration camps. The comprehension and acceptance of the limits of knowledge must not obscure the traces of the violence exercised in the name of rationality. The task of reason, after all, is to realize its own reasonableness just as its self-critical proponents cannot afford the sentimental lapse Horkheimer describes with, yes, wisdom: "that we do not know everything does not mean at all that what we do know is the nonessential and what we do not know the essential" (Horkheimer 1972, 39).

". . . an objectless inwardness": Philosophies of Identity

In "The Revolt of Nature," Horkheimer asks that nature be treated "as a text . . . that if rightly read [by philosophy] will unfold a tale of infinite suffering" (Horkheimer 1947, 126). I have already discussed Horkheimer's conviction that knowledge of the object must account for the power that the subject/concept wields over the object. Adorno shares this refusal to allow the concept to have the last word on the object in both discursive and material terms, and he elevates it into (appropriately enough) the substance of his philosophy. The subjugation of nature (as privileged signifier of the lowly status of the object) becomes, in Adorno's work, the informing (allegorical) principle of his monumental attempt to "give thought the density of experience" (Adorno 1967, 240).

In challenging the autonomy of thought, Adorno's philosophical discourse effects a radical departure from the vanity of all forms of epistemology that collapse the distinction between knower and known in the complacent conviction that the authority of consciousness reflects the reality of being. Adorno's critique of philosophical discourse can be described as the attempt to subsume the particular in the universal, the fact in the category, and the object in the subject. This critique has obvious resonances for the production of postcolonial discourse, because postcolonial discourse attempts to posit an object of knowledge that will elude the universalizing and anthropological pretensions of orientalist or occidental discourse, which produces the other in its own image.

The epigraph to *Against Epistemology—A Metacritique: Studies in Husserl and the Phenomenological Antinomies* reads: "A mortal must think mortal and not immortal thoughts" (Adorno 1982a, 3). This quotation from Epicharmus, fragment 20, encapsulates the sustained materiality of Adorno's thinking even as it suggests his disdain, not unlike Nietzsche's, for a mode of philosophy that aspires to system or that fancies itself as the point of departure for all thinking. Adorno attacks the transcendental subject of knowledge, whose forms and categories constitute the conditions of possibility for thought and the world. Adorno's familiar critique of identity thinking entails a radical undermining of epistemology as both the practice and principle of thought.

The phenomenological enterprise, for Adorno, serves as the model of *prima philosophia,* of the search for an irreducible first principle. As Adorno explains, the content of this first and final ground is not the issue; rather, what is at stake is "the very concept and legitimacy of such a foundation" (Adorno 1982a, 6). Although Adorno uses Hegel against Edmund Husserl, his analysis serves to dismantle the claim of spirit to contain matter. In other words, Hegel's method holds valid despite his own claims for *Geist* being called into question. Adorno traces the legacy of German idealism in Husserl, even though phenomenology, as its name indicates, styles itself as a philosophy of concretion.

Adorno subjects Husserl to an "immanent critique" (Adorno 1982a, 5). The procedure involves turning Husserl against himself or using the strength of Husserl's own premises against his conclusions. Adorno adopts this technique from Hegel, who claimed that genuine refutation was not achieved "by . . . defeating [the opponent] where he is not" (Hegel, as quoted in Adorno 1982a, 5). Adorno's intention is to demonstrate the "ghostliness of all phenomenological concretion" (1982a, 85); that is, Husserl's attempt to pierce the veil of conceptual reification through the intuitive glance that would reveal objects in their singularity confuses "the schema of order imposed on objects by human consciousness" with "the order of the objects themselves" (1982a, 76).

Husserl's argument is riven with this contradiction because he attempts to render the first principle "unmediated and immediate" (Adorno 1982a, 7). As Adorno shows, the intuitive glance that reveals the naked sense datum is itself mediated just as it mediates the object it re-presents. The materialist turn in phenomenology is ill served by a "scientific" method that "substitutes hypostatized fact for hypostatized essence" (Adorno 1982a, 105). Husserl rightly chafes against a conceptual veil that obscures the object; he errs when he fails to reflect critically on his own epistemological method and accords that method's products the status of unmediated phenomena, of things in themselves.

The phenomenological reliance on irreducible first principles is an example of what Adorno calls the "identity hypothesis" (Adorno 1982a, 7), which seeks to ground all phenomena even as it proclaims its own groundlessness. Adorno rejects not only the foundationalist aspirations of thought but also its claim to completeness. Philosophy that has recourse to first principles must paradoxically divest "itself of any relation to things" (11) in order to function as the guarantor of their being. Moreover, such an epistemological procedure "confiscates what is unlike itself and makes it the same, its property" (9). The exposure of the logical contradiction of a *prima philosophia* that must abrogate its relation to things in order to function as their explanatory principle spills over here into a preliminary sensitivity to the violence of the concept, which will permit nothing to escape its definitions. Identity thinking finds its locus in the knowing subject that functions as the a priori of the profession and pretensions of epistemology.

Adorno's indebtedness to Nietzsche is perhaps nowhere more evident than in this work, which proceeds to excoriate the "sickness of spirit" (18) that debilitates the discourse of philosophers. The difference is that, as Adorno explains, "Nietzsche undervalued what he saw through" (19). Adorno elaborates on this underestimation of the "honourable idolaters of concepts" (Nietzsche, as quoted in Adorno 1982a, 19) on two levels: one teases out the social bases of the victory of spirit over matter, and the other harnesses Nietzsche's perception that "nothing real escaped [the] grasp [of concept-mummies] alive" (Nietzsche, as quoted in Adorno 1982a, 19) to a dialectical reconstitution of the relation between method (spirit/concept) and matter.

In the manner of Marx, Adorno turns the interrogation of philosophy into a critique of ideology. Identity thinking, in Adorno's terms, reflects a social situation in which mental labor is effectively split from manual labor. The boundlessness of spirit, its capacity to contain what proceeds from it, manifests itself as the "fanatical intolerance" (Adorno 1982a, 13) of an epistemological procedure that transforms the particular into an abstract repetition of the universal rather than acknowledging precisely its nonidentity. Adorno relates the power of method to the supremacy of the principle of exchange in capitalist relations that reduces the relation between subject and object to one of equivalence.

This is a familiar enough Marxist critique of reification, but it gains provocative dimensions when Adorno claims that the principle of reification corrodes the practice of epistemology itself. Adorno's vision of philosophers is cruel indeed; the discourse of the peddlers of the identity hypothesis, he writes, is

> the self-deafening roar . . . of those who neither contribute to the real reproduction of life nor actually participate in its real mastery. As middlemen, they only commend and sell to the master his means of lordship, spirit objectified into method. (Adorno 1982a, 15)

This passage demonstrates the metaphysical character of Nietzsche's own damnation of philosophers for relying on concepts that evaporate reality. Adorno correctly emphasizes that the sickness of spirit afflicting philosophy "arises from real lordship" (18); that is, the subject can set itself up as better only because it is the victor in the struggle with the object. The object, Adorno argues, thus becomes victim of the irrefutable logic of violence: "What survives has more right on its side than what perishes" (18). Adorno therefore confirms Horkheimer's sense of the essential dualism of bourgeois philosophy, a dualism inextricable from the subject's assertion of its identity and mastery.

Adorno is careful, however, not to oppose, as Nietzsche sometimes does, a logic of becoming to that of being. The hypostasis and intolerance of being is not to be overcome by a Dionysiac lapse into the regenerative powers of the chaos of becoming—the object that merely confirms or reflects the unity and identity of the subject is just as much the latter's creation as the object that opposes its chaotic fury to the rational self-mastery of the subject. Despite his unfailing eye for the posturings of identity and the hubris of epistemology, Adorno never reneges on his conviction that "criticizing epistemology also means . . . retaining it" (Adorno 1982a, 27).

It seems important to point out (in however sketchy a fashion) the implications of the vigilance Adorno demands, paradoxically enough, of the philosopher, of precisely the "man" who may "kill" and "stuff" what "he" pretends to revere (Nietzsche, as quoted in Adorno 1982a, 19). Adorno describes this vigilance as the ability to distinguish between the truth and untruth of epistemology:

> Epistemology is true as long as it accounts for the impossibility of its own beginning and lets itself be driven at every stage by its inadequacy to the things themselves. It is, however, untrue in the pretension that success is at hand and that states of affairs would ever simply correspond to its constructions and aporetic concepts. (25)

The necessary distinction between concept and object is responsible, in a sense, for the "thought of identity" (32) that permeates their inevitable relation. Adorno demonstrates how the contingency and unfamiliarity of the object is perceived as a threat to the self-mastery of the subject. The subject's intolerance of contradiction and dissension is translated into an attempt to overcome the object's negativity. Instead of drawing the subject out of its isolation and imprisonment, the object suffers the loss of its own nonidentity and particularity and is subsumed in the familiarity of the concept.

The violent transformation of difference into identity reflects the inadequacy of an epistemological procedure that refuses to be surprised, and that seeks, instead, to explain the unknown by the known (Adorno 1982a, 32). This point will gain its due importance in Spivak's formulation of the inevitability of catachresis, of the necessity of a name for that which cannot function as the literal referent of the designation but which simultaneously demonstrates the limits of such signifying. An epistemology grounded in first principles cannot afford to acknowledge the irony that vitiates its claim to truth; a philosophy that comprehends everything thus comprehends nothing (35). Adorno's double-edged formulation is crucial because it illustrates not only the emptiness of concepts but their indispensability to the philosopher mindful "of the suffering that sedimented itself" in them (39).

Standing consciousness on its head entails more than the classic materialist ploy of linking the products of rationality to the forces and relations of capitalist production. The "miscarriage" of concepts constitutes "a bit of unconscious transcription of history"; more to the point, the suffering produced by that miscarriage carries the promise of salvation in the moment of the concepts' ruin (39). Adorno describes this moment of ruin, with characteristic aplomb, as the moment in which the idea of philosophical critique is born. A dialectician to the last, Adorno celebrates the birth of thought at the very moment that it contemplates the dissolution of the concept (as well as of itself) in the recalcitrance of the object.

Adorno's supple sense of a subjectivity that "is historically formed and yet not reducible to historical determinations" (Schroyer's foreword to Adorno 1973b, xii) accompanies his scathing, if humorous, denunciation of the deification of *Dasein* in the writings of Heidegger and like-minded existentialists. Adorno is simply impatient with gestures of autonomy or spontaneity that ignore the "objective context of unfreedom" (Schroyer in Adorno 1973b, xv). The Hegelian *Aufhebung* manifests itself in the figure of *Dasein,* which, in Heidegger's terms, exceeds the opposition between fact and essence (xvi). Adorno is immediately suspicious of any entity that claims to produce historicity while remaining exempt from historical determination.

The Jargon of Authenticity was conceived, Adorno writes, as "a kind of propaedeutic" (Adorno 1973b, xx) to *Negative Dialectics.* It reveals, therefore, a common interest in the disintegration of philosophical discourse into words that signal authenticity without containing it. In other words, neither the claims of authenticity nor the jargon that evokes it can be subject to rational critique because both are elevated above "the realm of the actual, [the] conditioned, and [the] contestable" (Adorno 1973b, 11). This contempt for the "ontic" (20) contributes to the reactionary nature of authenticity. As Spivak continues to argue, however, strategic essentialism escapes this reactionary quality because it specifies the politics of location and functions precisely as a strategy rather than a theory. In this sense, authenticity becomes a reclaiming of a hitherto obscured historical possibility.

Adorno's bald statement that "Man is the ideology of dehumanization" (Adorno 1973b, 59) captures the jargon's clever attempt to divert attention from "men" and their struggle against "conditions which are made by [them] and which harden into opposition against them" (60). Because, as Adorno argues, the emphasis is on an ineradicable essence of Man, the critique of social conditions, like its object, is deemed all too shallow for being historically bound. As the category of authenticity must rely on the givenness of things, it becomes "a possibility that is prefixed to and foreordained for the subject, without the subject being able to do anything about it" (127).

Thus authenticity only confirms the powerlessness of the contingent individual, who must "puff himself [*sic*] up into selfness" (163–64) in the face of a determining objectivity that denies "the absolute disposal of the individual over himself" (128). Moreover, if authenticity is prefixed to the subject, it can readily become indistinguishable from the prevailing social order that precedes and determines the individual. The jargon of authenticity fails to address the question of wholeness as an unquestioned good because it cannot afford to acknowledge that the brandishing of wholeness might only serve to "atomiz[e] . . . those who are without power" (142) or those for whom reality is, precisely, heteronomous.

Adorno categorically rejects the "specious humanism" (Kellner 1974, 185) that the jargon endorses in creating an antidote to alienation. The solution it offers is no consolation for the wrongs of the world, because it enables the "authentic ones" to cut themselves off from the travails of the ontic while "at the same time [they return] to the everyday world inwardly transformed" (189). The attempt to salvage subjectivity in the works of both Heidegger and Kierkegaard destroys the empirical content of that subjectivity beyond recall because pure identity, as Hegel well knew, is death. To concur with Hegel, one has only to remember that Kierkegaard's insistence on radical inwardness concludes in a theology of sacrifice, or that Heidegger's desire for the nonrepresentable power of Being manifests itself as a relation to death as a mark of authenticity (see Murphy 1977, 190–92). The complicity of the philosophical discourse of German idealism in the brutality to which men and women are subject, one needs no reminding, resides in its belief in "the lordship of spirit" (Adorno 1982a, 20), a belief that prepared the way for fascism.

The dismantling of the claims of identity and of epistemology converges in the book Adorno wrote with Horkheimer, *Dialectic of Enlightenment*. The ambitious nature of the project has rendered its contentions questionable, in that it proposes to offer a diagnosis of the malaise of Western civilization itself. The authors undertake, in a sense, to reduce historical processes to an "epic" struggle between "man" and nature. The analysis of domination therefore remains unrelated to specific social relations or modes of production because the authors wish to trace the progress (or regress) of consciousness itself. Yet the provocations of *Dialectic of Enlightenment* cannot be ignored, and its value, then as now, resides in its attempt to come to terms with the legacy of the Enlightenment.

The central concern of this work might be seen as the attempt to trace the process Weber called *Entzauberung* or demagicization; that is, "the elimination of all that is unpredictable, 'irrational,' qualitative, sensuous, and mysterious from both theoretical explanation and the practical conduct of life"

(Arato and Gebhardt 1990, 191). Peter Gay points out that the Enlightenment did call for a "disenchanted universe" (Gay 1966, 145), but, as he argues, it is a mistake to "ridicule" the philosophes of the Enlightenment as
mere "system makers and shallow rationalists" (182). Despite its savage indictment of "civilization as rationalized irrationality" (Horkheimer 1947, 94),
Dialectic of Enlightenment offers a useful corrective to those prophets of post-
mod-ernism who claim sole responsibility for the crisis of Reason. Adorno
and Horkheimer, while acknowledging themselves "both patients and physi-
cians" of the disease of Enlightenment rationality (Caton 1974, 1308), are not
so sure that the disintegration of reason is cause for heady celebration.

   Dialectic of Enlightenment is founded on the insight that the "history of
man's efforts to subjugate nature is also the history of man's subjugation by
man. The development of the concept of the ego reflects this twofold history" (Horkheimer 1947, 105). The authors wish to indicate that "man's"
urge to dominate nature is also responsible for the birth of reason itself. "The
first man's calculating contemplation of the world as prey" (Horkheimer
1947, 176) signifies not only the birth of reason and of the self, but also their
dis-ease. The triumph of reason (the attempt to control the environment)
produces the familiar split between subject and object:

> On the one hand the self, the abstract ego emptied of all substance
> except its attempt to transform everything . . . into means for its
> preservation, and on the other hand an empty nature degraded to
> mere material, mere stuff to be dominated, without any other pur-
> pose than that of this very domination. (Horkheimer 1947, 97)

The authors reject what they call instrumental reason, which "either eulo-
gizes nature as pure vitality or disparages it as brute force" (126), in the interests of a reconciliation between man and nature. This reconciliation is an
attempt to reject the manner in which instrumental reason becomes inseparable from "the acknowledgment of power as the principle of all relations"
(Adorno and Horkheimer, 1972; 1993a, 9).

   The authors' interest in the legacy of the Enlightenment is, on one level,
a consequence of their experience of Nazism. They perceive the transformation of the liberating power of reason into a repressive regime as endemic to
the constitution of Enlightenment rationality. The rise of fascism is represented in their work as the revenge of a nature that has not been subdued but
merely repressed. If the history of reason is inseparable from an ethic of domination, the "pathogenesis of the Western rationalist tradition" (Held 1980,
89) can be discerned in the very process by which reason continually col-

lapses into repression. Reviewers comment on the fragmentary nature of the work as a reenactment of the history it traces, but it seems pertinent to note the manner in which the "history" of the collapse of reason reverts into a myth or tale of the prolonged oppression of external nature and the subsequent repression of inner nature.

Adorno and Horkheimer write that the formation of subjectivity is contingent on the choice between the subjection of the self to nature and the subjection of nature to (and within) the self. The progress of the Enlightenment only confirms the process that began with Odysseus: nature becomes an inanimate object that "man" invests with significance or dominates at will. Odysseus, in the authors' eyes, seems already aware of Bacon's insight that one must obey nature in order to master "her."

As Connerton explains, Odysseus, in the episode with the Sirens,

> wants to discover a formula for rendering to nature what is nature's, and yet betray it in the very process. He must find an arrangement by which he as a subject need not be subject to it. This he does by a double strategic act of force. One possibility he reserves for himself. He listens, but while bound impotently to the mast. . . . The other possibility he prescribes for his men. . . . They are able to survive because they are unable to hear. . . . Odysseus has found a stratagem for resisting the temptation while listening to it, and so is able to control the power of nature: but only at the price of doing violence to his own inner nature, and of establishing social domination. He must forcibly restrain his instinctual drives . . . and he must force obedience upon those who travel with him . . . which in turn is only possible because he deludes them. (Connerton 1980, 68–69)

The authors' unusual interpretation of this familiar episode is the basis for their use of Odysseus as the prototype not only of "bourgeois renunciation" (Connerton 1980, 69), but of Western civilization, which they characterize as the introjection of sacrifice. The duplicitous character of sacrifice is evident in Odysseus's act because he is capable of self-surrender and self-preservation at the same time. The rational control of nature, or the exercise of instrumental reason, is bought at the price of the denial of desire for and the masking of the fear of precisely what one seeks to control.

Paradoxically, myth already contains a moment of enlightenment in that both are motivated by fear of the unknown and the desire to preserve the self. The difference is that the mythic conception of the universe does not entail a radical separation between self and world, and includes a moment of wonder in the angst that the human self experiences. The mimetic relation between self and world implicit in the ritual reenactment of natural forces is transformed, within the dialectic of enlightenment, into the relation to a world of quantifiable and manipulable objects. This emphasis on utility and calculability disenchants the universe and represses the instincts.

The "mere idea of outsideness is the very source of fear" (Adorno and Horkheimer, 1972; 1993a, 16). It is not difficult to connect this argument to Adorno's description of the lordship of spirit or of identity, which manifests itself as rage against otherness. *Dialectic of Enlightenment* draws startling conclusions from what might appear to be flimsy evidence. The transition from the domination of nature to the domination of "men" seems hasty and ill defined to critics like Connerton, whereas the mimetic relation between discursive concepts and instruments of technological mastery, they argue, seems overblown.

Adorno and Horkheimer seem less inclined to undertake specific analyses of historical situations; however, I think the importance of this (in many ways) aleatory work lies precisely in its *paradigmatic* status. The use of myth to destabilize reason makes the simple enough point that enlightenment is in danger of reverting to myth, that reason has lost, paradoxically, its self-consciousness in its newfound slavery to the dictates of necessity. That the categories of reason are no less subject to historical revision than the "facts" of existence bears repeating, if only because, as Adorno and Horkheimer are well aware, the development of history has not changed the fact of domination.

Without depreciating the value of historically and socially differentiated analyses, I want to assert that the recognition of the thread that links, as Adorno says, the slingshot to the bomb has a simultaneously bracing and sobering effect. We dismiss, at our peril, the authors' searing sense that, in Habermas's words, "the history of civilization arises . . . from an act of violence which humans and nature undergo in the same measure" (Habermas 1983, 100).

Adorno and Horkheimer argue that *Dialectic of Enlightenment* offers a "theory which holds that the core of truth is historical, rather than an unchanging constant to be set against the movement of history" (Adorno and Horkheimer 1972, ix). The previous paragraph might be said to be arguing exactly the opposite. My point is that the method of this work has implications for the diagnostic character of colonial discourse analysis, which seeks to situate the domination of the concept in the history of colonialism while simultaneously suggesting the self-contained or systematic character of the discourse of modernity that produced, so to speak, the colonizing imagination. Postcolonial discourse, in short, needs to suggest the historical consequences of a specific cultural discourse as well as the universalizing impulse of that discourse, which becomes the corrosive principle of thought itself. Precisely because "Enlightenment excises the incommensurable" (Adorno and Horkheimer 1993a, 12), it produces in the objects of that discourse "the condition of pliable trust in the objective tendency of history" (41). This trust and pliability are what the writings of Ashis Nandy and the Subaltern Studies Group, for example, reject in favor of a mode of knowledge that produces "the dissolution of domination" (42).

". . . the preponderance of the object": Negative Dialectics

I have contended that a return to dialectical thinking will serve the cause of the representation of the feminine and ethnic object because the concept of difference has its limits and is much too liable to recenter the Eurocentric self even within the realm of postcolonial discourse. The following brief detour through Hegel seems crucial to delineate the contours of Adorno's attempt to wrest Hegel's "truth" from his "untruth."

The figure lurking in the interstices of my discussion of Adorno's oevre thus far has, of course, been Hegel's. Adorno's challenge to the legacy of German idealism draws its inspiration from the dialectical principle that matter and method are inseparable; that is, as Adorno demonstrates in his analyses, the philosophies of identity dissolve into the very antinomies they seek to resolve. The philosophy of Hegel is not exempt from the charge that it posits an identity between object and concept.

Hegel presupposes an identity between "the contentless concept and the unthought object" (Friedman 1981, 116) even though he must begin with an acknowledgment of the *empirical* difference between concept and object. The task of philosophy, in Hegel's terms, is to transcend this empirical difference in the speculative unity of thought and thing. Consciousness, one remembers, produces or renders an account of the world through a process of self-reflection. This explains the circularity of the Hegelian dialectic; the mind becomes the locus of a reconciliation between thought and thing where the object is brought to the level of the concept (see Dubiel 1985, 141–42).

The problem for proponents of materialism is that Hegel presupposes the moment of identity without seeking a *historical* resolution of the problem of alienation. Hegelian Reason becomes "affirmative, even before reality itself is affirmed as rational. . . . The Hegelian solution seems a purely private assertion, a personal peace treaty between the philosopher and an inhuman world" (Horkheimer 1972, 204).

The immanently contradictory nature of the object of knowledge should apply equally to the thinking subject. Hegel neglects this possibility, or even actively obscures it, so that the subject's experience of contradiction is only a momentary stumbling block in its process of self-recognition. As I have suggested, the subject comes into its own when it recognizes the other as itself. Adorno deploys this self-contradiction in Hegel's text in the interests of the object of knowledge. Not only does he accord the moment of contradiction or of negation "primary" status, he manipulates the "impenetrable resistance of matter" to reconstitute the object of knowledge ("matter") not as "the manifestation of 'spirit,'" but rather [as] its essential *limit*" (Marcuse, as quoted in Feenberg 1981, 251; emphasis in original).

Adorno transforms what might be perceived as an internal inadequacy in Hegel's reasoning into its enduring strength. He takes Hegel's interest in the self-movement of the object seriously, as he does Hegel's contention that the most important principle of the dialectic is " 'to surrender to the life of the object,' to express and represent the 'coming-into-being' of reality itself [because] 'what the historical object has been, . . . what it is becoming, and what it is not' . . . all contribute to its character" (Hegel, as quoted in Held 1980, 229).

Adorno chooses to concentrate on the process of dialectical *mediation* between the extremes of form and content, nature and spirit, theory and praxis, freedom and necessity, thing in itself and phenomenon in order to avoid reading Hegel's philosophy in purely "affirmative" terms, as an ideology that reinforces the irrationality of social relations in the process of protecting the rationality of the absolute subject. This emphasis on the process of mediation elicits the "real" import of Hegel's critical reflections:

> The poles that Kant opposed to one another—form and content, nature and spirit, theory and praxis, freedom and necessity, the thing in itself and the phenomenon—are all permeated through and through by reflection in such a way that none of these determinations is left standing as ultimate. In order to be thought, and to exist, each inherently requires the other that Kant opposed to it.

Hence for Hegel mediation is never a middle element between extremes . . . instead, mediation takes place in and through the extremes, in the extremes themselves. (Adorno 1993b, 8–9)

How is consciousness to be attuned to the vitality of the object? Despite Adorno's defense of Hegel, the self-cognition of the object is difficult to distinguish from the movement Dubiel describes in which the object is brought to the level of the concept. Perhaps a different approach to the issue is possible if the reciprocity of subject and object is understood, in Gillian Rose's explanation, as a situation in which "the subject is part of the object to be apprehended, but that the subject does not construct that object" (Rose 1978, 57). Fair enough, but, as Rose herself admits, the object, in the sense of material reality or social processes, must then be seen to contain as well as condition our experience of it (61).

I think that Adorno wishes to retain the moment of nonidentity between concept and object to avoid granting priority to either, and to exploit it as an accurate reflection of society as an antagonistic rather than a harmonious totality. This nonidentity nevertheless enables his antinomic endorsement of totality as a critical rather than affirmative category. In these terms, the vantage point of totality serves to throw the contradictions of capitalism and of humanism into sharp relief; simultaneously, totality remains a "utopian" concept that vanishes when besieged (see Jay 1986, 226) and that, when spelled out, bears a remarkable resemblance to Hegel's alarming claim that the real is the rational. Adorno explicates this vanishing concept of utopia in "A Portrait of Walter Benjamin" when he writes that faith in the contours of possibility, a possibility that will become visible in the moment of reconciliation, only "reveals the chasm separating that day [of reconciliation] and life as it is" (Adorno 1967, 241).

Adorno is critical of this messianic strain in Benjamin's thinking, one that he aligns with the surrealist attempt to produce, as it were, objects out of a hat, set adrift from their anchoring in social reality. Adorno sees this desire to rescue the immediacy of objects as resignation to, rather than liberation from, reification. Reality is never simply there—it is irreducibly mediated. Finally, the realization of the concrete will occur, in Adorno's terms, only when the concept becomes identical with its object. This is not to be construed as a Hegelian appeal to the postulate of rational identity but, once again, as a desire to produce in discourse the singularity and, therefore, heteronomy of the object.

At this stage, I want to make a somewhat unorthodox use of "A Portrait of Walter Benjamin" to reconstruct Adorno's reflections on the status of the object. This touching and accurate tribute is, in its very respect for the elusiveness of its subject, paradoxically much more revealing about Adorno himself. Perhaps it is best to begin with the moment of divergence between Adorno's and Benjamin's thinking. Adorno states that Benjamin "transformed himself into a supreme instrument of knowledge on which the latter had left its mark" (Adorno 1967, 229). Although Adorno's own style reflects this attempt to battle the subjectivism of philosophy, he is less inclined to dispense with the subjective dimension itself. This aspect of Benjamin's philosophy, for Adorno, "is no less a source of terror than a promise of happiness" because its "inhumanity against the deception of 'the universally human'" rightly inveighs against the jargon of authenticity that compromises bourgeois ideology (135–36); however, Benjamin also succeeds in exploding the potential autonomy of the particular, contingent, or empirical individual in whose name his diatribe against Man is performed.

Yet, Benjamin's compulsion to "break the bonds of a logic which covers over the particular with the universal or merely abstracts the universal from the particular" (Adorno, 1967, 230) forms the guiding principle of Adorno's own thought. Philosophy, in Adorno's terms, needs to divest itself of the urge to define, to classify, and to abstract; in short, it is no longer to be rendered synonymous with speculation. The interest in the material that might throw the reality of the idea into doubt is linked to the irreducibly historical dimension of thought and experience. In a manner analogous to that of Marcuse, who conceives of essence as a historical concept (see the first section of this chapter), Adorno appreciates the sleight of hand by which Benjamin refuses to use historical objects as mere illustrations of concepts. Instead, the uniqueness of things demonstrates the historical character of ideas themselves while serving as poignant reminders of a reality that is always in eclipse. Benjamin's gaze does not elicit the substance of a thing; instead, his loving attention to the object intertwines its substance with its historical fate. The substance of things, then, is precisely that which eludes, in a nice touch, the ephemera of *concepts*.

This fidelity to the object produces the fragmentary quality of Benjamin's thinking, which, like Adorno's, refuses to submit to the exigencies of system. Benjamin's interest in a scarred and fractured substantiality is reminiscent of Adorno's micrological procedure. Adorno and Benjamin share a "methodological hostility to systems" (Fekete 1978, 193) that they express as a defense of the particular. The object's challenge to the dominion of conceptuality is represented stylistically in the form of fragments, aphorisms, and essays. As Fekete explains, "the aphoristic fragment sets its own horizon. It does not develop an epistemology of discontinuity. As a way of seeing the world, the aphorism both implies a greater whole and yet is complete as a fragment" (193).

Adorno is careful to indicate that Benjamin's talent did not lie in an unprecedented access to the immediacy of objects, a rare ability to intuit their presence. Instead, he characterizes Benjamin's fragments as extraordinary attempts to surrender to their object while simultaneously asserting the incommensurability of thought and thing. Benjamin's singularity, then, lies in his manner of seeing, which renders the familiar strange. More to the point, Benjamin's thought, in pressing close to its object, seeks to transform itself so that the stringency of his thinking is matched only by the density of the experience it contains and communicates (Adorno 1967, 240).

In a classic antinomial formulation, Adorno describes Benjamin's writing as the desire to invest conceptuality with what was previously denied it. Lest this desire be misconstrued as one that turns the philosopher into a creature privy to manifestations of a most theological sort, Adorno represents the task of philosophy as an "impossible possibility" (Adorno 1967, 241), as the elucidation of the possible reconciliation between concept and object but possessing, as the only means of such elucidation, the very concepts that render that "radical reduction" of distance (240) impossible.

It must be asked wherein the force and application of this projected reconciliation between concept and object might lie. I think the answer might be sought initially in an as yet inadequately highlighted aspect of objectivity. Habermas suggests that the primacy of the object must also denote the world, which confronts the subject as alien and threatening or simply opaque and inexplicable. Adorno interprets the process of self-reflection, therefore, as an attempt to ward off suffering (Habermas 1983, 106). Philosophy is innately fallible (106) because it cannot escape the objective context in which it finds its place; however, the power of reflection interrupts the course of necessity in its recognition of contingency.

The rejection of the purely speculative dimension of thought entails "not mere contemplation but praxis" (Adorno 1967, 150). In other words, Adorno restores the constructive dimension of thought, its ability to take cognizance of what is without sacrificing the desire for and awareness of possibility (Adorno 1993b, 10). Poststructuralist epistemology, on the contrary, turns the perception of the limits of knowledge into empty consolation for the fragility of thought and existence. History can be rewritten from the point of view of the vanquished only if the postcolonial historiographer, for example, can break the spell of what is in favor of what might be or of what was denied existence.

Adorno remains true to his project of producing the kind of thinking that resists paraphrase (Jay 1984a, 11). It is with due trepidation, therefore, that I proceed. *Negative Dialectics* abounds in paradoxical (Adorno thought this a weak word to explain his technique) formulations that enact the "impossible possibility" of a philosophical method that substitutes "for the paramountcy of the supra-ordinated concept . . . the idea of what would be outside the sway of such unity" (Adorno 1973c, xx). A philosophy that might serve "authentic concretion" (xix) cannot be articulated without addressing the radical separation of subject and object that epistemology takes for granted.

"The fallacy of constitutive subjectivity" (xx) has produced a state of affairs in which the subject, once "radically parted from the object, . . . reduces it to its own measure; the subject swallows the object, forgetting how much it is an object itself" (Adorno [1969] 1990, 499). The transcendental subject is self-grounding and, as such, fails to recognize itself as the very form of objectivity. In claiming to engender the world, the transcendental subject can "brag of [its] captivity as freedom" (504) because, as always, ideology is at pains to conceal that consciousness is determined rather than determining.

This need to acknowledge that "Man is a result, not an *eidos*" (511) cannot afford to ignore the fact that "the antithesis of universal and particular . . . is both necessary and deceptive. Neither one exists without the other; the particular only as defined and thus universal; the universal as the definition of something particular, and thus itself particular. Both of them are and are not" (510). Adorno therefore does not wish to reverse the relation of constitutive primacy; instead, he seeks a mode of cognition in which the subject would function as "the object's agent, not its constituent" (506).

This cognitive mode would involve reading the particular "not in the light of the universal, but rather in the light of the very contradiction between universal and particular" (Jameson 1990, 32). Adorno conceives of a philosophy whose very proximity to its object ironically confirms its distance *from* that object. Negative dialectics is born in the intolerable tension between these two positions.

The claim to constitutive subjectivity is responsible for "the sense of identity of a mind that repressively shapes its Other in its own image" (Adorno [1969] 1990, 499) and thus reveals the reality of reification. Adorno wants to emphasize the historical truth contained in this separation of subject from object, that the object has continually receded from consciousness because the subject's claim to supremacy over the object ironically "defrauds" it of the object (507). The subject, in this scenario, casts a spell over the object instead of entrusting "itself to its own experience" (506). *Negative Dialectics,* it might be said, seeks to "[rend] the veil [the subject] is weaving around the object" (506).

The opening pages of *Negative Dialectics* describe Adorno's project as one that uses "the strength of the subject to break through the fallacy of constitutive subjectivity" (Adorno 1973c, xx). This declaration sets the pace for the vertiginous effect of a dialectical method that has and seeks no alternative to using philosophical concepts to cope "with all that is [by definition] heterogeneous to those concepts" (Adorno 1973c, 4). Critics of Adorno can hardly be blamed for considering *Negative Dialectics* the epitome of all attempts to paint (write) oneself into a corner; in my estimation, however, Adorno's virtually comprehensive sense of the difficulty of his task in no way vitiates either its necessity or his conviction that it is undertaken for the sake of the possible.

Adorno admits that the continued currency of Hegelian dialectics needs defending, and he proceeds to offer this defense by getting rid of the dialectic's affirmative traits. The anachronistic character of a dialectical method that posits the negation of negation must be asserted, without, however, denying the value of contending with the contradictions that Hegel's failure brought to light. How, then, does Adorno propose to represent the moment in which "philosophy is obliged ruthlessly to criticize itself" (Adorno 1973c, 3)?

Adorno begins a thoroughgoing analysis of the logic of identity in the process of reconstituting the dialectical method. He observes that dialectics is haunted by the realization that "objects do not go into their concepts without leaving a remainder" (Adorno 1973c, 5) and that the relation between knowledge and its object can no longer conform to a norm of adequation. Adorno redefines the principle of contradiction as the mute reflection of the "untruth of identity, [of] the fact that the concept does not exhaust the thing conceived" (5). Because Hegelian dialectics operates according to a principle of unity, it necessarily renders the object "divergent, dissonant, [and] negative" (5) until the object is forced to reflect the unity and identity of the subject.

The project of *Negative Dialectics* is radical because the logic of identity is the failure not only of Hegelian dialectics but of thought itself. Adorno's philosophy relies on a reversal that discerns the irrationality of reason (Buck-Morss 1977, 7). This complex position implicates the categories of rationality in the antinomial social reality to which they bear witness. Negative dialectics, in this context, is thought in which thinking itself, in equal measure to the contents of thought, is under scrutiny (see also Jameson 1971, 45).

The irreconcilability of concepts and reality enables one to penetrate the reified appearance of reality while questioning the adequacy of concepts that capture that reality. The real cannot coincide with the rational in thought unless an objective reconciliation of social contradictions can be foreseen. The principle of nonidentity reveals itself in the process of a thinking that enacts what Adorno calls a "logic of disintegration"; that is, the micrological procedure Adorno uses in his critique of philosophies of identity is reproduced in *Negative Dialectics* to make the categories of reason self-destruct (see Buck-Morss 1977, 63–64). Only this practice of immanent criticism would ensure that philosophy became the enemy rather than the ally of the course of history.

"To think," Adorno says uncompromisingly, "is to identify" (Adorno 1973c, 5). The difference between subject and object, particular and universal, has hitherto been dictated by the universal so that unity is conceived as the measure of heterogeneity (5). Adorno seeks to destroy conceptuality as we know it in the interests of what he calls nonidentity, the "insight into the constitutive character of the nonconceptual in the concept" (12).

What might the consequences of such an insight be for the practice of epistemology? What would a substantive philosophy look like? Adorno calls for a philosophy that "would truly give itself" to the diversity of objects that impinge on its consciousness "rather than use them as a mirror in which to reread itself, mistaking its own image for concretion" (13). The respect for objects would coalesce with a concession to the finite and incomplete character of knowledge.

Adorno's aversion to systems becomes explicit here because, to his mind, categories, systems, and theorems only attest to his conviction that "no object is wholly known" (14) and that the truth of philosophy resides in its simultaneous admission and exposure of error. This conviction seems endemic to the construction of postcolonial discourse, whose province is composed of absences, silences, and distortions that must nevertheless be interpreted in order that history might acquire the character of revision.

This desire to surrender to the life of the object must nevertheless contend with the concept, "the organon of thinking, and yet the wall between thinking and the thought" (15). In one of his many succinct, yet opaque, characterizations of the principle and practice of negative dialectics, Adorno declares that philosophy "must strive, by way of the concept, to transcend the concept" (15). Why does Adorno cling to the concept, to what he tirelessly ridicules as the nemesis of philosophical discourse?

His statement serves, to my mind, as a prelude to his desire to retain a speculative moment within thought. The danger of thought's pressing itself close to the object is that it might mistake ideology for reality. The primacy of the object might reinforce the division between subject and object because one would be deemed wholly abstract and the other wholly concrete. If the object is conceived as "pure material," it becomes a "dead thing" and loses its power of predication (91). Materialist thinking would then dwindle into a metaphysics of matter; the informing principle of this metaphysics would be commodity exchange. After all, reification is precisely the consequence of forgetting the labor congealed in the commodity. Adorno, once again, wants to retain a dialectical emphasis that permits the philosopher occasionally to accuse the world of being inadequate to the concept.

Adorno insists that negative dialectics is not a negative theology that "hypostatiz[es] the concept of nonconceptuality"; instead, it constitutes the "self-critique of the concept" (136). His very allegiance to dialectical thinking precludes this hypostasis because the deferral of identity ensures that concept and object are always restless moments of their own opposites. Adorno wishes to break the stranglehold of an epistemological procedure in which subject and object "solidly confront each other" in favor of one in which "they reciprocally permeate each other" (139).

Adorno conceives of this reciprocity as existing within a *Kraftfeld* or force field, "a relational interplay of attractions and aversions that [constitute] the dynamic, transmutational structure of a complex phenomenon" (Jay 1984a, 14). This juxtaposition of elements resists reduction to "a common denominator" and forms, instead, "a dialectical model of negations that simultaneously [construct] and [deconstruct] patterns of a fluid reality" (Jay

1984a, 14–15). Despite this emphasis on mutuality, Adorno posits the "preponderance of the object" as a gesture of resistance to the relations of force that merely logical contradictions obscure. Adorno, in other words, is interested in the fractured rather than the fluid dimension of reality.

Although Adorno indicts thought for its alleged purchase on infinity, he refuses to relinquish his belief that the pursuit of reason will explode the existing order (Adorno 1973c, 37). There is room for a *political* purchase on ideas because the notion of the world as a self-regulating mechanism is itself the product of capitalist ideology. Philosophy rests its claim to comprehension, in Adorno's terms, on the duplicitous character of society that "is full of contradictions and yet determinable; rational and irrational in one, a system and yet fragmented; blind nature and yet mediated by consciousness" (quoted in Jay 1984a, 99). The very exercise of thought, as Horkheimer knew, is already a sign of resistance; the paradox, as Adorno points out, is that the freedom of thought must point unforgivingly to the unfreedom of existence (Adorno 1973c, 18). The difficulty of practicing a philosophical procedure that will "allow the method neither quite to absorb the contents . . . nor to immaterialize them" becomes particularly evident when one recognizes that "the principle of dominion which . . . rends human society" reproduces itself in the principle that "causes the difference between the concept and its subject matter" (Adorno 1973c, 48).[1]

There is no reason to elevate this difference that manifests itself as social antagonism and as logical violation into an ontological condition. Negative dialectics dissolves the congealed character of concepts and things when it reads both as "text[s] of their becoming" (52). Negative dialectics elicits this inner history to revoke the immediacy of objects and to expose the untruth of concepts (52). Adorno makes the political dimension of negative dialectics explicit when he writes that shattering the spell of reification entails adumbrating the "possibility of which their reality has cheated the objects" (52). This possibility is visible only to thought that has the courage to think against itself (141). To reveal the contradictions within reality is, as I have argued, to produce a philosophy that sets itself up as a contradiction *against* reality (145).

If negative dialectics has the principle of identity as its point of departure, its practice teases out the desire that grounds the repressive regime of the concept: "Living in the rebuke that the thing is not identical with the concept is the concept's longing to become identical with the thing" (149). Appropriately, therefore, nonidentity contains identity, confirming for

Adorno the "truth moment of ideology, the pledge that there should be no contradiction, no antagonism" (149). In a courageous and strategic move, Adorno turns the desire of the concept to be one with the thing against itself; negative dialectics is propelled not by the desire of the concept but by the "resistance which otherness offers to identity" (160–61).

Adorno's rejection not of the content of identity but of its very idea gains credibility because he never wavers from his conviction that "an appetite for incorporation" always combines "with an aversion to what cannot be incorporated, to [ironically] the very thing that would need to be known" (Adorno 1973c, 161). The object becomes the nonidentical, that which remains immanent to identity even as it is pushed out of it (162). Lest this conception of the subject as more than what it is lead once again to an appropriation of the nonidentical, Adorno accords the object a moment of resistance. The object's identity constantly militates against its identifications (161) so that it is "irreducible to—although not entirely unmediated by—an active subjectivity" (Jay 1984a, 63). The "groping for the preponderance of the object" (Adorno 1974c, 183) on the part of the subject that wants to cast off the carapace of identity becomes, in turn, the latter's salvation (277).

Negative dialectics is too often perceived as a "fraud" because Adorno's refusal to sacrifice the *Kraftfeld* or dialectical interplay of contradictions in favor of an ontological postulate seems to condemn the "advance" his critique makes to "retrogress[ion]" (Kracauer, as quoted in Jay 1986, 232). One way of defending Adorno's refusal of "generative first principles" (Jay's phrase) is to represent his text as standing "in the very river of history itself" (Jameson 1971, 50), as a footnote "to a totality which never comes into being" (52). Adorno, I think, would refuse the pathos of this stance even though he would be in accord with its spirit.

Kracauer's comment underestimates the radical quality of Adorno's enterprise, its diagnosis of the

> boring imprisonment of the self in itself, crippled by its terror of the
> new and unexpected, carrying its sameness with it wherever it goes,
> so that it has the protection of feeling, whatever it might stretch out
> its hand to touch, that it never meets anything but what it knows
> already. (Jameson 1990, 16)

Regression is an ever-present possibility within the neurosis of identity, of course; nevertheless, the persuasiveness of Adorno's work, for me, resides in its remarkable capacity to evoke the fragility of a new self committed to "imagining what [it] can by definition not yet imagine or foresee; what has no equivalent in [its] current experience" (Jameson 1990, 16).

In the texts of Spivak and Said might be glimpses of what Jameson calls "another side, an outside, an external face of the concept" (Jameson 1990, 25) or of what Adorno, in a predictably enigmatic fashion, names the "inextinguishable color from nonbeing" (1973c, 57). The negative impulse, in Said's and Spivak's view, would emanate from the (feminine) object of the discourses of patriarchy, capitalism, and Empire, which has hitherto been condemned by the logic of identity to function as what Adorno would style a systemic excrescence. Excrescences, as the text of *Negative Dialectics* demonstrates, shatter the pretensions of conceptual logic or of the mania for systems whose rage against otherness manifests itself as the unity of identity.

"Frankfurters and French Fries": Adorno and Poststructuralism

This project is an attempt to change the subject of theory and of political practice, at least insofar as it has remained the creature of poststructuralist discourse. The suitably disseminated subject still wields power and requires, therefore, rather more rigorous scrutiny than has often been given it. The philosophy of Adorno offers an "epistemological 'break' that simultaneously changes the subject and the very discourse in which change is being theorized" (to adapt Radhakrishnan 1990, 126). Nietzsche's destruction of any necessary connection between interest, agency, and insight has been reproduced in poststructuralist theories of the subject that celebrate the latter's (putative) death.

The problem, in short, is that the poststructuralist subject is radically dehistoricized, and can therefore hardly be called upon to assume its role in the context of revolutionary agency. Within Derrida's writing, for example, the contextualization of the empirical individual in terms of specific histories of oppression collapses all too often into yet another opportunity to expose the continued hegemony of logocentrism. In contrast to Derrida's emphasis on *différance* as an ethic of particularity, Adorno's consistent focus on the contingent, empirical, particular individual in an administered world transforms damaged lives into the radical negativity of situated consciousnesses whose epistemology is inseparable from political commitment. Adorno, too, understands that the production of knowledge reinforces the status of the subject as an effect of ideology, but he does not discount the possibility of revolutionary change.

Adorno can make this claim with such confidence because the moment of negation occurs in the very gap between ideological reality and possibility. Without discrediting the vexed relation between epistemology and politics or between theory and practice, it is time to determine whether the *conflation* of epistemology and politics might serve strategic or "revolutionary" ends. As I have indicated in my readings of Althusser and the members of the Frankfurt school, both knowledge and reality are tied to specific processes of production. Indeed, for these theorists, the production of ideology is inseparable from the reproduction of capitalist relations. To use Marx's familiar terms, consciousness is determined by matter and not matter by consciousness.

In the work of Adorno and Horkheimer, the progress of reason is inextricable from the instrumentalization of nature and labor; hence their sustained attempt to discover the traces of instrumental rationality in discursive concepts. Within this scenario, the vaunted asymmetry between the categories of rationality and the constraints of capitalist relations seems untenable. The asymmetry is to be located, rather, in the gap between the claims of capitalist ideology and the reality of capitalist relations, a gap that comes to be inhabited by critical negation.

The interrupted relation between politics and epistemology that needs posing is precisely what poststructuralism cannot bring about, because its discourse is part of the problem and not of the solution. Rather than take the familiar road to political success by investing the discourse of poststructuralism with historical specificity, I want to address the possibility of, yes, a radically *different* practice.

Poststructuralist epistemology lapses only too readily into what Adorno pungently describes as "risk without hazard" (recall my comments on the strategic and adventurous character of *différance*), into privileged contemplation of the pathos of subjectivity in which, "at the cost of any possible answer, the radical question becomes what is substantial unto itself" (Adorno 1973b, 29). How, then, might epistemology's inevitable implication in and relation to the ethicopolitical be deployed to ensure that "a difference in theory [is] translated into a difference in history" (Radhakrishnan 1990, 148)?

The difference between poststructuralist texts that reduce the function of epistemology to "a knowing reiteration of [their own] impossibility" (Osborne 1991, 41) and Adorno's own "enterprise . . . always teetering on the brink of blowing itself up" (Eagleton 1990a, 341) is that the latter is undertaken *for the sake* of the possible and is never perceived as an excuse to stop thinking. Negative dialectics is "a *rational* critique of reason" (my emphasis) because the survivor of Nazism could not afford to forget that "when men are forbidden to think, their thinking sanctions what simply exists" (Adorno 1973c, 85). The "posture of incessant harrying of an unbeatable enemy" (Dews 1987, 44) should not obscure the privileges of a position that is not obliged to explain the source of the authority of a discourse that questions the status of all discourses (see Godzich 1983, xvi).

My explication of Adorno's attempt to reconstitute the relation between subject and object seeks to emphasize his representation of this relation not only as the other's difference from, but as its resistance to, the hegemony of identity. The very writing of *Negative Dialectics,* thought's attempt to think against itself, disperses the subjectivist mist in which the object has been enveloped and gives the abstraction of thought the form of "authentic concretion." The subtle negotiation of the terrain between a "'bad' immediacy of the object and the false self-identity of the concept" (Eagleton 1990a, 341) enacts the dialectical mediation of the epistemological and the ethicopolitical because the reification of thought reproduces the spell (the principle of commodity exchange) that bewitches "men."

Adorno is cognizant of the limitations of philosophy in that an abstract negation of the course of the world in theory often accompanies its blind affirmation in praxis (Nägele 1982–83, 65). He is reluctant, therefore, to effect any easy transition between epistemological and ethicopolitical revolution, though he insists that one cannot proceed without the other.

I want to state here categorically that what is in crisis is not the subject but the object. The indiscriminate celebration of otherness, difference, and radical indeterminacy within academic discourse has precluded precise accounts of the growing backlash against minorities (as defined in terms of race, gender, or sexual orientation) as well as fostering a dangerous inattentiveness to the existence and possibility of resistance. The guardians of "radical" discourse within the academy, in an uncanny imitation of the purveyors of authenticity in Adorno's day, "ominously [strike up a] concerned tone: no answer would be serious enough; every answer, no matter of what content, [is] dismissed as a limiting concretization" (Adorno 1973b, 29).

This refusal to "pin [themselves] down" is passed off as a concession to the dynamism (the play of *différance*) of the world (Adorno 1973b, 29); instead, it serves as a sobering reminder of Horkheimer's contentious sense that "mankind [*sic*] [is] not betrayed by the untimely attempts of the revolutionaries but by the timely attempts of the realists" (Arato and Gebhardt 1990, 106). The valorization of difference, in facile versions of poststructuralism, has turned into a gesture of autonomy without content, while the insight into the speciousness of the ideology of humanism is threatening to destroy even the desirability of subjectivity. It seems important, once again, to indicate the disingenuous conjunction between the displacement of the subject and the desire for subjectivity on the part of the object.

My use of Adorno's critique of Heidegger to expose the vulnerability of poststructuralism might seem inappropriate at first glance. I have been concerned to show how poststructuralism reinforces the hierarchies it deconstructs. In these terms, I would suggest that poststructuralism's challenge to authenticity does not escape the jargon of authenticity. The bind in which poststructuralism finds itself, the loss of the subject as the ground and authority of knowledge and practice, reveals its failure to articulate a mode of discourse in which the subject's inevitable complicity with ideology does not necessarily connote paralysis. Negative dialectics, on the contrary, "knows" that to "put [one's] cards on the table . . . is by no means the same as playing the game" (Adorno 1973c, xix).

The political context of Adorno's own philosophy, that of Nazism, gives him a different take on the problem of subjectivity. For him, the undermining of the authority of identity occurs in the name of those condemned to acquiesce to a logic of definition that produces otherness as its negative term. Adorno never forgets that relations of difference are also differential relations of power. Moreover, the poststructuralist subject may not have escaped the confines of the dialectic of enlightenment, in which self-assertion and self-surrender are complementary necessities. The introversion of sacrifice (recall the example of Odysseus) that produces instrumental rationality as well as identity seems to have become, ironically enough, the motto of the poststructuralist subject (as I have mentioned in discussing Cixous; see also Derrida 1978, 257–58).

It has become customary to label Adorno a *déconstructeur avant la lettre* (see, for example, Jay 1984a; Ryan 1982; and Eagleton 1981), but the work of disentangling negative dialectics from the clutches of the strategy of *différance* has only recently begun. The parallels between deconstruction and negative dialectics are, of course, not readily dismissible, but one cannot help wondering at the fugitive evolutionary impulse within the discourse of poststructuralism, shown by its demand that all roads lead more or less coherently to a postmodern/poststructuralist universe.

Peter Dews was one of the first to undertake a systematic analysis of the differences between Adorno's project and that of poststructuralism (Dews 1987, 1991). Not confining himself to Derrida, Dews includes Lacan, Foucault, and Lyotard in his interpretation. I shall limit my consideration to those elements I find pertinent to the reconstitution of the postcolonial subject in the discourse of Spivak and Said. Because Foucault and Derrida might be said to be of prime importance in the work of Said and Spivak, I have dealt with Foucault and Derrida almost exclusively in my own writing.

Adorno and Derrida share a paradoxical admiration for and repudiation of Hegel as well as an interest in the place and function of alterity in relation to identity; however, deconstruction all too often lapses into an empty and ahistorical affirmation of contingency and particularity at the expense of a cogent analysis of the system of determinations that produce that alterity. Similarly, their shared concern with the relation between concept and reality is represented in Derrida as one of "necessary antagonism" rather than as a recognition of the fact that the antagonism is itself the product of "an historically obsolete imperiousness of consciousness" (Dews 1991, 14). Despite Derrida's sensitivity to the way in which boundaries between conceptual opposites remain infinitely transgressible, he posits the logical priority of non-identity over identity (17) because *différance* is the dialectic of oppositions' condition of possibility. This tactical maneuver does not permit the step Adorno's negative dialectics takes: the assault on the inadequacy of the concept is equally an indictment of the irreconcilability of the object (see also Osborne 1991, 28). Adorno has been responsible, along with Hork-heimer, for extended analyses of instrumental rationality, which renders the object identical with the concept. As I have suggested, Adorno does not wish to dispense with concepts altogether; his quarrel is with the kind of thinking that subsumes the particular in the universal, that relies on a mimetic correspondence between reason and reality.

This desire to render reason substantive assumes different proportions in the rhetoric of Derrida, which, as Barbara Foley points out, also claims to move beyond the realm of textual exegesis to produce "an epistemological practice possessing the capacity to expose and disrupt the ideological stratagems by which advanced capitalist society legitimates itself" (Foley 1985, 121). Foley's essay, however, disproves this claim.

The idiom of subversion, resistance, and displacement is no more than a cover, once again, for textual exegesis, for a revelation of the internal contradictions of a discourse and for an undermining of the said discourse's claim to epistemological authority (Foley 1985, 120). Foley asserts that unless deconstruction "takes to task not the existence of opposed categories qua categories, but their historically specific contents," it "cannot—will not—provide the grounds for a rupture that is, finally, anything more than discursive" (128–29).

Foley traces the "political bankruptcy" (113) of deconstruction to Derrida's continued deferral of his confrontation with Marx as well as to deconstruction's refusal of mastery. Foley rejects Spivak's and Ryan's attempts to annex Marx to the discourse of deconstruction because she says they offer, as a consequence, a radically revised Marx who refuses "to master—in practice—the text of capitalist domination" (133). The reliance on dispersal and heterogeneity defuses the value of *oppositional* politics because such a politics requires "determinate analysis . . . pursuing determinate results" (129).

Foley remarks that "binary oppositions are dialectical rather than static—historical rather than epistemological" as she criticizes deconstruction for its desire to "freeze in time its act of epistemological transgression" (129). Adorno's emphasis on mediation, as I have been insisting, avoids this problem because the nonconceptual functions as the concept's *immanent* contradiction. Because Derrida advocates the *logical* priority of nonidentity, *différance* cannot itself be differentiated by *what* it differentiates.

Because history, for Derrida, always assumes the character of a telos, deconstruction cannot be construed as historical. Instead, deconstruction poses the problem of history; *différance* serves to constitute historicity itself. For Adorno, the problem with epistemology is that, by engaging in disquisitions on the origins of historicity, it deliberately diverts attention from the historical determinations of epistemology. Negative dialectics is a logic of disintegration because it is committed to tracing the historical trajectory of the object: its change, disintegration, and multiple modality.

If deconstruction elicits a *reality* in eclipse (history as the category of alterity), negative dialectics counterposes the richness of things (constellations of particulars) to the transience of *thought*. Although Adorno is well aware of the inadequacy of categories, he does not seek to "bypass the order of apprehension" (Derrida's phrase). If "we" have no other form of apprehension, how can thought proceed as it always has, but with a difference? The trick, for Adorno, is to produce "a set of guerrilla raids on the inarticulable, a style of philosophizing which frames the object conceptually but manages by some cerebral acrobatics to glance sideways at what gives such generalized identity the slip" (Eagleton 1990a, 342). Negative dialectics moves beyond deconstruction because concept and object are not merely incommensurable but *"determinate* in their irreconcilability" (354; emphasis in original). Eagleton's point is important, because Adorno's reiteration of the social dimensions of epistemology enables him to transcend deconstruction's Nietzschean assault on the *inherent* violence of the concept. Besides, negative dialectics incorporates the insights of deconstruction without reducing itself to a naive faith in the stolidity of the real.

I could be accused, thus far, of confusing notoriously conservative misappropriations of Derrida with the "master" himself. I therefore want to address (in necessarily sketchy terms) the premises of Derrida's own philosophy to determine whether they can become grounds for the articulation of political resistance. Derrida's work has of course been a running concern in my text, but some direct confrontation might be useful as a prelude to my reading of Spivak's allegiance to deconstruction and of her desire to make deconstruction the ally of the disenfranchised "Third World."

Peter Dews echoes Foley's objection to the relentless Manichaeism of Derrida's world, the reduction, as he perceives it, of Western thought into "a set of perfunctory dualisms" (Dews 1987, xv). The emphasis on undecidability obscures this premise of Derrida's thought, which also fails to relate the antinomies of thought to the relations of production in the manner of Marx and Adorno. Even if one quarrels with Dews's reading by pointing out that Derrida is concerned with the tradition of Western metaphysics, there are enough indications that Derrida means to topple the structure of thought itself.

Dews first inquires whether the radical claims of deconstruction are borne out even in epistemological practice. He contrasts Adorno's and Derrida's readings of Husserl to illustrate his contention that Derrida offers us "a philosophy of *différance* as the absolute" (Dews 1987, 24). Adorno questions the very concept and possibility of the transcendental reduction regardless of its content. His reading of Husserl uncovers "the reef of facticity on which any transcendental enquiry must run aground" (Dews 1987, 16).

Derrida too discovers this internal contradiction within the discourse of phenomenology, but argues that what *"appears* to be the result of the intrusion of facticity and historicity, is the effect of a transcendental structure more fundamental than that of consciousness" (Dews 1987, 18; emphasis in original). Adorno's impulse is to reveal the intertwining of subjectivity with

the realm of facticity; Derrida seeks the ground of transcendental consciousness itself. Irene Harvey explains Derrida's contradiction of Husserl thus:
"the moment of evidence, the foundation of all truth and objective knowledge is a result of a 'more fundamental' absence—indeed the movement of
différance itself" (Harvey 1986, 10).

This move produces *différance* as an "ungrounded ground of ground, or
that which allows for the constitution of the notion of ground itself and in
turn for the notion of constitution itself"; it is a " 'more originary' origin,
which is profoundly not an origin for Derrida" (Harvey 1986, 20). *Différance,*
one remembers, does not contradict identity but 'grounds' the very opposition between identity and difference. In this sense, deconstruction as a practice of reading can only "lay bare" the structure of contradictions that constitutes a text; it cannot oppose or change it. Derrida's quest for the effaced
nonmetaphysical ground of metaphysics allows him to illustrate "the limits
and conditions of the possibility of metaphysics. . . . It does not prohibit in
the slightest the continuation and indeed paradoxical affirmation of that same
history" (Harvey 1986, 14).

Deconstruction's attempt to think radical contingency, curiously
enough, does not imply that it undergoes the logical progression from the
contingency of knowledge to the revisability of knowledge (Dews 1987, 37).
As Dews points out, Adorno's awareness of the reciprocal determination of
consciousness and materiality makes it possible for knowledge to "learn from
its objects" (37). Negative dialectics maintains a more complex position,
which states that "there is something *given* in experience, and that there is
nothing given *immediately*" (41; emphasis in original)—that is, the fact of reification does not preclude the attempt to shatter it. Deconstruction is
tempted, as I have maintained, to eschew the possibility of reference and to
reduce subjectivity to a textual effect to offset the universalizing pretensions
of the subject as the source of all knowing.

With these preliminary remarks in mind, I want to address the implications of Adorno's dismantling of the logic of identity (one that he
systematically relates to the logic of equivalence produced by the exchange
relations of capital) for the not merely different but *dissident* subject of feminism and of postcoloniality. Karen Newman's provocative essay "Directing
Traffic: Subjects, Objects, and the Politics of Exchange" makes a plea for
a reappropriation of Adorno's "Subject and Object" inflected with a feminist politics. She describes this procedure as a "politics of the negative"
(Newman 1990, 48).

Newman appreciates Adorno's attempt to perceive subject and object as mutually constituted because, as he was well aware, the point is not to enthrone the object but to abolish the separation and inevitable hierarchy of subject and object. Neither the identity nor the antithesis of subject and object tells the whole story. Newman makes a case for a relation between subject and object in which power circulates rather than congeals, and in which neither subject nor object occupies a fixed position (50).

While I am sympathetic to Newman's desire to complicate the relations between ideology and sexually and racially differentiated subjectivity (I make a similar argument in the Introduction to this book), I am less comfortable with her tendency to privilege the fluidity of the *Kraftfeld* at the expense of Adorno's own trenchant sense of its tensions and contradictions, of what I call its fractured dimension. The fluidity of boundaries could, in short, preclude the acknowledgement of active transgression.

This elision of the *conflict* between self and other misses Adorno's crucial reformulation of the movement of dialectical mediation as "unassuaged unrest" (Adorno 1973c, 203). The dialectic is no longer informed by the subject's desire; instead, it is animated by the opacity of the object. Newman defuses the political import of Adorno's audacious maneuver because she readily forgets that the circulation of power and of subject positions must nevertheless foreground who regulates whom. The marriage of epistemology and ethics/politics can occur, as I have argued, only if the mutual constitution of subject and object does not mystify their historically produced antagonism. It is impossible, therefore, to make grand gestures that simply cancel the subject. Newman's desire to lose sight of the self must be expressed, instead, as an attempt to reclaim the subject "through a postulate of transgression" (Nägele 1982–83, 70). The circulation of power and fluid identities lacks ethicopolitical content unless it includes the subject as "both the resistance against and the principle of domination" (70).

4 /Gayatri Chakravorty Spivak: The "Curious Guardian at the Margin"

I insist that deconstruction is not neutral. It intervenes.   Jacques Derrida

Unfortunately, I understand everything I say.   Gayatri Chakravorty Spivak

The essay allows for the consciousness of nonidentity, without expressing it directly; . . . in refraining from any reduction to a principle, in its accentuation of the partial against the total, in its fragmentary character.
— T. W. Adorno, "The Essay as Form"

It is often said of Adorno that he is a thinker whom everybody knows and nobody reads. I think the same can be said of Gayatri Chakravorty Spivak, for perhaps a different set of reasons. I mean this comment literally in that, as far as I am aware, there is no extended study of her writings (Robert Young's *White Mythologies* devotes a chapter to her work but remains much too polite in its critical engagement), though her name is sprinkled liberally in texts that attempt to politicize deconstruction or that engage with the postcolonial subject.

    Adorno's penchant for aphoristic formulations has led, as Fredric Jameson and Gillian Rose, for instance, have pointed out, to egregious errors of interpretation because the "quotable quote" is plucked from its context and then marshaled as evidence. Because Adorno attempted to write sentences all equidistant from the center, as it were, this strategy of interpretation could lead to embarrassing blunders. More to the point, the fragment, in Adorno's and Benjamin's terms, both conjures up the whole of which it is a part and fractures or defers it. The fragment, in other words, is not an illustration of an idea; it is, instead, a constellation of particulars a momentary illumination of the object's history of suffering as well as of the possibility that has been denied it thus far.

But what has all this to do with Spivak? More than might be evident at first glance. Spivak, too, is cited often, and is always, it seems, embodied in the phrases that appear to encapsulate her often complicated and precious arguments. I want to explore the possibility that critical engagement with Spivak's oeuvre has limited itself to these "simple" phrases because the scope of her critique seems both alarming and unconvincing.

Critics who accept Spivak's generalized pithy (and witty) formulations can congratulate themselves on their sense of humor but can avoid familiarizing themselves with the specific charges she makes. The "global" connections she makes in the context of transnational capitalism then appear as leaps in logic inevitable in one with an ax to grind. Reading Spivak's work, however, also produces the opposite problem. If, as she claimed in a presentation at University College, Galway (May 23, 1992), she never, except unknowingly, overdresses a simple idea, what is the value of the often impenetrable prose in which her analyses are couched? If her contentions are readily condensable into the succinct assertions she periodically introduced into her speech, could these contentions have been made without subjecting her audience to occasional bewilderment?

It probably seems curious that my interpretation of Spivak begins with random remarks on style, but such a consideration is crucial in relation to a corpus that has suffered puzzling *critical* neglect in the same instant that its author garners public attention. Spivak is more often used to bolster arguments, confirm surmises, or confer authority than she is patiently analyzed. Given this situation, it might prove fruitful to broach the problematic of her critiques with Adorno's cautions in mind.

In *Negative Dialectics,* Adorno writes that "philosophy is not expoundable" and that the "crux" of philosophy "is what happens in it, not a thesis or a position" (Adorno 1973c, 33). Is it possible to read Spivak in this light? She calls her essays "interventions," a word that served as title for one of Adorno's own collections of essays, implying thereby that hers is a form of praxis irreducible to theory. By the same token, one must ask whether anything happens in Spivak's essays, whether her privileging of the position of "gadfly" (Spivak 1985a, 147) stirs other than discursive trouble.

Could my demand for lucidity be a function of my desire to collapse the means of representation with the representation itself or to confuse communication with representation? Do Spivak's texts wrestle with the "paradoxicality" of language of which Adorno speaks: that every attempt to communicate is haunted by the sobering awareness of the commodification to which knowledge is subject? To speak, in this sense, is necessarily to misrepresent, to sell out to those whom Spivak has recently called "clarity fetishists" (Spivak 1993, 121). Would Spivak, however, concur with Adorno's contention that "truth is objective, not plausible" (Adorno 1973c, 41)?

In "Imperialism and Sexual Difference," Spivak adopts a theoretical model borrowed from Paul de Man. She writes that according to this model "the basis of a truth-claim is no more than a trope" or what she later calls "a politically interested figuration" (Spivak 1986, 225). Feminism performs a "tropological deconstruction" when it recognizes that woman or the racial other has been produced with reference to, but nevertheless unlike, the "truth" of man (225). Feminism's attempt to establish this recognition as truth is immediately confronted with the problem that its discourse "is marked and constituted by, even as [it] constitute[s], the field of [its] production" (225). Spivak then goes on to show that even as feminists "discover the troping error of the masculist [*sic*] truth-claim" they "perform the lie of constituting a truth of global sisterhood" (226). She describes the "substance" of deconstructive concerns as "the blindness of truth-telling" (226). This blindness is a consequence of ignoring what deconstruction "knows" only too well—"that 'truths' can only be shored up by strategic exclusions, by declaring opposition where there is complicity, by denying the possibility of randomness, by proclaiming a provisional origin or point of departure as ground" (226).

Adorno, too, acknowledges that "cogency and play are the two poles of philosophy" (Adorno 1973c, 15), but he warns specifically against turning philosophy itself into a work of art. Adorno refuses to "authorize some brusque exorcism of the concept" (Eagleton 1990a, 355) and asks, rather, that the conceptual and the aesthetic "keep faith with their own substance

through their opposites" (Adorno 1973c, 15). To collapse the distinction between language and truth (the aesthetic and the conceptual) is to forgo the
value of each. Art's resistance to its meanings is matched by philosophy's refusal to clutch at any immediate thing (15).

Spivak does not consider the possibility of this active negotiation of
truth and trope, just as she does not suggest how the modulating of opposition into the recognition of complicity might change things. Is the blindness
of truth telling more than a pious disclaimer? I have already indicated that
this deconstructive insistence on blindness can itself become a form of superior insight. Commenting on the interweaving of truth and trope in "a general configuration of textuality" (Spivak 1987, 78), Spivak writes that literature "displays that the truth of a human situation *is* the itinerary of not being
able to find it" (77; emphasis in original). She then argues that the unavail-
ability of unified solutions is often not confronted (78). Critical theory, one
assumes, enacts this repeated confrontation.

I want to examine the traffic between the modesty of theory and the
puzzling authority of the theorist a bit further. The critic cannot hold the
key, because "the moment of evidence, the foundation of all truth and objective knowledge is a result of a 'more fundamental' absence—the movement of *différance* itself" (Harvey 1986, 10). Derrida traces the birth of metaphysics to the effacement of its ground, that is, the role of writing in the
constitution of Being. Because the meaningfulness of the sign inheres precisely in the absence of subject and object, interpretation opens on to an
abyss in which the oppositions of metaphysics have "their secret copulating
relationship" (Harvey 1986, 18).

Spivak presumably has this argument in mind when she demonstrates
the impossibility of feminism's oppositional stance. But who "knows" that
this is the case? The deconstructor? As Harvey explains, the question that
seeks to determine what is proper to the practice of deconstruction is itself
improper. Deconstruction's reliance on "both-and" formulations, and its insistence that, if it can be described within metaphysical determinations, such
descriptions do not constitute "the *essence* of deconstruction" and are instances of "incomplete determination" (Harvey 1986, 24; emphasis in original) still do not explain how deconstruction has managed to escape the distinction between truth and falsehood, or what one is to do with an answer
that shatters the question. In other words, to ask what deconstruction is entails setting up a response within the domain of metaphysics that deconstruction has already effectively undermined/exceeded.

If the critical negativity of deconstruction cannot be aligned with the affirmativity of (feminism's) politics, then Derrida's and Spivak's claim that deconstruction is not neutral can be understood only in terms of its complicity with, rather than its opposition to, power. If truth and epistemology are to be situated elsewhere, or at least also elsewhere, deconstruction must confront the epistemological status of a discourse that exposes the vanity of epistemology. How is the "presence" of deconstruction to make a difference if intentions are intrinsically nonfulfillable and the object always escapes (see also Harvey 1986, 25, 28)? Besides, deconstruction seems in danger of banality when so much of the discourse produced in its name seems to overlook the distinction between the impossibility of unified truth and the provisionality of truth(s).

Adorno's philosophy, to put it crudely, adopts for its premise deconstruction's conclusion. Adorno writes that in principle, "philosophy can always go astray . . . which is the sole reason why it can go forward" (Adorno 1973c, 14). The "untruth" of epistemology, in other words, is the condition of possibility of its "truth." Rather than read Adorno's declaration (truth is objective, not plausible) as a species of objectivism or as a desire to resurrect a metaphysics of presence, it seems appropriate to construe the term "objective" in relation to the status of the object in Adorno's philosophy.

If one recalls Adorno's solemn assertion that "the need to lend a voice to suffering is a condition of all truth" (Adorno 1973c, 17–18), then the "objectivity" of truth inheres in the world that weighs on the subject. The "truth" of Spivak's texts lies in her capacity to contest the plausibility of patriarchy, capitalism, and Empire, inasmuch as their discourses simultaneously invest and occlude the dispossessed colonial subject. The objectivity of her texts resides in the visibility she accords those constituted as others or as objects of these discourses.

Adorno is to be understood literally here: truth is objective because it tells the tale of the object and seeks to redeem the object in its alterity. This alterity cannot be elicited without charting its historical trajectory, the relations of determination that conspire to produce alterity as the object of a certain discursive practice. Nevertheless, Spivak's task, as Adorno's interest in concretion bears out, is to explore the contingency of the object as not only the sum of its determinations, but also their excess. Spivak, in short, attempts to reveal the heteronomy of the feminine and ethnic object of the "subject of the West, or the West as Subject" (Spivak 1988, 271).

In warning against confusing truth with the plausibility of explanations,

Adorno deprecates the epistemological model that represents knowledge as the possession of truth. Adorno is leery of the commodification of knowledge, the process in which, as Susan Buck-Morss explains, "the medium of language [is] seen as the truck that [takes knowledge] to the market, where the 'exchange' of ideas mean[s] simply the transmission of information" (Buck-Morss 1977, 87). Spivak, particularly because of her precarious position as native informant, shares Adorno's wariness.

She traces her discomfort with the emergence of the "Third World" as a privileged signifier within radical criticism to the tendency "to think of the Third World as distant cultures, exploited but with rich intact heritages waiting to be recovered, interpreted, and curricularized in English translation" (Spivak 1985a, 128). Hence, her work on the Third World or what she deems a particularly "hallowed" signifier, that of the Third World Woman, has been devoted to exploring "the difficulties in fixing such a signifier as an object of knowledge" (128). This chapter reads Spivak's continued reluctance to "fix" the Third World Woman against Adorno's affirmation of "the preponderance of the object," of epistemology as the process in which the object, not the subject, takes the lead (see Buck-Morss 1977, 88).

Does focusing on the Third World Woman as an object of knowledge leave no choice but to objectify her? Can epistemology avoid the perils of information retrieval? Can the "realized difficulty of knowing" (Sangari's phrase) constitute a kind of object lesson? Should the language of philosophy content itself with indicating how the object always escapes? If intelligibility is a function of the absence of subject and object (because meaningfulness inheres in signs), how is the diagnosis of power relations to be conducted? After all, the nexus of power-knowledge requires a hierarchical relation between subject and object, just as discourses, which in Foucault's terms are responsible for rendering an object manifest, nameable, and describable, are not anonymous. If the intelligibility of the signifier is always in doubt, how can it nevertheless bespeak an oppression that "radical" critics use as a stick with which to beat the hegemony of interlocking systems of social order? These questions frame my critical scrutiny of Spivak's interruptions of the texts of transnational capitalism, patriarchy, and Empire. I hope to delineate the possibility of a relation between native informant and Third World Woman that does not require the denegation of the active, interpretive powers of the subject and that simultaneously brings the fate of the object at the hands of the subject to the fore.

I would like to recapitulate briefly some of the contentions that I have made in chapter 3 in order to clarify my interest in Spivak's work as in some ways an exemplary execution of Adorno's plans for negative dialectics. Adorno's philosophy simultaneously forms the basis of my critique of Spivak's methodological assumptions and procedures. I have no desire to turn my engagement with Spivak into a conflict of interpretations; her essays, as Adorno might have said, are the occasion and not the point of my critique (see my discussion of Adorno's micrological procedure in *Against Epistemology* in the second section of chapter 3).

In other words, I do not wish to claim the superiority of my analysis of the texts she reads over hers—what is at stake is the viability of the strategies she employs and the tenability of the conclusions she draws. More to the point, I want to determine the political consequences of adopting a (deconstructive) epistemology that "does not wish to officiate at the grounding of societies" (Spivak 1985a, 147) but prefers, instead, to rest easy in "a radical acceptance of vulnerability" (Spivak 1990b, 18).

Adorno argues that the identity accorded the subject has been the consequence of a constitution of the object as radically other. Adorno rescues the dialectic from critical orthodoxy when he claims that the movement of the dialectic is animated by "the resistance which otherness offers to identity" (Adorno 1973c, 160–61). This desire to reclaim the object or the other from the inexorable progress and sublation *(Aufhebung)* of the Hegelian dialectic grants the object a new status. The object is no longer merely instrumental to the subject's self-realization but remains *immanent* to identity as objective resistance and as "unassuaged [somatic] unrest" (Adorno 1973c, 203).

Spivak imbues the object in (merely) philosophical discourse with historical specificity. The object that Adorno describes as being immanent to but coerced by the subject becomes, within the confines of Spivak's discourse, the "subaltern" as sexed subject and ethnic other. It might also be said that she extracts the other from the epistemological confines within which Derrida asks that philosophy think *its* other and reintroduces the other into history. It remains to be seen whether Spivak accomplishes more than "a pointing toward that which can *never* be reached" (Harvey 1986, 131; my emphasis) or whether she manages to elude the slippage between "that which language can *never* capture" and "that which language seems to kill" (136; my emphasis).

The world that weighs on the subject is the discourse of orientalism and of racism, whose epistemic violence ensures that the subaltern does not "speak." As Derrida explains in "Racism's Last Word,"

> the point is not that acts of racial violence are only words but rather that they have to have a word. . . . [Racism] institutes, declares, writes, inscribes, prescribes. A system of marks, it outlines space in order to assign forced residence or to close off borders. It does not discern, it discriminates. (Derrida 1985b, 292)

Spivak's own "blueprints of an interminable analysis" (Spivak 1987, 110) trespass on forbidden ground to carve a representative space from which the subaltern might speak. These blueprints might be said to be of a piece with yet another dimension of Adorno's sense of the objectivity of truth. Not only does Spivak "lend a voice to suffering"; she produces, in the course of doing so, "truth" that "critically challenge[s] the course of history rather than merges with it" (see Snow [Buck-Morss] 1977, 115).

Spivak's work raises questions that theoretical discourse prefers to evade: Who or what inhabits/appropriates the category of the subject? How might the insertion of philosophy into history make it possible to trace the (de)formation of the subject to "the conditions of material production" (Adorno 1973c, 284)? If one reads her texts as vital deployments of a negative dialectic between a masculine and Eurocentric self and its feminine and ethnic other, the significance of Adorno's rethinking of the discourse of the subject from the standpoint of the object becomes clear.

Spivak situates theoretical consciousness in "the arena of cultural explanations that question the explanations of culture" (Spivak 1987, 117). In doing so, she seems to endorse Adorno's assertion that the mind does not lie "beyond the total process in which it finds itself as a moment" (Adorno 1973c, 200). If Adorno's critique of identity hinges on the split between mental and manual labor, in which categories of rationality inadvertently reproduce the constraints of capitalist relations, Spivak's essays repeatedly draw attention to the collaboration of intellectuals, institutions, and "advanced capitalist technocracy" (Spivak 1987, 107).

This displacement of the opposition between mental and manual labor (except insofar as intellectuals, in their institutional allegiances, collude in the exploitation of the latter) is crucial if intellectuals are to avoid consigning Third World Women to "questions of daily survival" while they lament the fact that "women of privilege . . . have the luxury to contemplate woman's writing and voice" (see Przybylowicz 1989, 299). I shall return to this problem in connection with Spivak's privileging of women who have no access to the culture of imperialism and for whom, she claims, entering the labor force is not an unquestioned good.

Given this hasty attempt to put Adorno and Spivak into what I hope will be a productive relation, it is now possible to consider the value and efficacy of Spivak's effort to turn the negativity of the subaltern, who has hitherto been reduced to a systemic excrescence, into occasion for critique and resistance. The subaltern woman, in Spivak's texts, becomes the "effective and as yet unthought limit" (Derrida 1985b, 298) of the self-consolidating discourses of Empire and humanism. Spivak has no desire to produce more versions of the subaltern as a "programmed near-[image] of [the] sovereign self" of Europe (Spivak 1985a, 128). Instead, she seeks a mode of writing that will transfigure philosophy (theory) itself into "the prism in which [the inextinguishable color from nonbeing] is caught" (Adorno 1973c, 57). Spivak does not simply oppose, in complementary fashion, the lost self of the colonized to the sovereign self of Europe. If self-definition produces otherness as its negative term, the nonbeing of the other challenges the very terms of the definition.

If Spivak's trajectory can be described as the unsettling inhabitation of master discourses by a differential female subject of color, how does the catachrestical nature of her predicament or the unevenness of her discursive interruptions enable the re-presentation of the feminine/ethnic object? If it is true that "to be lost, to encounter impasse, to fall, and to desire both fall and impasse" is "what happens to the body in theory" (Trinh 1989, 42), what might the fate of the body of and in the real be?

Benita Parry's "Problems in Current Theories of Colonial Discourse" (one of the very few essays that devote reasonable space to Spivak) identifies the achievements of deconstructive analysis in the field of colonial discourse while trying to ascertain the "truth" of its radical claims or the superiority of its diagnosis of the "dispersed space of power" (Parry 1987, 29) to the "adversarial rhetoric" (28) more common to the writings of critics like Fanon. Parry summarizes the tenets of deconstructive decolonization as follows:

> In the territory cleared of metaphysical divisions, undifferentiated identity categories and ontological absolutes providing the ideological justifications for colonialism's system, criticism . . . reveals for analysis the differential, variously positioned native—for some crit-

ics a self-consolidating other, for others an unconsenting and recalcitrant self—and in place of the permanently embattled colonial situation constructed by anti-colonialist theory, installs either a silent
place laid waste by imperialism's epistemic violence, or an agonistic
space within which unequally placed contestants negotiate an im-
balance of power. (29)

Although Parry does not want to accuse "criticism" of political quietism,
she is rightly troubled by its inability to translate a politics of reading into an
adumbration of "native" resistance. She is equally concerned that the homogenizing impulse evident in, for example, Spivak's use of terms such as
the "axiomatics of imperialism" obscures the diversity of Europe's self-pre-
sentation. In Parry's terms, Spivak attributes absolute power to colonialist
discourse and simultaneously rejects the value of representing the role of
the "native" as a combative historical subject committed to the quest for
an-other knowledge (34).

Parry argues persuasively that Spivak's writing out of years of actual historical and political struggle on the part of the colonized is a consequence of
the very sensitivity of her micrological analyses, which transform brute
power into an insidious process wherein the "native" colludes in his or her
own objectification. Parry "masterfully" describes this disturbing transition
in Spivak's work:

Where military conquest, institutional compulsion and ideological
interpellation was, epistemic violence and devious discursive nego-
tiations requiring of the native that he [*sic*] rewrite his position as
object of imperialism is; and in place of recalcitrance and refusal enacted in movements of resistance and articulated in oppositional
discourses, a tale is told of the self-consolidating other and the dis-
articulated subaltern. (36)

My engagement with Spivak echoes Parry's perspicacious observations,
but I hope, with the help of Adorno, to "redeem" Spivak's oeuvre. This desire involves examining the implications of interpreting her interventions as
performances of a negative dialectic between colonizer and colonized rather
than only as tropological deconstructions. My critique tries to come to terms
with what Spivak does before faulting her for what she fails to do. In articulating the limits of her "perilous" and "interrogative" (deconstructive) epistemology Radhakrishnan's phrases, I hope to invoke the beginnings of "another knowledge" (Parry's phrase) that allows "the method neither quite to
absorb the contents . . . nor to immaterialize them" (Adorno 1973c, 48).

The "seeds" of this other knowledge exist in the interstices of her own work—in the logic of its matter, as Adorno might have said.

Despite Spivak's problematic adoption of a deconstructive epistemology, her interest in the *politics* of marginality makes it difficult to dismiss her readings out of hand. Even though she identifies truths with tropes, she continually emphasizes that these truths or tropes are politically interested figurations. Her tropological deconstructions, therefore, indicate the exclusions that shore up truth-claims. If Derrida lays bare the structure of contradictions that constitutes a work, Spivak reveals "what inhabits the prohibited margin of a particular explanation" (Spivak 1987, 106). She argues that the nature of the prohibited margin exposes the politics of the explanation in question.

She chooses to inhabit the excluded margin of cultural explanations in the name of difference. Her cultivation of marginality, it must be noted, is strategic; that is, it involves more than pointing an accusing finger at the center (107). Spivak defends the complexity of her position in deconstructive terms—she does not want the margin to exchange places with the center (this desire is to be read in conjunction with her rejection of oppositional politics) but to displace the opposition between margin and center.

By implicating herself in the center, Spivak accuses *it* of marginality while allowing herself the freedom and flexibility to act as a "shuttle" between margin and center who "thus narrate[s] a displacement" (107). Spivak does not confront the privilege the postcolonial intellectual must possess in order to roam the corridors of power at will, all the while proclaiming her marginality. Besides, does her privileging of those women who have no access to the culture of imperialism as objects of knowledge mean to imply that resistance can come only from those lucky enough to be "shuttles" rather than victims?

In the paper Spivak presented at Galway, she assumed an inevitable split between theory and practice when she admitted that the language of what she called "high theory" was of no use in her dialogues with women in Algeria. There, she said, the work of revolution proceeds in the way it always has, meaning, I suppose, in a language replete with pragmatic considerations. I think there is more to this than a courageous concession to the irrelevance of theory.

Through much of her speech, which described the process of gendering as internalized constraint perceived as choice, Spivak seemed oddly surprised that disenfranchised women nevertheless exercise their right to make ethical choices. Some of the members of her audience alighted on this perception as a novelty, as if "survival" does not involve the rational adjudication of truth-claims. I dwell on this problem at some length because the apparent sensitivity to the mutual implication of politics and epistemology rarely seems to avoid the patronage of a stance that leaves the "real" work of revolution to the "other" while intellectuals confine themselves to refining epistemological categories on the other's behalf (see also Foley 1985, 121; Spivak 1988).

At this point I want to reiterate Adorno's designs for a radical philosophy in the context of an essay I have deliberately failed to mention. This hitherto silent essay, though possibly the instrument of Spivak's "redemption," will not serve to resolve the sometimes impossible contradictions of her work into a spurious harmony. Both Spivak and Adorno hold that "no object is wholly known" and that "knowledge is not supposed to prepare the phantasm of a whole" (Adorno 1973c, 14), so I hope this absence of closure will be forgiven.

Adorno shatters the dichotomy between politics and epistemology because he believes that reification bewitches both concept and object. Social contradictions, therefore, reappear as the distortion to which philosophical antinomies subject thought. Immanent critique incites the self-liquidation of concepts or the process of dialectical negation, which holds concepts accountable for effacing the suffering that has sedimented itself in them.

The very transparency that concepts arrogate to themselves betrays them because it proves much too revealing of their being in the world. Materiality inheres in consciousness as the latter's immanent contradiction and thus renders absurd the belief that "the power of thought is sufficient to grasp the totality of the real" (Adorno [1931] 1977, 120). Nevertheless, Adorno emphasizes that even though the real functions as thought's essential limit, it is overpowered by thought's relentless desire to "rediscover itself" in the real. Thought then "veils reality and eternalizes [reality's] present condition" (120).

The lecture in which Adorno makes these points, "The Actuality of Philosophy" (1931), proves the surprising consistency of his rumination. It is his first attempt to refashion philosophy into a discourse whose primary task would be to relinquish the illusion "that being itself is appropriate to thought and available to it" (120). For Adorno, reason can hope to "come across correct and just reality," but "only in traces and ruins" (120). He aims to "burst . . . open" the relation between reason and reality (122).

Adorno transforms the stolidity and seamlessness of being into an "incomplete, contradictory, and fragmentary" text that philosophy must "read"

(126). Adorno is careful to distinguish the philosophical from the scientific method: the scientist, in his view, receives scientific findings as ahistorical and invincible, whereas the philosopher turns epistemology into the unriddling of signs, into a precarious mode of interpretation that seeks truth without ever being sure of possessing the key to it. This truth, being both fleeting and elusive, puts philosophy in the position of continually beginning anew. Philosophy alights on truth unexpectedly and momentarily and consequently does not envisage its task as the unearthing of an already existent meaning.

Adorno's indebtedness to Benjamin is evident here, particularly when he goes on to claim that the configuration of historical images constitutes unintentional truth, in contrast to the Hegelian assumption of the intentionality of history. The crucial difference, for Adorno, was that the historical dimension of truth did not prove the truthfulness of history. Adorno shares with Marx the desire to collapse the interpretation and abolition of given realities in the imagination of a constructive, not merely interpretative, philosophy.

The question that informs his lecture is how interpretative philosophy can "construct keys before which reality springs open" (130). The opposing modes of idealism and positivism use keys that are too large, or that fit in the lock but fail to open the door. Armed with the premise that being does not submit to the rationality of thought, interpretative philosophy welcomes the moments when "irreducible reality breaks in upon it" (132). The loss of security that the reliance on historical concreteness involves (that it is no longer possible to grasp the *totality* of the real), however, is not threatening to the modest hope that "it may be possible to penetrate the detail, to explode in miniature the mass of merely existing reality" (133).

Adorno's call for a "nonalienated mode of cognition" (Eagleton 1990a, 2), his desire to philosophize not about the concrete but out of it (see Nägele 1982–83, 74), requires the philosopher to dissolve the reified appearances of things in order to make their historical becoming visible and intelligible. Adorno wants to avoid the process by which reality that is no longer identical with its concept becomes opaque and inexplicable (Buck-Morss 1977, 72).

The particular, in his philosophical method, always exists in a dialectical, mediated relation to the totality of social relations, and its value lies in its contingency. The traces and ruins of which Adorno speaks are the loci of hope because their very resistance to categorization defies the existing order of things (Buck-Morss 1977, 76). This resistance mocks the classificatory and universalizing impulse inherent in the attempt to equate pigeonholing with knowledge (Buck-Morss 1977, 72). Adorno, in short, employs a philosoph-ical method whose "gaze [catches] the exception rather than the rule" (Buck-Morss 1977, 176), and the exception thus becomes a fugitive glimpse of the rule's most profound truths.

Can the Subaltern Speak?

Spivak's entire project can be described as a persistent vigilance to the, at best, objectification, and at worst, disappearance, of women in the Third World from discourses whose "focus remains defined by the [Western] in-vestigator as subject" (Spivak 1987, 150). She writes that the discontinuity between worlds must be confronted because an attention to sexual difference does not necessarily connote an antipathy to imperialism, however benevo-lent the impulse of Western feminism might be. This problem prompts Spivak's listing of questions she considers crucial to intellectual endeavor on the part not only of excommunicated patriarchs but also of canonized femi-nists, busily perpetuating the lie of global sisterhood:

> However unfeasible and inefficient it may sound, I see no way to avoid insisting that there has to be a simultaneous other focus: not merely who am I? but who is the other woman? How am I nam-ing her? How does she name me? Is this part of the problematic I discuss? (150)

In Spivak's acknowledgment of benevolence, she appreciates the decision on the part of Western feminists "to suspend their judgements . . . whenever the other is concerned," but she seeks to indicate that their recognition of the danger of speaking for the other also "serves as an excuse for their compla-cent ignorance and their reluctance to involve themselves in the issue" (Trinh 1989, 80). Spivak's own position as a postcolonial intellectual, colo-nized by the culture of imperialism, if not subject to the brute exploitation of multinational capitalism, is, she claims, nevertheless one of token power.

She describes her status within the institution as a product of the process by which "the putative center welcomes selective inhabitants of the margin in order better to exclude the margin" (Spivak 1987, 107). While I hesitate to accept her abject representation of her own access to power, I sympathize with her identification of the irony that attends that access. There is also something to be said for Spivak's experience as a diasporic intellectual, the "dehumanization of . . . relocation—reeducation—redefinition, the humiliation of having to falsify [her] own reality, [her] voice" (Trinh 1989, 80), which colors her sometimes remote theoretical formulations with an occasional personal urgency.

Spivak is too intelligent to attribute much of the pain that accompanies displacement to her own experience; after all, hers was not a forced relocation and she was not fleeing the horrors of the Calcutta that fascinates and repels Western imagination and fills Western media. But it is precisely this displacement of the "authentic" Indian experience within the dimensions of her self that informs her critical practice. Incidentally, the cover of Spivak's *The Post-Colonial Critic* sports an image of what one might call a "generic" Indian woman, replete with a tight braid, dangling earrings, and what the West likes to call a caste mark on her forehead. Although I do not imagine that this portrait is intended to resemble Spivak herself (at least I hope not!), the nature of the representation is, to say the least, significant. After all, it serves to introduce the reader to a woman who vigorously abjures every attempt to iron out her constitutive contradictions and homogenize her stubborn heterogeneity, one who always registers as other (Spivak 1990b, 79). Perhaps the juxtaposition is deliberate; that is, the conversations with Spivak serve to revoke the stereotyped image.

Spivak cannot "say" her reality even though she is angered by representations that distort it and compelled by the desire to stall the eager voices that rush "to fill in the blanks on [her] behalf" (Trinh 1989, 80). The chastening realization that her inability or unwillingness to say her reality has resulted in her being said (my deployment of Trinh 1989, 80) produces the repetitive and interminable nature of her analyses, their relentless pursuit of discourses that presume to say the other in order, predictably, to *unsay* those discourses.

Even if Spivak's practice of deconstruction cannot be consigned to the category of free play, there is no denying that she continues to situate her interventions (the very word gives her game away) within the inscription and de-scription of the "tried and true" codes of patriarchy and imperialism. To borrow Audre Lorde's words, Spivak uses "the master's tools [to] dismantle the master's house" and seems relatively content to do so, even though her tactics keep her trapped within the confines of "beat[ing] [the master] at his own game" (Lorde, as quoted in Trinh Minh-ha 1989, 80) and render her reluctant to promote genuine change.

For her, critique involves the unremitting exposure of complicity rather than the charting of opposition, the shifting of the ground under one's feet as a prelude to walking somewhere (see the description of Derrida's technique in Hobson 1991, 104). Spivak's method is analogous to that of Derrida, who says: "If I saw clearly ahead of time where I was going I really don't believe that I should take another step to get there [but this does] not mean . . . I never know where I'm going" (quoted in Hobson 1991, 104).

Postcolonial discourse, I submit, cannot be content with such artlessness (or artfulness); it must attempt at least a modest resolution of "the determinate tension between . . . the critical and the affirmative, the radically indeterminate and the intentionally determinate" (Radhakrishnan 1987, 214). That practice and principle might very well prove to be at odds is no excuse for not putting theory to the test of history, or for not letting "truth . . . enter . . . into configurations and causal contexts that help to make it evident or to convict it of its failings" (Adorno 1973c, 42).

Spivak's readings occur "within a shifting and abyssal frame," continually confronted with the proverbial choice that is no choice at all: "To choose not to read is to legitimate [hegemonic] reading, and to read no more than allegories of unreadability is to ignore the heterogeneity of the 'material'" (Spivak 1987, 28–29). Whether she admits it or not, Spivak can hardly wish that her efforts be construed as admitting to failure in advance. As Foucault might say, to argue that discourses transmit power is simultaneously to produce discourse that thwarts power. To rely on a discursive practice that does no more than reveal the field of its production is to succumb to what Spivak herself attacks as the conservative misreading and annexation of deconstruction. Surely her writing is a consistent battle against deconstruction's unfortunate fate: "What was once to surpass dogmas and the tutelage of self-certainty has become the social insurance of a cognition that is to be proof against any untoward happening" (to adapt Adorno 1973c, 35).

I should like to consider Spivak's contentious essay "Can the Subaltern Speak?" in order to suggest the parameters of the "radical" nature of her enterprise. Spivak's reluctant authority stems from her position as native informant "for first world intellectuals interested in the voice of the Other" (Spivak 1988, 284). Her tricky negotiation of the traffic between First and Third Worlds involves her distance as a privileged intellectual from those women with whom she nevertheless shares a common identity as "native." She must contend, therefore, with a proximity to those she seeks to represent, a proximity that paradoxically reveals itself as untraversable distance.

She uses this doubled sense of the subaltern subject as at once "irretrievably heterogeneous" (284) and uncannily alike to advantage in the construction of a theory that can no longer be placed in binary opposition to practice. Consequently, the instability of the object of knowledge undermines the possibility of a theory that is " 'of' something, [that] requires a genitive, a beat which it can police or process" (Hobson 1991, 103).

Her "intention" is to operate "like a map or graph of knowing rather than an individual self that knows, [thus inscribing] a limit to the claim to power of knowledge" (Spivak 1987, 258). Spivak therefore cannot produce a theory whose "beat, [or] area of application is *opposite, over against*" its object (Hobson 1991, 103). Instead, she offers two different options: that "the production of theory is also a practice" (Spivak 1988, 275) and that intellectuals practice a "vigilance precisely against too great a claim for transparency" (293).

These injunctions inform her analysis of "the relations between the discourses of the West and the possibility of speaking of (or for) the subaltern woman" (271). She begins with a critique, interestingly enough, of "those intellectuals who are our best prophets of heterogeneity and the Other" (272), her targets being Foucault and Deleuze. Spivak argues that the "theory of pluralized 'subject-effects' gives an illusion of undermining subjective sovereignty while often providing a cover for . . . an interested desire to conserve the subject of the West, or the West as Subject" (271).

She makes this claim because of the tendency in both these intellectuals to indulge in "an unquestioned valorization of the oppressed as subject" and to declare as their objective the establishment of conditions in which the oppressed themselves would be able to speak (274). Here Spivak seems to share Horkheimer's and Adorno's perception that the mere fact of oppression in no way serves as the guarantor of correct knowledge, as the wherewithal for crashing through the walls of ideology, or as incitement to insurrection.

Moreover, the "brandishing [of] concrete experience" could merely reproduce the division between "those who act and *struggle* [and are therefore mute and] those who act and *speak*" (275; emphasis in original). Within this scenario, the intellectual need no longer implicate "himself" in the constitutive contradictions of subject-formation or acknowledge "his" complicity with the dissemination of ideology. Spivak thus unveils the interested convergence of the representation of subalterns as "self-knowing" and "politically canny" with the representation of intellectuals as "transparent" (Spivak 1988, 275), as somehow untouched by the vast economic and political machinery that constitutes the "Other as the Self's shadow" (280).

Spivak draws upon Marx's attempts to defetishize the concrete in her rejection of Foucault's and Deleuze's desire to occlude the overdetermined process that produces the other as a subject whose attempts to knit together power, desire, interest, and agency are deliberately and "ruthlessly dislocated" (280). She traces this systematic dislocation to the imperialist project in which economic and epistemic violence coincide. Her essay questions the essentialist agenda implicit in the Western intellectual's ability to consider subaltern consciousness in isolation from the "palimpsestic narrative of imperialism" (281), in "his" positing of "an unrepresentable subaltern subject that can know and speak itself," thus allowing "him" to "abstain from representation" (285). Spivak's point is that this abstinence is itself a form of representation, of an undeceived subaltern consciousness in whom desire and interest unproblematically coincide.

Spivak has thus far called into question the place and authority of the writing/investigating subject, a strategy not unlike Adorno's critique of identity thinking. Like Adorno, Spivak rejects the predication of the possibility of knowledge on identity (254). Her essays adumbrate the "interruption" that characterizes the relationship between the theoretical ("no program of knowledge production can presuppose identity as origin") and the practical (the "need for claiming subaltern identity"), and that "persistently brings each term to crisis" (254).

She develops this strategy in order to point out that the narrative and history of imperialism cannot be contested merely by "substituting the lost figure of the colonized" (295). This substitution only sanctions the First World intellectual's ignorance, because this intellectual constructs "a homogeneous Other referring only to [his] own place in the seat of the Same or the Self" (288). In her own way, Spivak does as good a job as Adorno in rejecting the jargon of authenticity, particularly insofar as it serves to ground "counterhegemonic ideological production" (307).

She resists the temptation to masquerade "as the absent nonrepresenter who lets the oppressed speak for themselves" (292); instead, she offers a nuanced position in which intellectuals do not "represent *(vertreten)* [the other] but . . . learn to represent *(darstellen)* [themselves]" (289). I want to examine briefly what such a position involves and what it implies for the future of postcolonial discourse. I want to suggest that this shift only apparently dissolves the subject who Spivak says presides by disavowal; in reality, under the guise of protecting the subaltern from being offered as "an object of seduction to the representing intellectual" (285), of refusing the epistemological hubris that renders the subaltern all too available and assailable, Spivak returns the focus squarely to the machinations of imperialist discourse, leaving the subaltern woman to shuttle between the twin terrors of patriarchy and imperialism, to fend for herself as well as a "pious item . . . in global laundry lists" can (308).

In "The Rani of Sirmur," Spivak makes an explicit statement of her lack of interest in engaging in counterhegemonic ideological production. She writes that to "nostalgically [assume] that a critique of imperialism would restore the sovereignty for the lost self of the colonies [and that] Europe [would], once and for all, be put in the place of the other that it always was" is a "revisionary impulse" doomed to failure. She prefers to produce "an alternative historical narrative of the 'worlding' of what is today called 'the Third World'" (Spivak 1985a, 128).

Spivak accords more value to the tracing of the itinerary of the consolidation of sovereignty and the concomitant effacement of subaltern consciousness than to the articulation of the latter's resistance. Even if one must reject "an essentialist, utopian politics" (Spivak 1988, 276), is the only alternative a sweeping assertion that "there is no space from which the sexed subaltern subject can speak" (307)? Adorno is only too aware of the dislocation and incoherence to which the subject under capitalism is prone, but he insists that the mutilation the subject suffers is also the beginning of the subject's different articulation of its self in relation to an administered world. Spivak rightly rejects the positivistic tendency to view the concrete as somehow indestructible and static, but fails to see that her own attempt to elicit the constitutive contradictions of subaltern consciousness might discover, not a *definition* of subaltern consciousness that encompasses its buried reality, but an active demonstration of the manner in which the subaltern disarticulates its determinations. The identity of the subaltern, in other words, exists in the subaltern's resistance to its identifications. Spivak seems to believe that because nothing is given immediately to experience or to representation, it must be deemed inaccessible.

Spivak wishes to illustrate that the subaltern on the other side of the international division of labor has, for far too long, served as superfluity, as a dispensable and disposable excess or by-product of the modes-of-production narrative rather than as a subject with autonomy and substance. It is therefore sentimental (because the subaltern has been denied even the respectability that attaches to a discernibly proletarian subject) to attempt to retrieve the subaltern self, or at least within the context of what Spivak calls "elite approaches" (Spivak 1987, 253), "the subaltern's view, will, presence, can be no more than a theoretical fiction to entitle the project of reading" (204).

Spivak views the subaltern as an indispensable "beginning" in Said's sense, as the name of that which authorizes a process of rereading or intervention. The subaltern enables the project of reading but is not itself its identifiable object. Spivak, however, gives up too easily. Even the estranged appearance of reality, in Adorno's terms, harbors, if nothing else, the truth of reification and thus can be unriddled to elicit something besides its deceptive appearance.

This condition might account for Spivak's sustained focus on the discourses and relations of material production that produce the subaltern as the object of knowledge. Her focus leads her to conclude, first, that there is no space from which the subaltern can speak because of the latter's subsumption in power relations, and, second, that the notion of the concrete is itself a limiting proposition, one that enforces slavish conformity to the dictates of common sense. The first conclusion puts Spivak in danger of what Adorno would describe as practicing critique that confirms rather than negates what it attacks (see my Introduction to this volume). The second leads her to underestimate her own accomplishment.

I have already commented on Adorno's notion of the object as containing both its history and its denied possibilities. Spivak's interest in the subaltern's geopolitical determinations, which deny the transparency of the subject of knowledge as well as of the object of cognition, resists the reification implicit in a commonsense perception of facts. What she does, therefore, in locating the "immense discontinuous network of strands" of which what seems to operate as a subject is part (Spivak 1987, 204), is to "bring the petrified [thing, that is, the subaltern as object of cognition] in flux and precisely thus make us aware of history" (Adorno 1973c, 130).

Spivak, appropriately enough, has discovered not the essence of the subaltern, but the concreteness (in Adorno's sense of the term) of the subaltern. This concreteness can be traced to the function of the subaltern not only as the unthought limit of Western epistemology, but as the unresolved contradiction of the ideology of Empire. What Spivak implies but does not assert is that "the aporetical concepts of philosophy are marks of what is objectively, not just cogitatively, unresolved" (see Adorno 1973c, 153). For the deconstructive critic, this by no means simpleminded relation between sign and referent is impossible.

Or is Spivak's point that the *Western* intellectual will be unable to hear even if the subaltern were to speak? If this is the case, Spivak seems to want to have things both ways. On the one hand, intellectuals who believe that

the oppressed can represent themselves are castigated as engaging in sanctioned ignorance of the subaltern's position "on the other side of the international division of labor from socialized capital, inside and outside the
circuit of the epistemic violence of imperialist law and education supple-
menting an earlier economic text" (Spivak 1988, 283). On the other hand,
her own attempt to "traffic in a radical textual practice of differences" shifts
the interest from "rendering vocal the individual" to "rendering visible the
mechanism" of silencing (285). In this context, the epistemic violence of imperialism becomes indistinguishable from the "general violence that is the
possibility of an episteme" (287).

The prospects for counterhegemonic ideological production seem bleak
indeed if the discovery that the colonized have no history within the context
of colonial production is matched by the contention that they cannot know
and speak for themselves. The postcolonial critic, in Spivak's terms, seems
confined to contesting the production of the colonial subject within *Western*
discourse. Her praise of Derrida, for example, has to do with his desire to de-
mote the subject of knowledge within the context of ethnocentrism (293).

The dangers of the assimilation of otherness are too familiar to warrant
comment. But is there room for (female) subaltern consciousness that is not
merely a "displaced figuration," "a violent shuttling . . . between tradition
and modernization" (306)? Must the colonized be forced, once again, to
read the narrative of imperialism, albeit this time inflected with "correct"
politics? For all its theoretical sophistication, Spivak's essay seems to be op-
erating with a schematic notion of power in which oppression seems merely
a matter of gullibility.

Despite her dismissal of the jargon of authenticity, Spivak is not above
privileging the sexed subaltern subject as the discourse of imperialism's unthought limit, or "the historical predicament of the colonial subaltern [as] the
allegory of the predicament of *all* thought, *all* deliberative consciousness"
(Spivak 1987, 204; emphasis in original). She retains the West, therefore, as
the point of reference for the voicing of the subaltern self. More to the point
is her desire to see "that inaccessible blankness circumscribed by an interpret-
able text . . . developed within the European enclosure as *the* place of the
production of theory" (Spivak 1988, 294; emphasis in original).

Is the voicing of subaltern consciousness then to become Europe's problem? Or is the subaltern now instrumental to the intellectual's unlearning of
privilege? (In Spivak's essay "Can the Subaltern Speak?" the subaltern, in the
words of "Imperialism and Sexual Difference," "cathect[s] the representative

space or blank presupposed by the dominant text" [Spivak 1986, 229], but in "Imperialism and Sexual Difference" that space is cathected by the native informant. This collapse of the distinction between investigating subject and subaltern object is never explained.) Why is the text of imperialism any more readable than that of the subaltern? If semiosis is to concern itself with what a text cannot say, why, quite frankly, would it bother? And why does the subaltern continue to recede while the narrative of imperialism overwhelms the vision?

Here Spivak's admiration for deconstruction does her in. Otherness is privileged as the anti-West or the West's limit-text, as the vanishing point of the intelligibility of the discourse of imperialism. The very strategy that enables her to indicate the ruthless effacement of subaltern history and consciousness leads her to privilege that absence and that silence. As a form of resistance, Spivak's method is of a piece with the movement of *différance* that "produces what it forbids, makes possible the very thing that it makes impossible" (Derrida 1976, 143). There is more to this than my frequently expressed distaste for deconstruction's political ambiguity, however.

In the first volume of *The History of Sexuality,* Foucault writes :

> This often-stated theme, that sex is outside of discourse and that only the removing of an obstacle, the breaking of a secret, can clear the way leading to it, is precisely what needs to be examined. Does it not partake of the injunction by which discourse is provoked? Is it not with the aim of inciting people to speak of sex that it is made to mirror, at the outer limit of every actual discourse, something akin to a secret whose discovery is imperative, a thing abusively reduced to silence, and at the same time difficult and necessary, dangerous and precious to divulge? (1980, 34–35)

He then explains that the curious conjunction of provocation and prohibition meant "not that sex [was consigned] to a shadow existence, but that they dedicated themselves to speaking of it ad infinitum, while exploiting it as *the* secret" (Foucault 1980, 35; emphasis in original). I suggest that this is exactly the process to which Spivak subjects the category of the sexed subaltern. Her derogatory comments on authenticity and her refusal to fetishize the concrete notwithstanding, Spivak keeps theory chained to the allure of an elusive subaltern being that is to be found neither in the text of imperialism nor in that of insurgency—indeed, not even between the two.

The "inaccessible blankness" of the subaltern, she says, is nevertheless what she would like to see installed as *the* place for the production of theory, as, in Foucault's terms, an incitement to discourse. She is careful to indicate that the disarticulation of the subaltern is to be understood as a violent aporia rather than a blank absence, but because the subaltern can neither speak the text of female exploitation nor unravel the strands of ideological mystification, her being doubly in shadow makes her all the more effective as theory's constitutive lapse as well as its potential salvation.

Spivak is right to spurn Western intellectuals' celebration of dispersion and heterogeneity without any concession to the active dislocation of identity contingent on the efficacy of imperialism, but, in doing so, I am not so sure she serves the political interests of the subaltern subject either. Because she fears that no theory escapes the marketplace (I borrow Adorno's idea here), and that the text of insurgency could readily freeze into an object of imitation or of investigation, she discerns resistance in the very intangibility of subaltern consciousness.

Does the intangibility of subaltern consciousness connote its impenetrability? its invulnerability? Here, once again, is an example of Spivak's vulnerability to the jargon of authenticity. The subaltern will retain a mysterious quality only because, as Adorno would say, it cannot "be laid down in definite contents that would give the meddlesome intellect something to latch on to" (Adorno 1973c, 61). Given the "secret copulating relationship" between prohibition and provocation, what is to prevent the continued proliferation of Western self-consolidation at the expense of the other that has now safely been deemed inconceivable?

On a different but related front, Spivak tirelessly attacks the prophets of heterogeneity who brandish concrete experience because they readily believe in their own transparency and in the uncomplicated visibility of the objects of their philanthropic radicalism. Curiously, she seems to want to deny the interpretive powers of the investigating subject altogether because of what she construes, in poststructuralist fashion, to be the inherent violence of the episteme. This position, however, would deprive her pronouncements of any validity whatsoever, because she, too, must be considered to conceive her objects as she conveys them (see Adorno 1973c, 206).

Because she wants to highlight precisely those whom the vast intellectual, political, and economic machinery has forgotten, as well as to let them function as a return of the repressed that wreaks havoc on the giant lie of imperialism, her representations of subaltern consciousness, however inadequate to their object, must not be allowed to fall by the wayside as manifestations of "the logic of translation-as-violation" (Spivak 1986, 235). The intellectual, it seems, can desire but not touch, re-present *(darstellen)* himself or herself but not represent *(vertreten)* the other, and, above all, violate but never know.

If I might make a "simple" restatement of my objection to Spivak's position, she supports "a *strategic* use of positivist essentialism in a scrupulously visible political interest" (Spivak 1987, 205; emphasis in original), but avoids tackling the *methodological* implications of an interest in concretion. The problem is that any endeavor that upholds the primacy of the object is immediately identified with positivist essentialism. She engages in a critical appraisal of the project of the historians/historiographers who comprise *Subaltern Studies* in these terms; that is, she applauds what she perceives to be their deployment of deconstructive methodology in their visibly and scrupulously political analyses.

She chooses to privilege their realizations that "subaltern consciousness is subject to the cathexis of the elite, that it is never fully recoverable, that it is always askew from its received signifiers, indeed that it is effaced even as it is disclosed, [and] that it is irreducibly discursive" (Spivak 1987, 203). These are edifying and necessary cautions, no doubt, because one must at all costs avoid the pitfalls of assuming that subaltern women/consciousness need/ needs the superior wisdom that sophisticated theory can offer or are/is unaware that patronage often masquerades as compassion. However, she offers them as methodological presuppositions, which add up to a theoretical practice that accounts for the deconstructive enterprise, always in some sense remaining vulnerable to the very assumptions it dismantles.

The importance of this generalized inscription of cognitive failure cannot, in Spivak's scheme of things, be stressed enough. In succumbing to the desire to restore autonomy, substance, and self-determination to the subaltern, the historiographers, she argues, would ironically objectify "him" because they reproduce, in this move, their transparency and "his" unproblematic representability.

I have already pointed to the tautological character of this move, an inevitable consequence of assuming that knowledge is necessarily analytical, that it partakes of the character of a proposition, a definition, or a statement. The possibility Spivak does not explore here is the one (naturally!) Adorno suggests. Spivak envisages a focus on the particular that fractures or defers the whole, one that does not admit that the particular might be capable of invoking (dare I say referring to?) a whole it cannot articulate.

But Adorno extends the role of the particular as he does that of totality. The impossible totality should function as a critical rather than affirmative category, but also (and this is particularly relevant here) its very deferment accords to "the particular present . . . concrete fullness" (Adorno 1989, 106–7). It is only thus that the reality of the idea or the episteme can be thrown into question. To "forge a practice which takes . . . into account . . . that what one is saying is undermined by the way one says it, radically" (Spivak 1990b, 20) Spivak should also advocate an openness to the undermining accomplished by the heterogeneity of materiality itself.

Spivak's repeated confusion of concretion with positivism is responsible for exhausting the particularity of the subaltern women in the seeming inexhaustibility of the category (the macronarratives of imperialism, patriarchy, and transnational capitalism or the international division of labor) and not the thing. One must regret that the eloquence she summons to the war against the sanctioned ignorance of the Western intellectual or even the native informant does not come to the defense of subaltern specificity more often.

Decolonizing Historiography

I might be accused of deliberately ignoring Spivak's contention that "the truth of a human situation *is* the itinerary of not being able to find it" (Spivak 1987, 77; emphasis in original), in order to force her to conjure a reality that, by definition, is invisible or unattainable. I hasten, therefore, to experiment with a different option. Could Spivak's forays into subaltern territory be accompanied by the "wisdom" that Roland Barthes claims "the action of love obtains": "the other is not to be known; [her or] his opacity is not the screen around a secret, but, instead, a kind of evidence in which the game of reality and appearance is done away with" (as quoted in Trinh 1989, 49)?

Adorno, too, draws upon Marx's inscription of sensual immediacy "in a systematic nexus of ideological deception" (Nägele 1982–83, 75) in his desire to provoke empirical appearance to tell the truth. When Adorno makes philosophical interpretation conform to the unriddling of signs he, in the manner of Nietzsche, Marx, and Freud, rethinks "the dialectic of appearance and being, of surface and depth" (75). Althusser's concept of overdetermination, of the structure of ideology as a process of condensation and displacement, is also, of course, valid here. Nägele's comments, nevertheless, are pertinent to Adorno's conception of philosophical interpretation as the shattering of the spell of reification. If estranged reality is all the philosopher has at "his" disposal, then the dialectic between surface and depth will simply not do. In other words, if surfaces can't be trusted, neither can depths or buried realities be elicited. What is crucial is a tracing of the process of displacement itself that produces this conundrum. In short, "the process of hiding *is* the structure of truth" (75; emphasis in original).

But if phenomena were themselves the truth, and there was no need to look behind them for the truth, how was this truth to be released? The world could not be changed unless it was interpreted first. It is not the elements themselves, but their configuration, that makes them cognitively accessible. In order to express the "logic of the matter," therefore, the subject resorts to an "exact fantasy" that is at once an attempt to "abide strictly within the material" (Adorno [1931] 1977, 131) and a desire to escape its confines insofar as the object is revealed in a new modality. In short, while the subject surrenders to the object, the latter does not remain unchanged by the encounter (see also Buck-Morss 1977, 86–90).

A similar process is at work in Spivak's writing. She seems to believe, with Barker, that postcolonial "discourse must search in restless pursuit of an imaginary goal which it will never reach because the lack of its indefatigable, if subterranean, desire is precisely the apparatus of the quest" (Barker 1984, 110). This belief informs the manner in which her interruptions burst open the relation between reason and reality and mock thought's desire to read the real as its reflection.

Her belief, moreover, contains a political desire to represent the truth of the situation of the subaltern as "the itinerary of silencing" of the subaltern (Spivak 1990b, 31) within the narrative of the West's history. The tracing of this itinerary foregrounds the negotiation between epistemological phenomena and structures of violence that cannot be contained within discursive realms (36). The subaltern, precisely because she functions as the vanishing point of the intelligibility of Western discourse, becomes the unintentional instrument of the deconstitution of its founding concepts, or, to put it more directly, functions as the excess that brings to light the rottenness at/of the core.

In "The Rani of Sirmur," Spivak proposes a reading of archival material in order to suggest the difficulties involved in any historical attempt to get the story straight. Her method, like Adorno's, distinguishes itself from one that seeks reality behind given data. The archival material itself needs considerable sifting and manipulation, and thus conforms, in Adorno's subtle imagining, to the typology of the philosophical text. It is important that Spivak proposes a *reading,* because the historical record is unprocessed and therefore presents itself to the theorist not as a graspable whole or an archaeological find, but as, in Adorno's terms, an "incomplete, contradictory, and fragmentary" text that Spivak must interpret, reconstruct, and reevaluate. She must proceed with due trepidation, because there is, as yet, no fixed object of investigation as well as no results that can be foreseen.

As Spivak makes clear, the historical/archival records "show the soldiers and administrators of the East India Company constructing the object of representations that becomes the reality of India" (Spivak 1985a, 129). She appreciates, as a consequence, Dominick LaCapra's warning against the privileging of archives, however textual their deployment. The archive, as LaCapra points out, inadvertently functions as "a stand-in for the past that brings the mystified experience of the thing itself" (quoted in Spivak 1985a, 130). Her intention is to read historical documents not merely as "quarries" (as LaCapra puts it) for facts, but as overdetermined relics of the "thematics of imperialism" (130).

In the context of "imperial governance" the object emerges as a "cross-hatching of condensations" (130) and, one assumes, displacements, if the Freudian thematics implicit in this essay are taken at face value. I think Spivak resorts to Freud because she wants to explore the relation between the epistemic violence that the subject of imperialism inflicts and the desire that the native informant feels for the lost object of her analysis. Spivak's procedure can, in Adorno's terms, be envisaged as an "unriddling," as an attempt to unpack the "astonishing entwinings" of desire, thought, and matter. She has, after all, only the refuse of an irrecoverable reality at her disposal; worse, this is the refuse of *imperial governance.* The object, that is the Rani, is already lost to Spivak's compassionate gaze; the Rani does not *exist* in any simple sense and neither has she been concealed in order to be made manifest by an intrepid explorer such as Spivak. But if Spivak's reader expects not the spirit or essence of the Rani but a "constellation" of the changing configurations of her "entwinings" with "native" and British patriarchy and Empire or, if one wills, a figure in the carpet, that reader is both satisfied and frustrated.

Spivak's project is unmistakable: "to inspect soberly the absence of a text that can 'answer one back' after the planned epistemic violence of the imperialist project" (131). It seems clear that even as she transforms ciphers into readable texts, Spivak does not permit herself a willingness to be surprised. In other words, the Rani's absence is a foregone conclusion. But, as Adorno might ask, is there a crack or a crevice within this pieced-together, but nevertheless formidable, collage of oppression, misinformation, misrepresentation, native collaboration, and the sheer weight of circumstances that conspire against the Rani, through which the "unintentional reality" of the Rani might seep? Sites of desire and representation, after all, do not have to reconstruct a *sovereign* self, the impossibility of which seems to be Spivak's beef against revisionary impulses or the language of nativism.

Because Spivak's attention remains trained on the construction of the Rani as the object of imperialism, her reading of dispatches, letters, and consultations concerning the deposing of the Rani's husband and the subsequent control to which she and her young son were subject is geared toward uncovering the "force" that can "make the 'native' see himself as 'other'" (133). Spivak produces a reading of the texts at her disposal that "masterfully" traces the process by which the alien is domesticated as Master and the native obliged, ironically, to "cathect the space of the Other on his home ground" (133). In this scenario, the contradiction between the colonizer pitching his tent on what he must represent to himself as uninscribed earth and the dependence of the intelligibility of "the narrative of imperialism-as-history" on "planned" (134) violence is never explored except to affirm the relationship as one of contradiction.

Here the confusion stems from what Adorno would call the phrase giving birth to the reality. The substantiality of the systematic control of land and the forcible removal of its natural or rightful inhabitants sits uneasily with the materiality of a representation in which the alien unintentionally deceives himself that he is occupying uninscribed territory. Of course, ideology is born in the contradiction between representation and reality, but at the risk of reintroducing intentionality into the trajectory of imperialism, I think this representation of matters between alien master and native slave seems unlikely.

The economic motives of imperialism were, after all, never in doubt, least of all to the scions of the East India Company. The conquest of territory, as the history of wars repeatedly bears out, is a logical consequence when trading rights are involved. Because imperialists use up a great deal of pen and paper to explain away their actions, it is a mistake to assume them to have been "unaware" that they were massacring hordes of natives to stake their claim on the land. In this instance, I think it fair to presume that the imperialists were the last to believe their own rationalizations. I do not want to suggest that imperialists were given to introspection or moral conflict; I think, merely, that there is something to be said for Marlow's comments on the colonists' devotion to efficiency in the opening pages of Conrad's *Heart of Darkness* (see also Said's *Culture and Imperialism*).

Spivak offers a competent analysis of the imperialist conspiracy that produces "an 'other' text—the 'true' history of the native Hill states" (135), but does not, in the course of this analysis, examine the effects of this conspiracy on the imperialist subject. A recognizable phase of the project of imperialism, as Marlow sees it, is one in which the colonist is no longer distinguished by his belief in the idea or his appetite for force. He is, instead, the quintessential bureaucrat who effects an inversion of means and ends; that is, colonization is a job like any other, and the colonist can be asked to do no more than his duty, to follow orders as best he can. The devotion to efficiency, in such a reading, produces a complex (imperial) subject, one whose non-monolithic status is not only a matter of class composition or social positionality (133), but whose agency is predicated on his instrumentality as, not surprisingly, an agent of Empire.

Spivak seems to recognize the importance of reconstituting intentionality as a devotion to efficiency, and the master as the subject of the instrumental rationality crucial to "the 'interested' science of war" (135) because, at this point in her essay, representation inexplicably assumes a "planned" status and loses its character as ideological deception. Spivak never distinguishes sufficiently between planned and overt representations, and her essay succumbs to an aporia on this score.

A dialectical approach would have served Spivak's interests admirably here: if the Rani's fate makes visible "unintentional reality," one that defeats the archival documents' "intention" to write her out of historical existence because the riddle of her absence demands interpretation, the intentionality of the project of imperialism can simultaneously be rewritten, not only as a telescoping of determinations, and certainly not as a deliberate(d) cause (136), but as the trajectory of truth in which the debris of history continually surfaces to ensure that conquerors are never redeemed by their unselfish belief in the idea (Marlow's phrase). Similarly, the relation between Birch (instrument as agent) and the Rani (instrument as allegory) is insufficiently explored, perhaps because Spivak tends to absolutize imperial governance.

Spivak wants to make sure that understanding is not construed as forgiveness (136); accordingly, she eschews the temptation to develop the strands of determination into a decipherable pattern or even a momentary illumination. Her traces and ruins consume any significance they might have for the understanding because she wants to retain the irreducibility of the epistemic violence of the narrative of imperialism. This position implies that imperialism is a form of displacement that serves to ground the race-class-gender determinations (137).

In order to resist the transformation of overdetermination into a species of determinism, Spivak removes, oddly enough, the narrative of imperialism from its grounding *in* history or from the function it has hitherto held, which is to tell the truth *of* history. Instead, the narrative of imperialism becomes akin to *différance,* a nonoriginary ground of the process of grounding sociopolitical processes in their race-class-gender determinations. Because the narrative of imperialism is a ground that figures an originary displacement, it troubles the process of narrativization itself, in which "the willed (auto)biography of the West masquerades as disinterested history" (131).

I wonder whether this discursive displacement of the material reality of imperialism puts the Rani at an even further remove, even though the effects of the brutal history that lies in truth are only too palpable on her person or in her lack of personhood. Spivak relinquishes the security that macronarratives offer in favor of what troubles the edge of hegemonic discourses, what is in danger of being destroyed by blundering instruments of conventional analysis that seek to explain events or determine causes rather than trace the relations that produce causes as effects of effects.

Her emphasis on the historicity and narrativity of events does not enable an engagement with historical images or particulars *in* their concreteness— or does it? Spivak identifies the stages that seem to draw her ever closer to the Rani, the mediations that envelop the Rani's subjectivity. Why does Spivak choose this figure, who appears to have little or no presence as an individual but whose instrumentality in the designs of Empire (Spivak says the dismemberment of Sirmur was in the cards) is only too plain? Her obscurity is instrumental to Spivak's own method, which seeks to demonstrate "the allegorical predicament" of the Rani "caught . . . between patriarchy and imperialism" (144).

Spivak rejects the desire to see the Rani as an individual: she emerges as an individual within the text of imperialism only because the English want Sirmur in the hands of "a weaker vessel" (142) who is guarding a young son. This individualistic focus would keep Spivak within the confines of discoursing *about* the concrete rather than from out of it. Instead, Spivak discovers the Rani amid the overwhelming defacement of the names of widows who suffered the fate of self-immolation and the correspondingly meticulous records of the names of the Company's cadets.

It is interesting that Spivak glosses over the record of the Rani's astuteness and generosity because the Rani's actions are "interfere[d] with . . . authoritatively" by the "young white man in her own household" (143–44). I suspect that Spivak wants to avoid lapsing into an individualistic focus that would render the real relations of power askew; however, it seems important that Spivak indicate why the Rani's actions do not count as "evidence" in her desire to touch "some remote substance" of her (147).

Once again, the Rani's declared intention to commit sati becomes the occasion for Spivak's reconstruction of her allegorical predicament. Spivak's comments on the relation between sanctioned suicide and subject formation are insightful and powerful. She writes that this counternarrative of women's consciousness and desire produced not only the imperialist motif of white men saving brown women from brown men (see Spivak 1988), but also served the suspect function of according free will to the sexed subject. The irony, of course, is that "free will" meant allowing oneself to be dissuaded by a British officer or choosing death as the signifier of female desire.

The records do not indicate whether the Rani did commit sati after all, but given the force and persuasion on the side of the British, it is unlikely that she could "choose" to die. Spivak offers the possibility that the English misread the Rani, but uses this perception merely to prove that the Rani "emerges only when she is needed in the space of imperial production" and to insist on the "textualization that violated [Spivak's] Rani" (146–47).

I have no quarrel with Spivak's concern with "the fabrication of representations of historical reality" (147), because she performs the invaluable task of connecting the interpretation of a given reality to the abolition of its oppressive power. Her interest in the Rani as an object of knowledge, as a historical particular, serves to expose the Rani's mediated connection to the totality of social relations. There is, as Spivak says, no real Rani to be found; however, even if the Rani cannot be presented whole and complete and delectable enough for the appetite for knowledge, is there a value to be accorded the brief glimpses one gets of her in Birch or the other imperial texts?

Might those moments when the Rani expresses a desire or performs an action (even if it was nipped in the bud) be construed as the moments when Spivak's traversal of the space of imperial production might have been brought up short, when "irreducible reality breaks in upon" the risky enterprise of unriddling signs? Could the modest hope of "penetrating the detail," the discarded piece of the imperial puzzle, be a genuine probability because the Rani's resistance is already beginning to crack the smooth facade of imperial discourse and power?

Spivak of course does not want to render the traces of the Rani merely opaque and inexplicable, but her own reading is an "exact fantasy" that abides within the archival material and transcends that material only to imagine the Rani "in her simple palace, separated from the authority of her no doubt patriarchal and dissolute husband, suddenly managed by a young white man in her own household . . . [and] caught thus between patriarchy and imperialism" (143–44).

That her "imagination" does not extend to the strain the Rani seems to have put on the patriarchal and imperial text that apparently contained her shows a puzzling neglect by a deconstructive critic who is, by definition, interested in loose threads that unravel a text. I want to conclude my discussion of the Rani with the "fantasy" (I am well aware of the remove at which my own rereading is placed) that a canny and knowing subaltern consciousness might be found in the political embarrassment the Rani's putative sati might have caused (146). Spivak herself admits the Rani was "astute," and it is this figuration of the Rani as the site of (to be sure, failed) resistance to epistemic violence rather than as the space of imperial production that I prefer to "imagine," or that is at least equally persuasive.

"Woman in Difference"

In contrast to the discourse of poststructuralism, which celebrates the language of the body in terms of an ineffable *jouissance* that bespeaks the body's pleasure, Adorno's desire to return thought to the palpable materiality of the body focuses on the capacity of the body to signal suffering. The unassuaged somatic unrest that thought seeks to reproduce within the confines of negative dialectics tells a "tale of scarcity and oppression" (Eagleton 1990a, 343) rather than of orgasmic pleasure or even aesthetic beauty.

This unrelenting interest in the body's suffering is a function of Adorno's ethic and politics of negativity as well as of his searing sense of the consequences of instrumental rationality, which renders the body both docile and productive. This vision of the body would be inevitable, as Benjamin might have said, in any attempt to rewrite history from the point of view of the vanquished rather than from that of the victors. The suffering *of* the body can be read *in* the body (and, no doubt, *on* its surface) to disclose the manner in which the enjoyment of pleasure can readily modulate itself into a "callous refusal to see" pain; indeed, into a "hardening of pains" that people endure (Adorno 1974b, 25–26).

Adorno's uncompromising belief that "there is no longer beauty or consolation except in the gaze falling on horror, withstanding it, and in unalleviated consciousness of negativity holding fast to the possibility of what is better" (Adorno 1974b, 25) informs my interpretation of the "strategic essentialism" that Spivak locates in the body of the subaltern woman. In his aphorisms on the construction of the feminine in *Minima Moralia*, Adorno comments that Nietzsche "fell for the fraud of saying 'the feminine' when talking of women. Hence the perfidious advice not to forget the whip: femininity itself is already the effect of the whip" (96). Spivak deploys the female subaltern body in the interests of disclosing how that body functions as both the effect and excess of the terror of the whip (in this case, that of colonialism). Because Spivak characterizes the figure of the subaltern as escaping the confines of the narratives of imperialism and decolonization (elite nationalism) even as it suffers their effects, the body of the gendered subaltern, in her view, can be interpreted to challenge the attempt to predicate subaltern agency upon the retrieval of subaltern consciousness. The doubled character of the subaltern body, as I have outlined it, enables it to emerge within or at the edges of master narratives as the sexual differential they seek to suppress.

Spivak elucidates the body's enactment of the relation between identity and difference through its resistance to patriarchal accounts of female sexuality that align the latter with reproduction or with the life of the species. Spivak identifies the theoretical dissimulation that produces "woman" as the conduit for the legitimization of the patronymic. This process upholds the uterine rather than the clitoral norm in the representation of female desire. Spivak's affirmation of the clitoris as that which exceeds the "reproductive orbit" (Spivak 1987, 151) invests the anatomical with an explicitly political function.

The rather fanciful dimension of this critique gives way to a complex representation of the gendered subaltern body, a body that bears the marks of the historical processes to which it is subject. The subaltern body, Spivak recognizes, functions as the site for the exercise of power, but she also wants to read that body as the discursive site for the production of the "Third World." This ambitious, even obscure, project entails a theoretical vigilance, one that discerns the absence and silence of the subaltern in the space that is routinely categorized as the "Third World" but that simultaneously renders that absence and that silence intelligible. The very heterogeneity of the sub-altern body can function as epistemological possibility, as the ground and ex-emplar of the object's suffering as well as of its historical becoming.

Foucault's influential analysis of what he calls a technology of the body can clarify the principles that inform Spivak's insertion of clitoral excess (one of many embattled emblems of strategic essentialism) into the conventional analysis of paradigms that operate the specific oppression of women in their bodies (see Foucault 1984a, 173). Spivak not only agrees with Foucault's sense of the body as simultaneously productive and subjected, but also seeks to make the subaltern body the site of the production of discourse—in short, to make the body "speak."

Spivak's rejection of the body as the instrument of knowing is contin-gent on the inevitable relation she perceives, in her best Foucauldian man-ner, between rendering a body analyzable and rendering it manipulable. Adorno's emphasis on the tale of oppression inscribed on the body's surface renders the body *intelligible* or decipherable for politically subversive ends. The political history Spivak hopes to write examines, to borrow Francis Barker's words, the status of the (female) body: "neither wholly present, nor wholly absent, . . . is confined, ignored, exscribed from discourse, and yet re-maining at the edge of visibility, troubling the space from which it has been banished" (Barker 1984, 63).

Spivak displaces the initial opposition she sets up between penis envy and womb envy in order to deconstruct the traditional Marxist emphasis on production. She investigates the subversive potential of her refiguration of the womb as a "tangible place of production" (Spivak 1987, 80). The oppo-sition between pleasure and pain, she argues, is overturned in the body of woman where productivity includes pain *and* pleasure. Spivak extends this argument to determine whether there might be room for the clitoris as the signifier of "woman"—of her status as, in effect, the excess not only of wage labor but also of the modes-of-production narrative that dismisses the active control exercised over women's pleasure in order to uphold uterine social organization as the basis of the nuclear family, the passage of property, and the legitimacy of inheritance.

For Spivak, then, the "suppression of the clitoris" signifies that "'woman' is indeterminate by virtue of [her] access to the tyranny of the proper" (Spivak 1987, 91). (Derrida's critique of "le propre" includes the patronymic, private property, and so on.) The clitoris would accord woman stature as a sexed subject rather than merely a legal and sexual object, and would be unexchangeable because it cannot be contained within the definition of the body as the producer of value.

I find this a provocative argument, at least insofar as it prompts a rethinking of Marxist categories that suppress the question of the engendering of bodies that produce use-value. I think, however, that Spivak's suggestive paradigms—clitoral excess, womb envy—function in the service of no more than a discursive technique of trouble, because they aestheticize the materiality of the body and institute a form of thinking that is evocative rather than analytical. This is not in itself a bad thing, but acting on the imaginary to change the real might dissolve the political technology of the body she is at such pains to explain.

A more productive deployment of bodily metaphors occurs in Spivak's essay "Woman in Difference: Mahasweta Devi's 'Douloti the Bountiful.'" Her sense of the subaltern as making and unmaking an identity in difference influences her choice of a story that foregrounds a "space that cannot share in the energy of" the colonization-decolonization reversal (Spivak 1989, 106). Devi identifies this space, which has no "established agency of traffic with the culture of imperialism" and which "is also outside of organized labor" (106), as the specific instance of subaltern heterogeneity.

Spivak explains that Devi releases the force of heterogeneity in order to "make visible the phantasmic nature of a merely hegemonic nationalism" (108) and to reject categorically the ideology of collective resistance. What is seemingly outside of hegemonic discourses comes to trouble the interior of those discourses, a "displaced shadow space" (109) that denies the global reach of the modes-of-production narrative or even of the static opposition between Empire and Nation.

Douloti's status as a bonded prostitute suggests that she has been sold to repay her father's loan. Her sexual slavery therefore cannot be extricated from the system, which thrives on usurers' capital. Her body, as Spivak points out, is simply the last instance of a chain of exploitation that destroys her father as completely as it does her. In this sense, the men responsible for her father's broken body are the proud owners of the "male flesh" whose "hunger" she "quenches" (Devi, as quoted and translated in Spivak 1989, 112). Douloti's pain is figured in the "spirals" of power and pleasure that invade her body and circulate in it.

In other words, her body becomes the brutalized terrain for the circulation of capital. Devi's poem reflects this curious conjunction of desire and capital: "The boss has turned them into land / The boss ploughs and ploughs their land and raises the crop" (Spivak 1989, 116). The obvious sexual pun serves to throw the ethic of labor and productivity into relief—Douloti has earned more than forty-thousand rupees for her boss in the course of repaying her father's loan of three hundred rupees, and factory and whorehouse become as one.

Devi wants to grant woman's body a separate place, an ability to be sexual otherwise. Indeed, within the bleak cruelty of the exigencies of bonded labor, the bond slave has no alternative but to reveal an aptitude for the very labor that increases her domination. But something interesting happens within this scenario. Douloti (her name implies wealth) encodes the female body in economic rather than affective terms because the family is no longer instrumental to her socialization and her pregnancies are the by-products of her copulation with clients, of her job as a prostitute. Spivak reminds us that another of Devi's characters, "Jashoda," accomplishes a similar objective because "the breast-giver" does not place patriarchal continuity in syntax but is witness to its excess, the labor of foster mothering.

In Devi's tales of subaltern heterogeneity, labor is not an unquestioned good. Jashoda's endless labor of professional mothering, her pride in her ability to suckle the world, meets its comeuppance in the cancer that destroys her breasts. The economic coding of the female body, in an interesting twist, serves once again to situate the female body beyond the pale because Jashoda's body appears to punish her for denaturing it. Spivak notices Devi's attempts to return the female body to the economy of nature, but does not develop sufficiently their subversive potential. The cancer is, of course, witness to the suffering of the female body, but given the near farcicality of the legendary stature her breasts acquire (myth serving to undermine their use-value), the cancer can be read as her body's refusal of her desire to *capitalize* on her breasts.

The final scene of "Douloti the Beautiful" in which Devi reinscribes the "official map of the nation by the zoograph of the unaccommodated female body" (Spivak 1989, 127) displaces the distinction between the "coding of intention into resistance and the resisting acceptance of victimization" (125) because Douloti's body, wracked with venereal disease, responds to a need for shelter, nothing else. Douloti's body, as the instance or figure of "the space displaced from the Empire-Nation negotiation," "comes to inhabit and appropriate the [schoolmaster's representation of] the national map" (127). Devi writes:

> Filling the entire Indian peninsula from the oceans to the Himalayas, here lies bonded labor spreadeagled, kamiya-whore Douloti

Nagesia's tormented corpse, putrefied with venereal disease, having vomited up all the blood in her desiccated lungs. (127)

Spivak aligns resistance with Douloti as "figured body" rather than as "intending subject" because her being "all over India" (128) is a function of the significance Devi's text as well as Spivak's reading accord her body's response to the need for shelter. Douloti's mockery of the nationalist agenda is unintentional; however, her body's misery is evidence of the text of (intentional) exploitation that she cannot read but nevertheless "knows."

"Woman in Difference: Mahasweta Devi's 'Douloti the Bountiful'" accomplishes at least two worthwhile objectives. It removes the female body from Spivak's premature interest in the "esoteric" area of women's pleasure to attend to the pain that pleasure conceals, and in projecting a global significance for the unaccommodated female body on decolonized terrain (Douloti is all over the map because "the traffic in wealth is all over the globe"), Spivak seems to be attesting to the "value" of the female body, not in its conformity to the ethic of productivity, but in the manner in which it belies the "profits" of decolonization. Here, at last, is a sensitivity to the palpable materiality of the object (the unaccommodated female body) that is not yet in danger of dissolving that body's *unrest.*

Spivak's strategic essentialism serves to displace the tyranny of the proper insofar as the excess of the female body is revealed to be a function of access to the proper. In other words, the body of woman figures subaltern heterogeneity because it cannot be accommodated either within the modes-of-production narrative or within the relay race between imperialism and independence (Spivak 1989, 107). Devi releases subaltern heterogeneity when she names tribal communities or restores the historical and geographical nomenclature of the heterogeneity whose point of reference is neither Empire nor Nation.

The case of the Rani is far from simple in this regard. The Rani, in Spivak's terms, has no name except her title. The insurrection of the "Goorkhas" compels the British "to have recourse to arms *in vindication of* [their] *insulted honour,*" so the Hill states refuse partisanship and thus allow the East India Company "the right to claim entitlement to the settlement of the states" (Spivak 1985a, 132; emphasis in original). Spivak can therefore manipulate the imperial textualization of the Rani to disclose a dialectic between the status accorded her by her title and the British right to deprive her of entitlement to it. Moreover, the Rani's namelessness and silence contrast with Birch's presence and utterance; his emergence on the landscape as agent and representative of Empire highlights the Rani's situation of token power.

Spivak would explain this contrast by the relation between the words "proxy" and "portrait" (see Spivak 1988). Both Birch and the Rani "stand in" for the might of Empire, but in different ways. The Rani's title also permits her to function as her husband's proxy, though she is prevented from acting in his name. Her role as proxy, however, confirms her status as "weaker vessel" within the system of native patriarchy and the native king's subject position as the object of imperialism.

The tyranny of the proper plays itself out in the manner in which the Rani's identity is predicated on her being an imperial possession. Here, the subtlety of Derrida's attempt to read the propriety of naming or the legitimacy of the proper name in tandem with the entitlement to property becomes evident. Spivak points to the female body as the thoroughfare of legal inheritance, and within the narrative of the fate of Sirmur, the Rani's motherhood only serves to play her right into the hands of the Company.

She functions, ironically, as the visible sign of the sovereignty of Empire, and emerges in history, as Spivak points out, only in the context of the territorial interests of the English. It is curious that Spivak does little with the Rani's struggle for the right over her own body as territory *she* chooses to sacrifice to fulfill her obligations to her husband, or so the Rani claims. If the native kings' right to their territories became rewritten within the space of imperial production, as their territorial obligations to the Company, then the Rani's desire to let the territory of her body go up in flames, so to speak, to fulfill her wifely obligations *entitles* her to her name, "the Rani of Sirmur."

5 / Edward W. Said

What sanctity attaches to this word "criticism," which is elevated by the term "oppositional" or "secular," but defiled by the term "Marxist"?
> Aijaz Ahmad, *In Theory: Classes, Nations, Literatures*

Edward W. Said's passionate and prolific intellectual career is well known within academe and, I suspect, within the ranks of the Central Intelligence Agency, which must be anxious to keep under surveillance such an outspoken and courageous critic of the neocolonial pretensions of the United States. Said is a particularly interesting exemplar of the "intellectual in emigration," because the humane, ethical, tempered, and (for the most part!) civil accents that distinguish his elegant and refined work are persistently in the service of a radical critique of violence committed precisely in the name of (Western) "virtues, humanism, morality" (Said 1988, 60).

The bulk of Said's writing bears the unmistakable stamp of a voice in the wilderness that refuses to be stifled, one strengthened by its intense awareness of the precariousness of the human condition. In this sense, Said's stance enables him to infuse historical categories with the personal and the palpable (to adapt Ahmad's phrase), to retain within critical discourse that has effectively banished the individual (a mere effect of the ideology of humanism, after all) the possibility that "the individual has gained as much in richness, differentiation and vigour as, on the other hand, the socialization of society has enfeebled and undermined him" (Adorno 1974b, 17).

Intellectuals, in Said's scheme of things, are capable of genuine critical negation only because they forget "neither the system's claim to totality, which would suffer nothing to remain outside it, nor that [they remonstrate] against this claim" (Adorno 1974b, 16). Said shares with Adorno the concern for "the liquidation of the particular" (17) endemic to identity thinking, to self-affirmation that presides at the expense of whatever that self constitutes as other.

This concern produces a critical corpus that privileges the voice of the diasporic intellectual, one who can be counted on to discern the politics of appropriation implicit in the desire to represent the colonized or to let them speak for themselves. Crucially, therefore, Said departs from poststructuralist practice in that his desire to dismantle the authority of the "subject of the West, or the West as Subject" is also a desire to *replace* that subject or usurp its prerogative. Far from being empty, the place of the subject in Said's discourse is that of the postcolonial intellectual, one in which this intellectual can be at home with homelessness. Besides, the process of decolonization gains its energy from the imminent demise of the West.

Said has often been charged with privileging critical consciousness, with a perhaps too sanguine reliance on the individual imprint that challenges collective torpor or culpability. I think, however, that the power and veracity of Said's work stem precisely from a stringent accounting for the system that stifles such individual accomplishment, a system that serves as the inescapable condition of intellectual production. Said's work can be read in terms of Adorno's doubled (not merely paradoxical) sense of the dependence of critical consciousness on the very institutions it aims to subvert. Permitting oneself to think in a totalizing universe, then, becomes a compound of freedom and shame. The intellectual "middlemen," precisely because of their indirect relation to the reproduction of capitalist or colonizing relations, are granted freedom to think against the grain in the very moment that they collude in the dissemination of ideology.

Said translates this "shame" into a code of intellectual conduct. Said's texts gain their power from the uncompromising realization that the fact of Empire radically corrodes the claims of Western civilization. It is not possible, as Adorno well knew in the context of Nazism, "to defame barbarism and rely on the health of culture. Rather, it is the barbaric element in culture itself which must be recognized" (Adorno 1967, 71).

The diagnostic character of Said's intellectual labors is a function of his insistence on worldliness, on the self-implicating mode of knowledge production in which the intellectual's entanglement in the travails of existence produces a deep-seated commitment to the mitigation of those travails. Adorno and Said share the position of the intellectual émigré, whose experience of displacement translates into the loss of history, language, and identity, but whose very "damaged life" becomes the occasion for reflection on the conditions that produced that "mutilation." Adorno and Said privilege a particular form of critical consciousness rather than the category of thought itself; for them, the position of exile makes the intellectual vitally attuned to suffering, which enables a different articulation of one's position in the world. In short, the immersion in suffering produces its own repudiation in critique.

Adorno describes this form of intellectual contemplation as "distanced nearness" (Adorno 1974b, 90), conducted, or so he hopes, without velleity or violence. The implications of this position require further scrutiny. What is the value of Said's insistence on the situatedness of human knowledge? Is it more than a trivial acknowledgment of human failing? Is there a contradiction between Said's epistemological model, which relies on being-in-the-world, and his intellectual posture, which privileges displacement, even detachment? How can the content of knowledge include the transformation of material reality? How does Said's historical and critical consciousness acquire the immunity to worldly taint for which it applauds itself? In this sense, the serenity and poise that make his style instantly recognizable might contain an inability to acknowledge that he can afford to talk because others can't.

I have no intention of impugning Said's unimpeachable intellectual integrity; I merely wish to address the contradictions of the intellectual's situation, particularly those of the postcolonial intellectual who takes up cudgels on behalf of the vanquished and against the victors. These are considerations that trouble Said himself, and I hope to use them to elicit Said's distinctive brand of critical and determinate negation. I employ Adorno's pronouncements on the simultaneous necessity and injustice of intellectual labor somewhat liberally here, because Said makes several appreciative references to Adorno's critique of identity and plans for dialectical negation without, for the most part, relating Adorno's thinking explicitly or systematically to his own intellectual praxis, political desires, epistemological models, or lambasting of poststructuralism.

"Secular" Criticism:
(Dis)Placing the Postcolonial Intellectual

The essays in Said's book *The World, the Text, and the Critic* strive to project a future for intellectual production in which "textuality" will no longer function as the "exact antithesis and displacement of what might be called history" (Said 1983, 3). Said takes to task the institutional contexts that encourage the continued "divorce" between "the cultural realm and its expertise" and "their real connections with power" (2) in the name of professionalism. He advocates, instead, a radical embrace of all "that is worldly, circumstantial, or socially contaminated" (3) in the interests of reconstituting the relation *between* "texts and the existential actualities of human life" (5). What this entails is the refusal to "accept uncritically the conventional opposition between methodology and material knowledge" (Adorno 1967, 8).

The critic comes to figure that shadowy place between text and world, charged with the unenviable task of forging anew the links between criticism and its "constituency, the citizens of modern society, who have been left to the hands of 'free' market forces, multinational corporations, the manipulations of consumer appetites" (Said 1983, 4). Critics must adjudicate the rival claims of dominant culture and totalizing critical systems, so that their constituency might have more on its mind than textual aporias. Said seems unembarrassed by this rather tall order for the critical consciousness, and he proceeds, with a nice combination of vigor and circumspection, to discover what taking account of the world might mean.

In the essay that opens the collection, Said turns the example of Erich Auerbach's exile from fascist Europe into the allegorical predicament of the critical consciousness he envisages. This consciousness transfigures the "concrete dangers" of the exiled condition into "a positive mission" (6–7). Said reads Auerbach's exile as resonant with implications for received notions of nation, culture, community, and milieu.

Auerbach's exile in Istanbul, Said notes, is particularly significant because that city connotes, in occidental imagination, a metaphysical opposition to, and alienation from, Europe. Auerbach's major work, *Mimesis,* therefore, is a product of the fact of homelessness, its affirmation of the Judeo-Christian tradition inseparable from the experience of "agonizing distance" (8) between critical consciousness and the nurturant influences of tradition. Said's essay indicates the worldliness of *Mimesis* through the attention he pays the circumstances entailed by the text itself (4).

The negative dialectic between exile and affirmation that Said discerns in the conditions that produced Auerbach's "definitive" work becomes the occasion for an incisive analysis of the predication of ideas of culture, nation, and milieu on the affirmation of identity and the exclusion, silencing, or domestication of alterity. Contrary to routinely benign conceptions of culture as the name for that which fosters a sense of belonging and community, Said offers "culture" as that which aggressively fortifies itself against what "it believes to be not itself" (12).

Said argues that culture, far from signifying the apotheosis of humanity, is a system of evaluations or coercions that discriminates, prescribes, and proscribes. Said also dissolves the familiar distinction between culture and society or civilization in favor of an expanded sense of culture as the natural ally of the state, busily perpetuating national identity through a wrested victory over every perceived difference from itself. Where, in this battleground of alterity and identity, is the critical consciousness to be located? Said carves a space for individual consciousness (predictably enough, I suppose) "at a sensitive nodal point" in which belonging does not connote conformity and functions as critical distance (15). The critic, whose consciousness inhabits the world just as it exists in its body, becomes the site of a dialectical interplay between what Said calls "filiation" and "affiliation" (16), an interplay that disturbs the complacency of those working hand in glove with institutionalized authority and that renders the boundaries of nation, culture, and selfhood infinitely transgressible.

Said's argument thus far seems to conform to liberal humanism at its best, upholding the values of belonging and conformity even as it keeps the spirit of inquiry alive. Nevertheless, it is an explicit contradiction of the ideology of humanism, insofar as the normative value of Man is predicated on the domination of "men" who dare to deviate from that norm. Said's interest in methodology, moreover, is at odds with what he tirelessly criticizes in poststructuralist methodology and the academic Left—the skeptical tendency to call everything into question and criticize nothing (in Adorno's phrase). Moreover, he takes considerable pains to distinguish his interest in the social, economic, and institutional contexts of intellectual production from a mere sociology of knowledge, because the latter fails to identify who regulates whom. In short, for Said critical theory "is a theory of human relations only to the extent that it is also a theory of the inhumanity of those relations" (Adorno 1967, 41).

The provocative aspect of his exploration of the connections between exile and belonging becomes evident only when he suggests that the customary understanding of belonging conceals the repressiveness of culture as the affirmation of the known at the expense of the knowable (Said 1983, 22–23). Said demonstrates that the "natal" ties binding the individual consciousness to culture obscure the processes of incorporation that underpin the rootedness of culture. In this scenario, the individual consciousness readily loses its critical detachment and serves as a willing accomplice in the legitimization of conformity and assimilation. For Said, culture becomes the savior of society, the domain in which consciousness ironically expresses its disaffection for prevailing reality in the very categories of rationality that reality has produced.

Said describes this transition from a negotiated treaty between detachment and belonging to the uncritical affirmation of dominant culture as the willed irrelevance of criticism (25). This affirmation reflects the common conception of ideas as regulative truths rather than as themselves implicated in the guilt of society. His plea for "secular criticism," therefore, entails a consciousness that is "always situated . . . skeptical . . . reflectively open to its own failings . . . [but] by no means . . . value-free" (26).

This rather academic (antiseptic?) conception of criticism is, at the close of the essay, aligned with "oppositional" practice, one that populates the mere efficacy of method with alternative acts and intentions (29). Despite this belated sop to the coercive character of cultural affirmation, the dignified humanity and "mastered irony" (89) that characterize Said's essay curiously empty secular criticism of political urgency. In other words, Said seems more interested in adumbrating an intellectual ethic (as a Stephen Daedalus figure, perhaps, who is the conscience or consciousness of his race?), in critical protocol or decorum, than in the politics of critical (dis)engagement (see also Foucault 1984a, 373–81).

What, precisely, is at stake in reinforcing the known at the expense of the knowable? How does the text's "worldliness," its combination of "sensuous particularity as well as historical contingency" (Said 1983, 39), contribute to its status as event? If Said's claims for secular criticism transform texts into objects "whose interpretation . . . has already commenced and [that are] already constrained by, and constraining, their interpretation" (39), how does the analysis of their determinate nature further our understanding of texts as "fundamentally facts of power" (45)? Said alights on a concept such as "worldliness" rather than, say, materiality, because he wants, like Spivak and Adorno, to transform facts into "processes of infinite mediation" (Adorno 1967, 7).

In raising these questions, Said makes cultural discourses the objects of secular criticism in order to achieve at least two aims. The urbane world of criticism is suddenly rent by matters "having to do with ownership, authority, power, and the imposition of force" (Said 1983, 48). Because culture can "cloak itself in the particular authority of certain values over others" (53), the notion of culture itself becomes indistinguishable from ethnocentrism. Said can then deploy the discursive situation as a paradigm of the relation between colonizer and colonized; or, rather less persuasively, use the relation between colonizer and colonized to interpret the discursive situation.

The reciprocity between these two options produces his second aim— to construe the worldliness of texts and of criticism as representative of historical contingency; that is, if I might borrow an idea of Benjamin, the traffic between text and critical consciousness embodies or reproduces "the present in the course of its articulation, its struggles for definition" (51) in order to explode the continuum of history. This explosion is possible because criticism is a process that articulates "those voices dominated, displaced, or silenced by the textuality of texts" (53).

The significance of texts, then, is radically contested terrain because the textuality of texts displaces their circumstantiality as it does the connections between ideas and social reality. Secular criticism is informed by the Foucauldian principle that texts are "an integral, and not merely accessory, part of the social processes of differentiation, exclusion, incorporation, and rule" (Said 1983, 215). As for intellectuals, they must disclose the systematic links between the legitimacy of knowledge and the instrumentality of power or, more specifically, they must remain particularly alert to those moments when the meaning of "to administer, study, and reconstruct" slips imperceptibly into the significance of "to occupy, rule, and exploit" (222), when cultural affirmation becomes indistinguishable from vulgar bullying.

But even as scholarship repeatedly takes "account of power, money, and colonial conquest" (265), it must continue to be imbued with a "modest (perhaps shrinking) belief in noncoercive human community" as well as with "an unstoppable predilection for alternatives" (247). This predilection infuses Said's vision of secular criticism with historical energy, with "work, intention, resistance, effort, . . . conflict" (245), and, finally, with adversarial passion rather than merely healthy cynicism or humane skepticism.

Said's conception of "secular criticism," however, seems less subtle than it might be. He does not address explicitly what Adorno calls "the process of neutralization" to which culture is subject (Adorno 1978a, 100). Said's per-

ceptive delineation of culture's complicity with, even culpability for, relations of power cannot bear to dispense with a space from which the voice of
reasonable dissent can be raised. Culture's uselessness is inexorably transformed into "tolerated negativity" (101) in a world subject to instrumental
rationality. Said seems reluctant to confront the institutional guarantees that
gird intellectual power. The institution certainly functions as his oblique
point of reference and he objects at specific moments to its unsavory political and economic allegiances; but he makes little attempt to unpack the
vexed relation between a generalized acknowledgment that the "claim to
being autonomous, critical and antithetical" can never be asserted "with total legitimacy" and the fact that the intellectual "is granted the space in
which to draw breath immediately by that power against which it rebels"
(102). The self-imposed marginality of the postcolonial critic, as I remarked
earlier, turns alienation itself into a profitable commodity.

Further, the emphasis in Said's writing seems to be on the worldliness of
the (potentially orientalist) critic; he is less inclined, therefore, to contend
with the "administration" (in Adorno's sense of the term) that "is not simply
imposed upon the supposedly productive [native informant] from without
[but] multiplies within this person" (104). To what extent is the no doubt
disaffected postcolonial intellectual implicated within the processes of material production? If, as Adorno argues, culture has become indistinguishable
from the "congealed content of educational privilege" (108), does colonization produce "a savage mind" equally content to function "as an administered supplement" to the processes of material production?

To return to the question of Auerbach's exile, Said testifies to the birth
of critical consciousness in the experience of displacement. This privileging
of exile is a concomitant to Said's interest in consciousness as the site of resistance and critique rather than of conformity. The dialectic of filiation and
affiliation, however, concedes too much to the pleasures and profits of displacement. What if Auerbach's capacity to negate his culture was a consequence of being "satiated with tradition" rather than displaced from it (I use
Adorno's idea here; see Adorno 1978a, 102)?[1]

I raise this issue to distinguish Said's negative stance from the procedure
of negative dialectics. Negation, for Adorno, is possible only if thought thinks
against itself. In this sense, the situatedness of knowledge is more than an ontological concession to the finiteness of things. In the context of the relationship between tradition and exile, Adorno argues that the negation of tradition

is not mere wholesale repudiation, but the embodiment of a desire to restore the vitality of tradition against its ossification and self-satisfaction (102).

Critical consciousness that wishes to oppose the continual imposition of the known at the expense of the knowable cannot hope to succeed unless it acknowledges that "it is only where that which was is still strong enough to form the forces [of tradition] within the subject and at the same time to oppose them that the production of that which has not yet been seems possible" (102). Said seems less inclined to explore the possibility that while Auerbach's "agonizing [physical] distance" from the Judeo-Christian tradition produced predictable self-consolidation at the expense of the other, the agonizing proximity of the culture within might also have been responsible for Auerbach's critical alienation.

The words Said chooses to describe critical consciousness—"skeptical," "open," "reflective"—tend to mitigate Adorno's tougher sense of the process of negation as one of struggle and conflict between equally strong forces, forces that, in equal measure, are imposed from without and multiply within. Said seems willing to admit that "orientalism" could be the nemesis of both colonizer and native informant, but the virulence of the latter's negation stems, Said implies, only from the consciousness of being victimized and alienated by "tradition."

Said, of course, wishes to retain, in the manner of Adorno, a moment of spontaneity for critical consciousness, wherein "reified consciousness begins to cede to a consciousness of reification" (Holub 1983, 286), and the critic "is still in a position to alter the function of the institution within which [the critic's] consciousness expresses itself" (Adorno 1978a, 108). However, if "secular criticism" is to avoid the all-too-easy process by which the fact and experience of colonization become tantamount to critical validity, or by which the colonized carry the wounds of Empire as if branded with social untruth, a rather more rigorous and unflinching confrontation with institutions becomes crucial.

Adorno would concur with Said that hope is to be located in difference understood as divergence from the totalizing claims of culture and the systems of knowledge it produces, but he is only too aware that the success of ideology confirms the unpalatable suspicion that, all too often, "domination is propagated by the dominated" (Adorno 1974b, 183). It is precisely this pessimistic contention that Said challenges in "Intellectuals in the Post-Colonial World." Said argues that because the meaning of colonial rule is

"by no means . . . a settled question" (Said 1986, 44), the analysis of colonization has produced "*a politics of blame*" (45; emphasis in original) that forces
the colonized to experience gratitude for modernization in the wake of colonization and that issues in regret for the loss of the colonial past. Although
non-Western peoples are themselves responsible for simple denunciation
(46), the "hatred of colonialism" (45) must not, therefore, be obscured.

The postcolonial intellectual, in these circumstances, becomes representative of the "constitutive limitations imposed on any attempt to deal with
relationships that are polarized, radically uneven, remembered differently"
(45). In other words, the dilemma of the postcolonial intellectual is precisely
"his" consciousness of inhabiting a no-"man's"-land between First and
Third Worlds, neither of which acknowledges "him" as its own. Said points
to those Third World intellectuals who collude in "a whole set of appeals to
an imagined history of one-way Western endowments and free hand-outs
followed by a reprehensible sequence of ungrateful bitings of that grandly
giving 'Western' hand" (47) and obscure the "recourseless submission" to
European superiority that the colonized continue to endure (48).

Said, even as he rejects the search for alternatives within a system that
has made unthinkable those very alternatives (49), wants to make room for a
process by which the postcolonial intellectual, situated at the juncture of this
world and a different one, can turn the narrative of history as imperialism
into history as the indictment of imperialism. The function that defines the
postcolonial intellectual is that which attests to "an experience of colonialism
that continues into the present" (54). In this sense, the vigilance of the postcolonial intellectual to the vestiges of colonization serves "utopian" ends—
"the formerly silent native speaks and acts on territory taken back from the
colonialist" (55).

Paradoxically, this vigilance keeps the postcolonial intellectual within the
confines of a rewriting of history that must, willy-nilly, take the conquerors
into account while they go on to other things. In this scenario, imperialism
is central to the history of the colonized but not to that of the imperialists themselves. For Said, this contradiction illustrates the inescapable relation between materiality and methodology, between politics and epistemology, because the relation is dependent on "the power to give, or withhold,
attention" (62).

Having come this far, however, Said concludes his essay with a gesture
of what might be perceived as a retreat into "the intellectual vocation itself"

in which resides "a resistant, perhaps ultimately subjective, component of oppositional energy" (64). Said's disillusionment with collective resistance, which, he says, manifests itself much too often as domination or coercion (64), is of a piece with Adorno's call for "open thinking," which "*is* actually and above all the force of resistance" (Adorno 1978c, 167; my emphasis).

Said removes intellectuals from the area of combat and charges them with the task of reexamining the issues completely (Said 1986, 70). Changing the situation, he would concur with Adorno, is possible only through "undiminished insight" (Adorno 1978c, 167). Said's representation of thinking as a vocation rather than a choice, financial convenience, or exigency moves it from the realm of contemplation to that of praxis. Rather than perceive this position as a retreat into intellectual elitism, Adorno and Said would argue that the critical thinker who does not submit to being "terrorized into action is in truth the one who does not give up" (Adorno 1978c, 167).

In Search of "New Objects for a New Kind of Knowledge"

My analysis of Said's *Orientalism* will address, as others have (including Clifford, Ahmad, and Porter), the paradoxes that plague Said's desire to collapse the distinction between pure and political knowledge; to relate the discourse of anthropology to Empire as an ongoing concern; to reject nativism, essentialism, and authenticity—indeed, "reality"; and to address the vexed links between power, discourse, desire, knowledge, intellectuals, institutions, and the state. In the spirit of my critique of Spivak, I want to explore the value of Said's method, which refuses to objectify what it seeks to know.

It is difficult to believe that Said's *Orientalism* was written seventeen years ago, given the controversy it continues to incite and the challenges it continues to weather. Perhaps the very familiarity of its central tenets is reason enough for me to offer only a brief summary before ascertaining the force and application of Said's contentions for the future of postcolonial discourse.

Said claims that the Orient "was almost a European invention" that served, appropriately enough, "to define Europe (or the West) as its contrasting image, idea, personality, experience" (Said 1979, 1–2). Said explores the place and function of the Orient as Europe's "cultural contestant," as "one of its deepest and most recurring images of the Other" (1) within what he calls the discursive practice of "orientalism." Because orientalism is based on "an ontological and epistemological distinction" between the Orient and the Occident, it is readily identifiable as "a Western style for dominating, re-structuring, and having authority over the Orient" (3). Said, taking his cue from Foucault, argues, in short, that the vast scholarship marshaled as evidence *about* the Orient served in fact to manage and *produce* the Orient (3).

This premise leads to the constitution of a dialectic between "Europe and its others" in which the object of knowledge becomes indistinguishable from the object of conquest. Said argues that the Orient as an entity cannot be thought apart from the barrage of "interests inevitably brought to bear on (and therefore always involved in) any occasion when that peculiar entity . . . is in question" (3). The emphasis in Said's book, then, is on the history and tradition of "thought, imagery, and vocabulary that have given [the Orient] reality and presence *in and for the West*" (5; my emphasis). With his Foucauldian credentials plain for all to see, Said concerns himself with "the internal consistency" of orientalism "despite or beyond any correspondence, or lack thereof, with a 'real' Orient" (5).

Orientalism as a system or body of knowledge, Said makes sure to reiterate, not only filters the Orient into Western consciousness but also carries with it "a considerable material investment" (6). The word "investment" creates a nice conjunction of the economic and the psychoanalytical, in that the logic of orientalism is not merely a lie fabricated by colonialists for material gain but a complex "battery of desires, repressions, investments, and projections" (8). That desire, knowledge, and violence coalesce in the subject's experience of the object collapses, for Said, the distinction between pure and political knowledge, particularly because knowledge about the Orient is immediately violated by "the gross political fact" (11) of imperialism.

Said wants to move away from a conception of orientalism as a lie that can be contradicted and toward an understanding of the ways in which the representations of orientalism actively displace the Orient in the imagination of the West. Moreover, the politics of distinctions between truth and falsehood are at stake in Said's discussion, as well as the material reality of ideas themselves. His book Orientalism produces knowledge and representation of the Orient or of the colonized; however, their identity is negatively determined. The nature of the object is contained in the inventory Said, in the manner of Gramsci, compiles of the infinity of traces deposited by the historical process in the self of the colonized and the geography of the Orient (Said 1979, 25).

Said questions the epistemological model of surveillance, the "increasingly profitable dialectic of information and control" (36) implicit in the discourse of orientalism. The object, in this scenario, is immediately rendered vulnerable to scrutiny and reduced to thinglike status, to a fundamentally ontological and stable fact over which observers have authority because they know the fact "and it exists, in a sense, *as* [they] know it" (32).

For Said, orientalism contains the Orient within its representations, classifies Orientals by Platonic essences that render them intelligible and identifiable, and constitutes not so much a vision of reality or a mode of thought as an irreducible constraint on thought with overwhelming political consequences. Said wants to refrain from reading the discourse of orientalism as an accessory of imperialism after the fact, as a mere handmaiden or even an accomplice of brute force. Instead, he reveals the way in which "vision and reality propped each other up" (44). This process involves the reciprocity between a political *vision* of reality contingent on the radical opposition between the familiar and the strange (the known and the knowable) (43) and a political *control* of the strangeness that "does not require that the barbarians acknowledge the distinction" (54) or that they might have a stake in the reconstruction and domination of their reality.

Said, in short, usurps the prerogative of orientalism to elicit, as Spivak does, the blank space at the edge of its text that troubles its interior, which is no less dangerous for being rendered silent. If orientalism is a self-contained system, how does Said's alternative text function as the empirical example that will penetrate the opacity of the surface of orientalism? Is Said too guilty of transmuting reality into textuality? Does Said reinforce the mystery of the Orient by reviling those who want it to "deliver up its secrets" (138)? What guidelines does he offer for considering the experience of otherness "as a salutary dérangement of . . . European habits of mind and spirit" (150)? If "the very act of construction is a sign of imperial power over recalcitrant phenomena" (145), what purpose has his reconstruction of Orientalism served? Are we any closer to the historical and empirical Orient, or is knowledge itself always "set apart from, and unequal with, its surroundings" (157)? How can the general category avoid limiting the terrain upon which the specific instance can operate (102)?

Said's *Orientalism* ably demonstrates the absurdity of the belief "that man [*sic*] plays no part in setting up both the material and the processes of knowledge" (300), but, as he admits at the closing of his book, his desire to let his work serve as a "reminder of the seductive degradation of knowledge" (328) keeps the book from being an argument "*for* something positive" (325; emphasis in original). It remains, therefore, a crucial clearing of space and of the throat in the area of postcolonial discourse.[2]

Said makes the puzzling claim that the scholars most likely to escape the dangerous seduction of orientalism are those who define their discipline intellectually rather than those who operate in a field defined canonically, imperially, or geographically (326). Isn't the whole of *Orientalism* devoted to collapsing the distinction between the pure and the political? Catherine Gallagher seems to be right in finding in Said's work a privileging of critical intellectualism for its own sake. The great value of a "skeptical critical consciousness" (327), according to Said, is its ability to subject its method to reflexive scrutiny and to let itself be guided by the material rather than any kind of "doctrinal preconception" (327).

This laudable aim I have been touting myself; however, where is the material of the Orient that is not obscured by the vision of orientalism? The study of human experience has moral and political consequences, and the intellectual failure of orientalism was also a human failure because the orientalists failed to consider the experience of the other a human experience (327–28). But Said has also spent the better part of his book inveighing against a humanizing impulse that relentlessly familiarizes or estranges the other.

His faith in the independence of scholarship, though for obvious reasons an attractive proposition, begins to wear a bit thin. Said wishes to suspend the division of labor that keeps intellectuals chained to the allure of professionalism, but his writing is often in danger of forgetting that "the class from which independent intellectuals have defected takes its revenge, by pressing its demands home in the very domain where the deserter seeks refuge [the university, the discipline, and so on]" (Adorno 1974b, 21).

Perhaps it might be best to appreciate the modesty of an enterprise animated by the intuition that "the expression of history in things is no other than that of past torment" (Adorno 1974b, 49). Said's position as an intellectual accords him the privilege of voice, not as the reward of the free spirit (Foucault 1984a, 72), but as a responsibility to constitute a new "politics of truth" (Foucault 1984a, 74). His position within the institutionalization of disciplines enables him to engage with the regimes that produce truth and grant authority to its pronouncements.

Perhaps the contradictions of Said's position are not his own but of the circumstances in which postcolonial intellectuals find themselves: the "renunciation of power [must be] one of the conditions of knowledge" and yet "power and knowledge directly imply one another" (Foucault 1984a, 175), at least within the tangled web of orientalist discourses and imperialist narratives. Could *Orientalism* then be read as an embattled attempt "to put into play [the] *enabling limits*" of knowledge (Weber 1987, x)?

Said's method avoids the static opposition between self and other in favor of the relation between the identity of the self and the nonidentity of the other. The concept of each is therefore not substantial but relational. In criticizing the tendency of orientalism to turn otherness into a Platonic essence, Said also institutes a mode of analysis in which "cognitive objects are henceforth to be identified not by reference to an intrinsic quality, their *form*, but rather in terms of their capacity to be *deformed* and *transformed*" (Weber 1987, xi; emphasis in original).

This notion prompts Said's investigation of the "process of selective accumulation, displacement, deletion, rearrangement" that produced the Orient of occidental imagination (Said 1979, 176). The consequences of this procedure involve the undermining of the concept of knowledge as adequation and the rendering of the real rather than the cognitive ambiguous. Of course Said is not given to anything that smacks of radical indeterminacy, but he is equally aware of the importance of demonstrating that the processes of determination within which the object finds its place or suffers displacement transform that object not only as an idea but as an empirical reality. There is simply no other way in which to understand texts as facts of power.

The value of Said's work, then, lies not only in restoring to the empirical phenomenon of the Orient its historical, dynamic, and transmutational character, but also in enacting the process of thought in quest of its object. The doubled character of *Orientalism* is worth noting: in the course of interpreting the paranoiac form of thought that relentlessly estranges the other, Said produces thought that breaks with its own frames to include the other. Far from being insensitive to the foreground of the institution in his work, Said reads orientalism as a figure of institutionalization itself, as the strategy that establishes identities and enforces lines of demarcation. In this context, where the imposition of limits is inseparable from the exercise of power, Said's text unravels how this imposition of constraints occurs.

Orientalism, in short, represents the logical transition from what Weber calls "the institution of specific interpretations" of the other, the Orient, and colonization to "the interpretation of specific institutions [those of orientalism and Empire]" (Weber 1987, 17). Said finds the limits of knowledge of the other enabling because he recognizes that the conditions of possibility of knowledge are also the conditions of imposability (Weber's pun) and, as such, can be thwarted, challenged, reread, and rewritten. He is not, however, concerned that the other remains negatively determined in his text, because that is precisely the function of alterity: to negate what we know and to indicate what we do not know. Besides, as Adorno argues, to insist on a reality behind the mists of ideological deception is to reproduce the opposition between appearance and reality.

Even though Said's corpus can be viewed as the attempt to stall the displacement of history by textuality, he is careful not to turn history itself into a kind of absent cause that controls texts. After all, he has the best example at his disposal of the ravages the capitalizing upon history produces. His is a flexible situating of critical consciousness inside and outside things, a situating that makes it possible for him to comprehend the internal consistency of orientalism as a discourse even as he insists on its material consequences and reality. The fictionality of the real cannot, in Weber's words, afford to obscure the reality of fictions (Weber 1987, 152).

But how is the "dialectical critic of culture" able "to both participate in culture and not participate" (Adorno 1967, 33)? Weber suggests the possibility of conceiving of the other not

> as someone to be eliminated in order that his place be taken and his property be appropriated—but rather as an *agent,* acting in the name of a transgressive desire acknowledged to be as dangerous as it is seductive: seductive because it is shared by all members of the community, and dangerous, because if indulged it would threaten the very bounds that structure that community. (149; emphasis in original)

I want to explore the potential for critical negation contained in representing the postcolonial intellectual as "terrorist," as the figure that, by definition, offends "Western heritage, morality and outraged virtue" (Said, 1988, 50) while remaining, paradoxically, negative and indefinable. This conception of the postcolonial intellectual might help take the sting off Said's antiseptic cosmopolitan humanism and suggest the possibility of reconstituting the postcolonial self as transgressive other and critical consciousness as the reversal of limits. I hope it is clear that I am not advocating acts of terrorism.

In "Identity, Negation, and Violence," Said calls to account the invidious thinking that produces the affirmation of identity at the expense of alterity. He alights on the concept of terrorism and its permanent and subliminal associations with Islam in the Western mind. Said's task is to "reconnect representations of 'terrorism' to contexts, structures, histories and narratives" from which they have been severed (47). In other words, Said refuses to consider the phenomenon and conception of terrorism in isolation or to attempt a definition of the term. Instead, he exposes the mechanism of othering that produces terrorism as endemic to Islam and as therefore impervious to historical change or social amelioration.

How can the postcolonial intellectual oppose the practice of terrorism and simultaneously challenge the historical and contextual factors that inexorably transform victims into terrorists? This question underlies Said's provocative and determinate negation of the invisible terrorism of neocolonial interventions that systematically transfigures itself into the "frightening visibility" of individual terrorists and the tragic confirmation of the irremediable corruption of the Islamic psyche. This species of negative dialectic between terrorism and putative democracy shatters the radical opposition between alien and isolated acts of aggression and the bastion of humanity or virtue that the Western state represents. Terrorism, then, is a function of the interplay between identity and alienation that produces cultural affirmation. Said sees virtually no difference between triumphalist assertion and the rush to protect what seems endangered (54). This identification might seem to dissolve the distinction between victim and oppressor unless one realizes that the logic of identity underpins both. Terror, in Said's terms, is the logical consequence of the rationalized and sanctioned violence of colonialism.

Said's essay does not just denounce the process by which any attempt to retell the facts of history, to provide alternative versions of the seeming inevitability of colonial intervention, is automatically characterized as terrorism; it also institutes criticism *as* "terrorism" that can "press the interests of the unheard, the unrepresented, the unconnected people of our world" (60). Interestingly, the accents of terrorism are also those of "personal restraint, historical scepticism and committed intellect" (60).

Said often expresses surprised displeasure when he addresses the absence of references to imperialism in the Frankfurt school's study of domination. Both Said and I have found the school's pronouncements on the ethic of domination eminently useful in the context of postcolonial studies. The school's specific attention to or deliberate abstention from the issue of colonization seems, therefore, a moot point. The unusual aspect of Said's deployment of Adorno is that he mutes the uncompromising edge of Adorno's work in his explicit adaptations of Adorno's musicology and enhances that edge when Adorno is no more than a fugitive, if strongly felt, presence in his early writings. If Adorno's work has to be read as a sustained meditation on the relation between the particular and the universal, Said moves from an attention to the critical negation inherent in the historical predicament of the colonized object (the particular) to the possibilities contained in intellectual praxis that is worldly, secular, and, in the best sense of the word, humanist (the universal as utopian vision). This latter emphasis on Said's humanism has nothing to do with his apparent privileging of the West as location and as cultural arbiter; it is simply a reiteration of Said's conformity to the Adornian subject—his intimacy, indeed love, for the Western tradition is responsible for the power that this quarrel with that tradition exudes.

The materialist and aesthetic strains in Adorno's thinking find their locus in *Musical Elaborations,* the latest example of Said's attempt to understand and interpret the connection between the private and public dimensions of aesthetic (musical) experience (12). This is a familiar focus in Said's writing—the desire to distill "the ideal purity of the individual experience" (xiv) from the "public setting" (xiv) in which it takes place. My interest in this appropriation of Adorno's aesthetic theory centers on the suggestiveness of Said's formulations for postcolonial intellectual practice as well as on his agonistic relation to (in his terms) the totalizing impulse of Adorno's work.

Said's tendentious, indeed, reductive, reading of Adorno fails to mask the very real similarities in their thinking, as I have continued to demonstrate. That Adorno's vision was limited by European, modernist horizons, or that he was given to ruminations of a dire and doleful sort, is, of course, not in question. Said's exclusive focus on Adorno's aesthetic theory and his dismissal of Adorno's allegiance to Marxism prevent him from acknowledging that Adorno hardly swallowed Hegel whole, that Said's warning to avoid elevating particulars into universals (55) is the motive force of Adorno's philosophical writings, or even that Said's interest in mapping ensembles of affiliations and transgressions (71) is of a piece with Adorno's and Benjamin's interest in force fields and constellations. I make these points briefly because I have already devoted ink to explicating their application in Adorno's and Spivak's corpus. The question, however, remains: if Said is not ignorant of these features of Adorno's work, what is it about Said's postcolonial intellectual identity and practice that make his excisions necessary, strategic, or troubling?

This interesting situation produces Said's privileging of the "aesthete" in Adorno at the expense of the heir to the Hegelian-Marxist tradition. Adorno himself did not believe that the achievements of culture could be thought in isolation from their propensity to "barbarism," so it is curious that Said would reject the specifically Marxist dimensions of Adorno's critique of the reification of culture in favor of "pleasure and privacy" (xxi). Said's desire here is understandable enough; he wishes to extricate a utopian dimension from the domination that Adorno believes to be total, to gesture, as he always does, to noncoercive community. Although Said's challenge to Adorno's narrative produces the possibility of transgression, it loses the force of Adorno's equal interest in the redemptive power of art.

Adorno makes the "pure quality" (13) of music the index of its social concern, its atonality the very sign of its rejection of commodification. The point, for Adorno, is not to retreat into the crevices where domination does not seep, but to revel in "the consistency of artistic technique" (13) in the thick of ideological coercion. Adorno, like Said, rejects the false choices that render music "reducible either to simple apartness or to a reflection of coarse reality" (71), but he is less sanguine about the individual's ability to refuse unquestioning assent to the totality (55). The struggle, for Adorno, always occurs from within ideology.

Two factors might help explain Said's departures from Adorno's exhortations. Said's consuming interest in the narrative of imperialism produces his stake in eschewing occidental historical teleologies as well as in espousing secular transgression. For Said, Adorno "is a creature of the Hegelian tradition" (xviii) and, as such, believes in dialectical temporal models (xix). The trajectory of imperialism, as well as the critique of ethnocentrism or orientalism, Said argues, cannot be accounted for solely in temporal terms. Instead, a spatial or geographical model seems more appropriate. This interest in the ideology of space attends the shift in Said's attention from Adorno's philosophy to his musicology. As for the transgressive impulse, it takes its inspiration from the conviction that "no social system, no historical vision, no theoretical totalization . . . can exhaust all the alternatives or practices that exist within its domain" (55). In this sense, the apocalyptic force of critiques of Western modernity issuing from the West conceals their ethnocentric assumption that the manifest destiny of the West in the East is the only history or teleology there is.

Said's position in *Musical Elaborations* is a function of his investment in tracing the lineaments of the figure of the postcolonial intellectual as, variously, amateur, nomad, and transgressor. Even as Said rails against the West's belief in its own unassailability, his own transgression cannot do without the cultural monuments of and to the West. Said assumes the guise of the artist-musician whose eclecticism and disdain for orthodoxy contribute to the cel-

ebration of diversity and noncoercive community. This belief in community, interestingly enough, is a consequence of his own nomadic condition
that articulates affiliation as transgression.

The nomad, in other words, attaches "himself" to communities without ever being of them (70) or understands affiliation as a testing of limits and
as an affirmation of heterogeneity (55). These laudable sentiments are as inseparable from a critical method as they are from a mode of being—the desire to "think things through together, heterophonically, variationally" (97).
While Said claims that this luxuriating in the unforeseen (55, 98) stems from
his memory of Arab music, he cannot help but return to Western versions of
this exemplary endeavor. Said's transgression here quite literally has to do
with his ability to cross over, to, appropriately enough, applaud those examples of classical music that return him to a home and community that was
never his but will always remain defined as such in memory. Said's privileging of pleasure and privacy, in this formulation, gains historical resonance in
the same moment that it loses sentimental appeal.

If *Musical Elaborations* alludes only evocatively to the pleasures and trib-
ulations of exile, and treats the private and public domains of aesthetic experience as, in the main, transactions between individual performance and the
establishment of community, *Culture and Imperialism* translates the ability to
"think things through together, heterophonically, variationally" into the indispensable arsenal of the postcolonial critic who seeks to interpret the connection between culture and society as the story of Empire. Here, too, Said
eschews Adorno's more stringent *dialectical* formulations on the domination
of the concept, the resistance of the object, or the ethos of modernity in favor of Adorno's endorsement of the *contrapuntal* technique in modern music
and of the critical sensibility in and as exile.

Let me suggest why this shift from a dialectical to a contrapuntal mode
of analysis, as well as the willing espousal of exile, is responsible for what I
perceive to be the success and failure of Said's renewed attention to the discourse of orientalism. This hasty statement is, no doubt, sufficient indication
of the uses of contrapuntal analysis! Said announces that *Culture and
Imperialism* is motivated by two large concerns: to demonstrate "the general
relationship between culture and empire" (xi) and to represent "a general
worldwide pattern of imperial culture" in conjunction with "a historical experience of resistance against empire" (xii). The first of these is immediately
rendered more specific—Said wishes to address the culpability of culture, to
contend with the disingenuousness of the aesthetic that enables it to retreat

from worldly concerns in the very instant that it influences the "formation of imperial attitudes" (xii). Said wants to expose Empire not only as a structure of feeling but also as a structure of attitude and reference (to replicate Said's adaptation of Raymond Williams).

Culture and Imperialism, thus far, is at its Adornian best in its proclivity for doubled formulations: culture cannot be thought without simultaneous attention to the "sordid" (xiii) practices of the society that engages in imperialist activity, and imperialism itself must be thought in conjunction with indigenous resistance to the march of Empire. Said is, of course, right to insist upon the simultaneous emergence of the imperialist self and the colonized, if resistant, other, but in inveighing against the static identities to which both are subject, he rejects the "linear and subsuming" historiographical narrative of imperialism in favor of a "contrapuntal and often nomadic" (xxv) narrative of the self that seeks alignments across borders. This move has specific consequences for the constitution of postcolonial subjectivity.

Said's own historical origins and predicament no doubt produce his configuration of exile, transgression, and restlessness as peculiar to the postcolonial condition, but his essays in *Culture and Imperialism* do not delineate the "gritty objectivities" (Basil Davidson's phrase) that make his vision of nationalism without nation viable. Instead, one is offered the person of the postcolonial intellectual that inhabits "both sides and [tries] to mediate between them" (xxiii). In dialectical terms, the colonizing impulse meets its comeuppance not in the resistance of the object but in the flexibility of the third term (the postcolonial intellectual as exile and shape-shifter). In contrast to Spivak, who wishes to retain the "subaltern" in the position of the Adornian object, Said introduces the postcolonial intellectual as the subject *and* object of postcolonial discourse.

The contrapuntal model, in opposition to Said's own intentions, reproduces the static positioning of subject and object because the spatialization of temporality (the relationship between subject and object is contiguous or complementary rather than reciprocal or dialectical) does not allow for movement between the two poles. Adorno's notion of mediation is exactly opposed to Said's. For Adorno, the split between the two poles of the dialectic needs to be challenged. Each pole of the dialectic needs the other in order to be; it is itself mediated by the other. If, as Adorno writes, mediation occurs in and through the extremes, Said's introduction of the postcolonial intellectual as the mediatory figure who adjudicates the transactions between the extremes destroys the dialecticization of the relationship between the poles. Because the exile *embodies* the contradiction between the colonized imagination and the resistant impulse, the motive force of the dialectic (contradiction as critical negation and historical antagonism) is lost. The constitution of exiled subjectivity, rather than being predicated upon contradiction as critical negation and as historical antagonism, contains (in both senses of the word) that contradiction. Because Said scorns dialectical temporal models, the exile exercises (to switch registers) the synchronic rather than the diachronic option. In this sense, the exile is doomed to enact rather than resolve "his" historical dilemma. Although Said hints at reciprocity when he speaks of "intertwined and overlapping histories" (18), he fails to acknowledge that this overlap did not occur at the behest of the colonized, and that struggles against global capitalism and for nationalism challenge the inevitability of this interdependency. Said here succeeds in reinforcing the notion that the narrative of imperialism is the only available historiography.

This interdependency gets articulated somewhat differently as the book progresses: the contrapuntal attempt to play experiences off each other is undertaken in order to "[expose] and [dramatize] . . . discrepancy" (33). This discrepancy is not ultimately productive because, for Said, "the rhetorical separation of cultures assured a murderous imperial contest between them" (38). Said fudges the issue here because it is not clear whether the imperial contest produced the rhetorical separation of cultures or vice versa. Once again, the spatial model intrudes upon historical analysis because Said's interest is in the production of narrative impositions upon history rather than upon historical struggle itself.

Postcolonial subjectivity, then, inheres in the trappings of exile, in the posture of defiance that accrues to "him," "he" who rejects a world "constructed out of warring essences" (229). Said wishes to transform exile into a normative mode of being. This strategy is consonant with Adorno's own emphasis on the mutilation the exile suffers, but it turns the loss of a historical dimension into the possibility of spatial freedom and movement. If, for Said, imperialism was "the struggle over geography" (7), the exile transforms dispossession into the espousal of nationality without lapsing into nativism (229). The struggle against identity thinking begins here, in the acceptance of affiliations over filiation, in the constitution of identity as atonal ensemble (318) rather than essence, and in, interestingly, the possibility of "universalism" (229). Said's reversal of Adorno's attention to the particular and the specific should be noted: the exile is everywhere and nowhere just as "he" combines the contingent and the possible.

My ruminations thus far serve as a prelude to a brief attempt to address Aijaz Ahmad's notorious essay on Said in *In Theory*. I don't wish to participate in the furious debates that have ensued since the appearance of Ahmad's book except insofar as his argument pertains to my own. Four major and interconnected strands (for my purposes) can be elicited from Ahmad's essay: Said is not Marxist enough; this absence of Marxist credentials contributes to his narratives of transhistorical continuity (Ahmad 1992, 187); Said deploys mutually incompatible definitions of terms simultaneously (166) and seems untroubled by contradictory positions that reject humanism as history in the same breath that they evoke humanism as ideality (164); Said exhibits an overpowering desire "for a location *in* the West" (211; emphasis in original).

Said's subtle allegiances to Adorno's thinking might help explain or alter one's perception of the stumbling blocks Ahmad encounters. On reading Said's interview (see Sprinker 1992), one sympathizes momentarily with Ahmad's impatience with Said's disavowals of and equivocations on Marxism. Said considers Marxism "extraordinarily insufficient" (259), as "more limiting than enabling" (260), as "less interesting than other theoretical and political possibilities" (262), and the various versions of Marxism as no more than historically important (261). None of these statements constitutes an actual critique of Marxism and Said also hastens to add that he has never been anti-Marxist either. Said seems to have a fairly conventional notion of Marxism demanding that one toe the party line and therefore rejects its possibilities in the name of open thinking.

My discussion has sought to demonstrate that Ahmad, rather than accusing Said of not being a Marxist of his persuasion, might have been better served by challenging the antidialectical nature of Said's thought. Ahmad, as Adorno might have said, attacks Said where he is not and has never claimed to be. This awareness of the antidialectical nature of Said's arguments as well as of his predilection for contrapuntal analysis would also have explained Said's comfortable residence in contradictions that complement rather than destroy each other. Despite Said's discomfort with the totalizing impulse in Adorno's work, he deploys, as Adorno does in *Negative Dialectics*, totality as a critical rather than affirmative category and, as such, is interested in the paradigmatic rather than diagnostic character of the discourse of orientalism. In this sense, Said's major work owes more to *Dialectic of Enlightenment* than to his acknowledged sources (Gramsci and Foucault). Finally, Said's privileging of the metropolitan location has more to do with his trenchant awareness of the West as "intimate enemy," of its role in the institutionalization of knowledge, and of his expressed concern with the colonial inheritance that renders the topography of indigeneity uneven, uncertain, and mobile. In this regard, the dignity of Said's position stems from personal dislocation as emblematic of the historical exile of a people, a dignity that Ahmad himself acknowledges in praising the "polemical verve" (162) with which Said defines exile. Despite Ahmad's sensitivity to Said's political passion, he splits the polemical verve of the Palestinian essays from the humane skepticism of Said's other works. Here, too, Adorno might help. Said's commitment has less to do with tendentiousness and more to do with the development of a critical attitude that resists the course of the world (see Adorno's essay "Commitment"). In this sense, he continues to focus on the interplay of aesthetic beauty with political calumny rather than impugn one in order to expose the other.

In the distance that he establishes from the continuity of the familiar, in his hesitation before either verification or speculation, in his capacity to be both inside and outside things, in his reversal of the conventional opposition between the subjective and the objective (the objective is actually the product of human cruelty and misery; the subjective is what breaches the facade of normality, normativity, familiarity, and facticity), Said strives incessantly to make the possible real.

My own deployment of terrorism seeks to invest his critical detachment with the promise of difference and with the tension of conflict. It is a sobering thought, no doubt, that culture functions as ideology, but Said's task is more difficult—he must prove that the notion of culture as ideology is itself in danger of becoming only ideology. In the voice of the postcolonial intellectual, therefore, can be discerned the clamor of "those things which were not embraced by [the historical] dynamic, which fell by the wayside" (Adorno 1974b, 151). Said, too, knows that it is "in the nature of the defeated to appear, in their impotence, irrelevant, eccentric, derisory" (151); he also knows that therein lies the means to outwit the historical dynamic that destroys them.

6 / Conclusion: ". . . the inextinguishable color from non-being"

Spivak's *Outside in the Teaching Machine* and Said's *Culture and Imperialism* have appeared since the conception of this project, both seeking, in a sense, to address the cognitive "failures" of the authors' signature pieces "Can the Subaltern Speak?" and *Orientalism*. Spivak describes her collection of essays as "interconnected attempts . . . at thinking through the shift from (anti-)essentialism to agency" (Spivak 1993, ix); Said admits that he left out "the response to Western dominance" (Said 1993, xii) in his most famous work. My book has been a sustained effort to heed the other side, to risk affiliation with the "enemy" in order to envisage the most effective mode of decolonization, at least within the realm of theory.

As Said, Spivak, and Adorno unfailingly remind us, however, the production of knowledge has always been an unsavory practice, implicated in the drastic dominion of Empire and serving as the latter's willing accomplice and justification. Although Adorno was relatively silent on imperialism per se, his attention to the hegemony of the exchange principle and his critique of identitarian politics have, I believe, become indispensable to the affirmation of otherness, the resistance to global capitalism (the particularly virulent contemporary form that colonialism has assumed), and, crucially, to the discourse of modernity that arrogates to itself the "regulative political concepts" (Spivak, 48) that encode the claims of nation within decolonized space.

The dialectic I have articulated between metropolitan theories and subaltern realities discerns the limits of theory in the interests of comprehending the dislocation of the subaltern object in the material processes of production and of challenging the subsumption of her identity in orientalist identifications. This desire to trace the lineaments of subaltern resistance rests on the following assumptions: the success of colonialism and the perceived failure of subaltern resistance do not connote the absence of that resistance; the reading of that failure might elicit a concomitant failure on the part of imperialist or elite narratives of history to record struggle.

These assumptions, in turn, raise the issues of location and address. For whom is the decentering of subjectivity a viable option? How does the inscription of irreducible cognitive failure (in various confessional and reflexive narratives) reproduce the "sanctioned ignorance" of the other of which Spivak speaks? From where does the dismissal of the naïveté of essentialism (strategic or otherwise) emerge? Can the empirical avoid being confused with essence? These questions have, of course, animated my work; I reiterate them in order to assert, once more, that decolonization inheres in the assumption of "responsibility to the trace of the other" (Derrida, as quoted in Spivak 1993, 22).

In other words, the epistemological practice that affirms the "preponderance of the object" recognizes that postcolonial intellectuals, like the subaltern in whose name they speak, cannot afford the luxury of cognitive failure; they can only undertake to risk such (im)possibility. This risk entails the reclamation of space that has hitherto been obscured by the action of epistemic violence and culpable ignorance. The paradox of this space is that it is simultaneously empty and overdetermined. This space has hitherto been unimaginable within the confines of identity thinking as well as unthinkable outside of those confines. It signifies the limits of occidental knowledge but seems unable to transform the catachrestical nature of concepts into respect for the singularity of objects. Most important, it bespeaks a history that has, for the most part, remained untold or unforgivably distorted. Despite these difficulties, however, I want to address the writings of Ashis Nandy and of the Subaltern Studies Group as preliminary realizations of the promise contained in the practice of negative dialectics within decolonized space.

Adorno's searing critique of the domination of the concept and his advocacy of a concomitant attention to the particular find their unconscious deployment in the work of the Subaltern Studies Group, which not only challenges conceptualizations of nationalism and decolonization with the difference and specificity of the Indian example but also renders the concept determinate; that is, the abstraction of the concept is endowed with the concreteness of a designation—the category of the West and its identifiable presence in/as the discourse of modernity.

I offer here a reading of Ranajit Guha's "Nationalism Reduced to 'Official Nationalism'" in the context of Adorno's desire for an epistemology that does not use objects as mirrors in which to reread the subject. Benedict Anderson's *Imagined Communities,* in Guha's scathing critique, emerges as a predictable exemplar of the West's "boring imprisonment" in its own categories and identifications. Guha demonstrates how Anderson deduces the theory and history of (Indian) nationhood from the experience of print capitalism and the concomitant spread of literacy in the West as well as, in the manner of Marx, from India's encounter with colonialism.

Anderson's notion of nationalism as a cultural artifact gives the game away because he reads that artifact in isolation from its location in the West. Anderson's comments on Indian nationalism, therefore, assume that the Indian situation will simply adjust its contours to those of Anderson's postulates. Guha's piece, in opposition to Anderson's, shows the ability to think concretely, to derive the idea and reality of the Indian nation from the specific contexts of elite privilege, peasant insurgency, and the absence of literacy.

According to Guha, the colonialist impulse that characterizes Indian nationalism as a pure product of the struggle between the British raj and the Indian elite ignores the presence of subaltern resistance that "had little to do with either the culture or the institutions of the Raj" (Guha 1985, 104–5). It is precisely Guha's attention to the facts and complexity of the Indian situation that makes it impossible to subsume peasant insurgency in (Western) liberalist narrations of nation. Guha's strategy functions as a negative dialectic because he questions the bases of the opposition between raj and nation by showing the emergence of a third term that functions as a contradiction against both.

Guha accomplishes a double negation: he denies the raj the sole prerogative of provoking nationalist sentiment and simultaneously challenges the privilege of the national elite, their desire to write the history of nation as exclusively their own. This is not a strategy only of deconstruction because, rather than remaining content with exposing the false basis of the initial opposition, it proposes an alternative that contradicts both sides. In this sense, Guha not only reveals the cognitive failure contained in Anderson's desire to read Indian nationalism as contingent on modernity (colonialism and print capitalism working in tandem), to use the Indian example as a mirror of Western liberal and national desire, but also exposes the complex modality of the object Anderson obscures, even distorts. More to the point, Guha focuses on the object's resistance to the subject's identifications—on, indeed, the imposed irrelevance of Western categories in the Indian context. Unlike Spivak, therefore, Guha reiterates the determinate rather than the irreducible nature of cognitive failure.

To my mind, Guha also avoids the coy pathos of Spivak's attempt to speak of the conjunction between Western theory and indigenous realities as a "bastard filiation" (see Spivak 1993). This conjunction becomes both provocative and productive in Guha, because he recognizes, like Adorno, the value of immanent critique, of wresting the "truth" of Indian reality from the untruth of Western categories. Guha attends to what lies beyond colonialist and elite historiography without reducing his own subject position to one of polite or apologetic self-effacement. Rather than confine himself to the unremitting exposure of the limits of knowledge, he realizes that the recognition of limits implies that one has, in a sense, already transcended them. Guha, in short, transforms his writing into a "constructive force that enters fully into what is, without sacrificing itself as reason, critique, and the awareness of possibility" (Adorno 1993b, 1–53).

The work of Guha and his compatriots in the Subaltern Studies Group represents, in Ashis Nandy's terms, the systematic diagnosis of the "colonialism which survives the demise of Empires," of the transformation of the West as a "psychological category" that exists "everywhere, within the West and outside; in structures and in minds" (Nandy 1983, xi). Although the Subaltern Studies Group resists both the models of conformity and those of dissent proposed by the category of the West, it does not, like Nandy, attempt to defend tradition against modernity or affect particular sympathy for the degradation of the colonizer. The members of the Subaltern Studies Group recognize the contradictions within indigenous reality rather than merely deploying that reality against Western categories, against the world without. Precisely because of the scrupulous political interest that earns them Spivak's praise, they lift postcolonial discourse outside of its metropolitan location and determination and direct the gaze of disaffected diasporic intellectuals elsewhere. This move is not to be understood as a sentimental return of sorts, for the international credentials of the group are well known; what is different is that postcoloniality is no longer at odds with nationhood. Here, in my view, is "strategic essentialism" at its best: the politics of identity are inseparable from those of history, culture, and location. Simultaneously, however, the struggle for nation, at least within the Indian context, is inseparable from its class, caste, and gender determinations. The preponderance of the object, then, produces an indigenous subject.

Notes

Introduction

1. See Jay (1988) for provocative elaborations of this claim.

2. I am extending the implications of Spivak's argument in "Theory in the Margin." Spivak describes this space or ground as "graphematic" (Spivak 1991, 175), but does not gloss this unusual word. Because Friday's tongue has been cut out (that this perception of Friday is Susan Barton's seems not to concern Spivak), and he has only a slate at his disposal, I understand Spivak to be using the word "graphematic" to indicate a form of inscription that is not necessarily of the order of language. She is also interested, I think, in establishing a relationship between Foe, whom she calls an "enabling violator . . . without [whom] there is nothing to cite" (175) and Friday's victimization, which he translates into agency by refusing inscription and thus *disabling* his potential violator. In this sense they both occupy a space that awaits inscription. At the same time, Spivak wants to avoid placing Friday beyond signification; therefore, she uses a term that embraces representation without conforming to the order of writing, except, perhaps, in Derrida's sense of the term.

3. I have in mind Edward Said's reflections in *Beginnings: Intention and Method,* where he elaborates on the ways in which "writing or thinking *about* beginning is tied to writing or thinking *a* beginning" (Said 1985a, xv; emphasis in original).

4. This phrase serves as the title of an article by Said in *London Review of Books* (Said 1984).

5. Gillian Rose defines "determinate negation" as follows: "Loosely, negation is criticism of society which is positive (determinate) in that it aims to attain and present knowledge of society insofar as that is possible, but not positive in the sense that it confirms or sanctions what it criticises" (Rose 1978, 150). See also *Marxism and Form* (Jameson 1971, 360) for clarification. The fleshing out of a strategy of negation as grounds for emancipatory critique is the fundamental concern of my text as a whole. I therefore only suggest its outlines here. The phrase in question is a staple of the Hegelianized Marxism of the Frankfurt school.

6. I am drawing upon Michel Foucault's writings in *Power/Knowledge: Selected Interviews and Other Writings 1972–77* here.

7. I am aware that Gandhi's relationship with the "untouchables" was, at the very least, problematic, and that Dr. Ambedkar, their leader at the time and still revered today, had much to say on Brahmins who sought to assuage their own guilt at the material expense of the human dimension of their cause. See, for example, Arun P. Mukherjee's thoughtful comments (Mukherjee 1991, 27–51). It should be clear that I have no wish to exempt my family in this regard.

8. Interestingly, Max Horkheimer's early book of aphorisms is entitled *Dämmerung* (1934), signifying both dawn and dusk and suggestive of his and Adorno's tenuous, yet tensile (tenacious?), optimism. In *Minima Moralia,* Adorno writes, "For no sunrise . . . is pompous, triumphal, imperial; each one is faint and timorous, like a hope that all may yet be well, and it is this very unobtrusiveness of the mightiest light that is moving and overpowering. This is why precisely the loveliest dreams are as if blighted" (Adorno 1974b, 111).

9. The affinities with Jacques Derrida's *pharmakon* and Paul de Man's complex of blindness and insight (the splinter in the eye, as Adorno calls it) are obvious.

143

10. Spivak uses the notion of privilege as loss as an informing principle in her writing. She sees the process, quite rightly, as active. I think she would not disagree that loss is inscribed in privilege construed as gain.

11. According to Jameson, who has helped me clarify my engagement with Spivak, the profound tautology that is a function of the dialectical mode dissolves the *dualism* that allows the subject to imagine itself as distinct from the object. Spivak is not guilty of this naive dualism; however, her engagement with the object remains apparent rather than real. Her argument is something like a logical tautology: what began as different entities turns out to have been the same thing after all. As the progress of her essay demonstrates, the object grows increasingly phantasmatic, and it is unclear how one is to distinguish between the colonial encounter with the other, which reconstituted itself as self-absorption, and Spivak's own acknowledgment of defeat in the face of the "wholly other." She transforms this "defeat" into a respect for the integrity of limits; however, such a ploy seems to me insufficient, because she loads the dice so heavily against the subject's desire to know and constructs agency as withdrawal rather than as re-presentation from a different standpoint (not to be confused with the standpoint of *différance*). In my detailed engagement with Spivak's oeuvre in chapter 4, I hope to delineate the potential of a negative dialectic that rejects, as Spivak does, the reduction of the object to the subject's measure without concluding that the object is unrepresentable or, what is worse, withdrawing, like Nietzsche's woman unconcerned with truth, from the arena of truth and re-presentation. The object is also occluded because the emphasis remains on a refinement of categories rather than on an engagement with facts that corroborate or contest these categories. Interestingly, even if one stayed within the limits of Spivak's own terms, and the object *is* no more than the subject's fantasy, it should be eminently representable because, like all fetishes, it is also fungible!

12. See Susan Buck-Morss's discussion of Ernst Bloch in *The Origin of Negative Dialectics* (Buck-Morss 1977, 76) and Adorno's "Notes on Kafka" (Adorno 1967) for the germ of my idea.

13. Adorno uses the phrase "logic of the matter" in his critique of Husserl. His phrase evokes the immanent critique in which negative dialectics engages.

14. I have included only part of the quotation, which Buck-Morss cites in full: "Only he who recognizes the most modern as the ever-identical serves that which would be different." Adorno explains the process of thought turning back upon itself in *Minima Moralia* (Adorno 1974b, 86). I will demonstrate later what I have been indicating here, that deconstructive gestures can reconstitute themselves into recuperative gestures of mastery or into repetitions of the problems they attempt to overcome. The question of negative dialectics as protodeconstruction will be taken up in chapter 3.

15. Both Said and I use Forster's text as a symptom of a larger problem. In other words, the novel serves as the occasion for critique. In "Representing the Colonized" (Said 1989), Said refers the reader to his *Culture and Imperialism,* which I shall discuss in detail in chapter 5. I am concerned here with what I consider to be a less than careful reading of Forster within the confines of this article.

16. The rest of this book is devoted to distinguishing epistemology from appropriation. In order to do so, the postcolonial intellectual must acknowledge what Forster describes as the claims of the other on the self. These claims must be understood as the resistance of the object that is immanent to but coerced by the subject. The crisis of the subject has thus far managed to exclude a rethinking of the object precisely on the grounds that any such epistemological desire is doomed to repeat the history of colonization (see chapters 1 and 2). Forster's comment suggests a mode of analysis that does not confine itself to philanthropic gestures but that takes responsibility for the subject's implication in colonization by furthering decolonization. The self, in other words, must learn to take its cue from the other. In the context of *A Passage to India,*

Fielding fails to realize that the power of Empire grounds his desire or love for Aziz—they (Aziz and Fielding) are both servants of Empire. Fielding must acknowledge Aziz's claim on his sense of political "fair play" before he can presume either to know or to love Aziz.

17. The editors of *The Essential Frankfurt School Reader* describe Robert S. Lynd's collaboration with the empirical research conducted by the Frankfurt school as being informed by the principle I have just cited, and add, "only history could verify such hypotheses—by realizing them" (Arato and Gebhardt 1990, 406).

1 / The End(s) of (Wo)Man; or, The Limits of Difference

1. In their introduction to *Post-structuralism and the Question of History,* Geoff Bennington and Robert Young remark that poststructuralism's facilitation of "the examination of differentiated and customarily marginalised histories—of phallogocentricism, of the fantasmic structures of colonialism and of fascism—is a measure by which its interrogation of a dialectical history's transcendence can be assessed" (Bennington and Young 1991, 7). I think postmodernism shares this interest even if the two discourses must, to some extent, remain distinct.

2. The contradiction between a historically constituted system of reference and the lateral or spatial determination of concepts/words/forces is readily enough explained. Derrida wishes to avoid the structuralist emphasis on closed systems whose essential relations can be plotted; therefore, he creates an open-ended system that is potentially unlimited and thus open to history. However, the teleological model of history offers another form of closure. As Derrida explains, "if the word 'history' did not [in and of itself convey the motif] carry with it the theme of a final repression of *différance,* we [one] could say that [only] differences alone could [can] be 'historical' through and through and from the start [from the outset and in each of their aspects]" (Derrida 1973, 141). *Différance,* therefore, "is no more static than [it is] genetic, no more structural than historical. Nor is it any less so [Or is no less so]" (Derrida 1973, 142).

3. Derrida's practice of reading might serve as an example. In "History Traces," Marian Hobson shows how Derrida's texts (as "parasites") are indistinguishable from the "host" texts off which they live. When one attempts to prise them apart, the dangers of Derrida's parasitic habitation become clear—the structure of the host text threatens to collapse upon itself (Hobson 1991, 103). It is in this sense that Derrida makes claims for his political purchase on ideas—his loving homage to the texts he reads bears all the marks of an implosion. I also hope to develop Teresa de Lauretis's suggestive remarks in *Alice Doesn't: Feminism, Semiotics, Cinema.* De Lauretis contends that the problem for feminist theory remains "how to theorize that experience [which is based on the fact of the oppression of one sex], which is at once social and personal, and how to construct the female subject from that political and intellectual rage" (de Lauretis 1984, 166). This rage, however, cannot be articulated without an understanding of the ways in which social structures and modes of representation form and *deform* femininity. Thus de Lauretis believes that "the most exciting work in . . . feminism . . . is not . . . anti-Oedipal [but] Oedipal with a vengeance, for it seeks to stress the duplicity of that scenario and the specific contradiction of the female subject in it, the contradiction by which historical women must work with and against Oedipus" (157). Subsequent chapters will attempt to develop the notion of repetition with a vengeance in the context of the theory of dialectical negation (which eschews mere opposition) at stake in this volume.

4. In *Discerning the Subject,* Smith argues that "the imaginary is emphatically not, as Althusser implies, the opposite of the real or its direct product. The imaginary is that set of representations and identifications which supports an illusory plenitude of the ego . . . and the real is what . . . stands outside of all symbolization and is unknowable" (Smith 1988, 20).

2 / Rethinking the Object

1. The context for this distinction between category and substance is twofold. Kant shifted the emphasis from error as the distortion of truth to the conditions of the possibility of knowing. This shift made it possible to understand that "conditions of truth [were] regulative ideas and categorial forms through which, and only through which, we perceive sense data as particular objects or events" (Arato and Gebhardt 1990, 380). Kant's emphasis on the incommensurability of the subject with the reality that it knows is what Lukács wished to transcend in his demand that the subject be substance. The Viconian legacy in the definition of commensurability as the conjunction between knowing and making is particularly evident in Lukács's conceptions of alienation and reification. The dialectical unification of subject and object would occur in the proletariat, the only subject that was also an object (the object of capitalism would become the subject of communism; see Feenberg 1981, 116). The proletariat "comprehends reality in the very act of transforming it (Kolakowski 1978, 271). The rest of this chapter will continue to clarify relations between category and substance in the course of adumbrating a different mode of cognition. Foucault and Derrida are equally interested in the conditions of knowledge that place limits on that knowledge. Just as Kant grants a priori status to these categories or forms that determine the mode in which reality appears to the subject, Derrida and Foucault treat them as discursive practices that delimit the sayable or the thinkable. In other words, they treat these limits as *inherent* to the order of conceptuality. Because, in their scheme of things, the stability of the self is inseparable from the "will to know," epistemological failure becomes consonant with a subjectivity, in Foucault's terms, that writes in order to have no face. This effacement of self is reproduced in Derrida's appreciative reading of Bataille. The "ultimate subversion of lordship" occurs when sovereignty (of identity) "no longer seek[s] to be recognized" (Derrida 1978, 265). This subversion is possible only when sovereignty can "expend itself without reserve, lose itself, lose consciousness, lose all memory of itself and all the interiority of itself" (265). This posture of the self establishes a relationship to an "unknowledge" that will be "the absolute excess of every *épistémè*" (268; emphasis in original). Adorno, however, holds that the category of the subject is indispensable to such self-transcendence. He does not succumb to the temptation to bypass "the order of apprehension" (Derrida 1981b, 4); instead, Adorno seeks to expand the limits of the intelligible to include, precisely, the perceived incommensurability of the sensible.

2. In *Of Grammatology,* Derrida "domesticates" Hegel thus: "All that Hegel thought within this horizon [of absolute knowledge], all, that is, except eschatology, may be read as a meditation on writing. Hegel is *also* the thinker of irreducible difference" (Derrida 1981b, 26; emphasis in original). Under the guise of acknowledging his debt to Hegel, Derrida effects a curious reversal by which dialectics becomes indebted to *différance* and Hegel is legitimated as "the first thinker of writing" (26).

3. Compare, for example, the opening paragraph of Derrida's essay, "From Restricted to General Economy: A Hegelianism without Reserve": " 'Often Hegel seems to me self-evident, but the self-evident is a heavy burden.' . . . Why today—even today—are the best readers of Bataille among those for whom Hegel's self-evidence is so lightly borne? So lightly borne that a murmured allusion to given fundamental concepts . . . suffice[s] to undo the constraint of Hegel. . . . And, contrary to Bataille's experience, this puts one, without seeing or knowing it, *within* the very self-evidence of Hegel one often thinks oneself unburdened of. Misconstrued, treated lightly, Hegelianism only extends its historical domination, finally unfolding its immense enveloping resources without obstacle. Hegelian self-evidence seems lighter than ever at the moment when it finally bears down with its full weight" (Derrida 1978, 251; emphasis in original). Adorno's reading of the ruses of Hegelian Reason, I shall go on to argue, shares Derrida's

sensitivity, but seeks to transform the "constraint" of its matter into the "freedom" of its method. Hyppolite's view of Hegel, in common with Adorno's, contends with the *possibilities* of the dialectic even as it critiques the "historical domination" of Hegelianism.

3 / Theodor W. Adorno

1. Lata Mani's work on sati might serve as a useful example here. Although she articulates the manner in which women's bodies functioned as the ground for debates concerning sati rather than as the locus of female subjectivity, desire, or agency, her recourse to solely imperialist texts as well as her sense of the self-contained character of nationalist discourse, which excluded women's voices, reproduces the silencing and effacement of the female victims on whose behalf she wishes to speak. In this sense, her method emphasizes the discourse at the expense of its contents—the women.

5 / Edward W. Said

1. See Bové (1986). I want to acknowledge here the similarity of his contentions regarding Said's (dis)placement of the intellectual. Bové argues that Said serves to legitimate critical practice because his critical strenuousness draws on the very tradition of critical humanism that he opposes. Adorno argues in "Culture and Administration" that one must be imbued with tradition in order to hate it properly. While Said wants critical consciousness to privilege exile, one cannot help wondering whether his resistance does not stem equally from his formidable scholarship and from the fact that he wears his learning lightly. Bové also delineates, with care and perception, the American reception of *Mimesis*. He describes how Auerbach became transformed from the man who attributed his own powerful revitalization of Western culture to the authority of tradition into the isolated titanic figure who singlehandedly synthesized the fragments of a declining Western culture. Bové discerns the residue of this predictable American emphasis on individual effort in Said's work.

2. See Porter (1983, 179–94) for a thoughtful critique. Said's dismissive reference to Porter's essay in "Orientalism Reconsidered" (Said 1985c, 89–107) seems a defensive, uncharacteristically graceless response. Porter is right, I think, to point to the inadvertent homogenizing of the West that takes place in Said's argument and to take Said to task for failing to discern the contradictions and distancings from stereotypical realism in the so-called imperialist texts. This problem crops up in the discussion that follows "Intellectuals in the Post-Colonial World" when Said brands Conrad an unregenerate imperialist and refuses to grant credence to the knowledge *Heart of Darkness* might offer at least of the imperialist subject. This reading is complicated in *Culture and Imperialism,* but Said continues to attack Conrad for being unable to escape the confines of the imperialist narrative, for confirming the power of the very system he understands so well. I am not sure, however, whether Porter's essay escapes the process by which (in Spivak's terms) the recuperation of the moments of aporia in manifestly ideological texts serves to legitimate the subject of the West or the West as Subject. Besides, Porter's privileging of aesthetic texts as the sites of "truth" that contest ideology once again begs the question that Said raises with such urgency: that culture's separation from what Adorno calls the guilt of society is precisely what needs to be addressed.

Bibliography

Abel, Elizabeth, ed. 1982. *Writing and Sexual Difference*. Chicago: University of Chicago Press.
Adorno, Theodor W. [1931] 1977. "The Actuality of Philosophy." Trans. Benjamin Snow. *Telos* 31 (Spring): 120–33.
———. 1939. "On Kierkegaard's Doctrine of Love." *Studies in Philosophy and Social Science* 8, no. 3: 413–29.
———. 1940. "Husserl and the Problem of Idealism." *The Journal of Philosophy* 37, no. 1: 5–18.
———. 1941. "Spengler Today." Trans. Charles Francis Atkinson. *Studies in Philosophy and Social Science* 9, no. 2: 305–25.
———. 1941. "Veblen's Attack on Culture: Remarks Occasioned by *The Theory of the Leisure Class*." *Studies in Philosophy and Social Science* 9, no. 3: 389–413.
———. 1966. "Was Spengler Right?" *Encounter* 26 (January): 25–29.
———. 1967. *Prisms: Cultural Criticism and Society*. Trans. Samuel and Shierry Weber. London: Neville Spearman.
———. 1968. "Is Marx Obsolete?" Trans. Nicolas Slater. *Diogenes* 64 (Winter): 1–16.
———. 1969. "Interview: Of Barricades and Ivory Towers." With *Der Spiegel*. *Encounter* 33 (September): 63.
———. 1973a. "Correspondence with Benjamin." Trans. Harry Zohn. *New Left Review* 81 (September–October): 55–80.
———. 1973b. *The Jargon of Authenticity*. Trans. Knut Tarnowski and Frederic Will. Evanston, Ill.: Northwestern University Press.
———. 1973c. *Negative Dialectics*. Trans. E. B. Ashton. New York: Seabury Press.
———. 1974a. "Lyric Poetry and Society." Trans. Bruce Mayo. *Telos* 20 (Summer): 56–71.
———. 1974b. *Minima Moralia: Reflections from Damaged Life*. Trans. E. F. N. Jephcott. London: New Left Books.
———. 1974c. "Wagner, Nietzsche, Hitler." *Kenyon Review* 9, no. 1: 155–62.
———. 1975. "Culture Industry Reconsidered." Trans. Anson G. Rabinbach. *New German Critique* 6 (Fall): 12–19.
———. 1978a. "Culture and Administration." Trans. Wes Blomster. *Telos* 37 (Fall): 93–112.
———. 1978b. "Metacritique of Epistemology." Trans. Michael B. Allen. *Telos* 38 (Winter 1978–79): 77–103.
———. 1978c. "Resignation." Trans. Wes Blomster. *Telos* 35 (Spring): 165–70.
———. 1980. "Bloch's Traces: The Philosophy of Kitsch." Trans. Rodney Livingstone. *New Left Review* 121 (May): 49–62.
———. 1982a. *Against Epistemology—A Metacritique: Studies in Husserl and the Phenomenological Antinomies*. Trans. Willis Domingo. Oxford: Basil Blackwell.
———. 1982b. "Commitment." In *The Essential Frankfurt School Reader*, ed. Andrew Arato and Eike Gebhardt. New York: Continuum. 300–318.
———. 1982c. "Freudian Theory and the Pattern of Fascist Propaganda." In *The Essential Frankfurt School Reader*, ed. Andrew Arato and Eike Gebhardt. New York: Continuum. 118–37.

————. 1982d. "Subject and Object." In *The Essential Frankfurt School Reader*, ed. Andrew Arato and Eike Gebhardt. New York: Continuum. 497–512.

————. 1983a. "Interview: Education for Autonomy." With Helmut Becker. Trans. David J. Parent. *Telos* 56 (Summer): 103–10.

————. 1983b. "Interview: On the Historical Adequacy of Consciousness." With Peter Von Haselberg. Trans. Wes Blomster. *Telos* 56 (Summer): 97–103.

————. 1984a. *Aesthetic Theory*. Trans. C. Lenhardt. London: Routledge and Kegan Paul.

————. 1984b. "The Essay as Form." Trans. Bob Hullot-Kentor and Frederic Will. *New German Critique* 32 (Spring–Summer): 151–71.

————. 1984c. "The Idea of Natural History." Trans. Bob Hullot-Kentor. *Telos* 60: 111–24.

————. 1985. "On the Question: 'What Is German?'" Trans. Thomas Levin. *New German Critique* 36 (Fall): 121–33.

————. 1989. *Kierkegaard: Construction of the Aesthetic*. Trans. and ed. Robert Hullot-Kentor. Theory and History of Literature 61. Minneapolis: University of Minnesota Press.

————. 1991–92. *Notes to Literature*. 2 vols. Trans. Shierry Weber Nicholsen. Ed. Rolf Tiedemann. New York: Columbia University Press.

————. 1993a. *Hegel: Three Studies*. Trans. Shierry Weber Nicholsen. Cambridge and London: The MIT Press.

————. and Max Horkheimer. 1993b. *Dialectic of Enlightenment*. Trans. John Cumming. New York: Herder and Herder. Reprinted, New York: Continuum.

Adorno, Theodor W., Else Frenkel-Brunswick, Daniel J. Levinson, and R. Nevitt Sanford. 1950. *The Authoritarian Personality*. New York: W. W. Norton.

Ahmad, Aijaz. 1992. *In Theory: Classes, Nations, Literatures*. New York: Verso.

Alford, C. Fred. 1988. *Narcissism: Socrates, the Frankfurt School, and Psychoanalytic Theory*. New Haven and London: Yale University Press.

Althusser, Louis. 1969. *For Marx*. Trans. Ben Brewster. New York: Pantheon Books.

————. 1971. *Lenin and Philosophy and Other Essays*. Trans. Ben Brewster. New York and London: Monthly Review Press.

————. 1976. *Essays in Self-Criticism*. Trans. Grahame Lock. London: NLB; Atlantic Highlands: Humanities Press.

————. and Etienne Balibar. 1970. *Reading Capital*. Trans. Ben Brewster. New York: Pantheon Books.

Anderson, Benedict. 1983. *Imagined Communities: Reflections on the Origin and Spread of Nationalism*. London: Verso.

Anderson, Perry. 1988. *In the Tracks of Historical Materialism*. London and New York: Verso.

Arac, Jonathan, Wlad Godzich, and Wallace Martin, eds. 1983. *The Yale Critics: Deconstruction in America*. Theory and History of Literature 6. Minneapolis: University of Minnesota Press.

Arac, Jonathan, and Barbara Johnson, eds. 1991. *Consequences of Theory: Selected Papers from the English Institute, 1987–88*. No. 14. Baltimore and London: The Johns Hopkins University Press.

Arato, Andrew, and Eike Gebhardt, eds. 1990. *The Essential Frankfurt School Reader*. New York: Continuum.

Ashcroft, Bill, Gareth Griffiths, and Helen Tiffin. 1989. *The Empire Writes Back: Theory and Practice in Post-Colonial Literatures*. London and New York: Routledge.

Attridge, Derek, Geoff Bennington, and Robert Young, eds. 1991. *Post-Structuralism and the Question of History*. Cambridge: Cambridge University Press.

Auerbach, Erich. 1968. *Mimesis: The Representation of Reality in Western Literature*. Trans. Willard R. Trask. Princeton: Princeton University Press.

Bakhtin, Mikhail. 1981. *The Dialogic Imagination: Four Essays.* Trans. Caryl Emerson and Michael Holquist. Ed. Michael Holquist. Austin: University of Texas Press.

Bann, Stephen. 1984. *The Clothing of Clio: A Study of the Representation of History in Nineteenth-Century France.* Cambridge: Cambridge University Press.

Barker, Francis. 1984. *The Tremulous Private Body: Essays on Subjection.* London and New York: Methuen.

———, et al., eds. 1983. *The Politics of Theory: Proceedings of the Essex Conference on the Sociology of Literature, July 1982.* Colchester, England: University of Essex Press.

———, et al., eds. 1985. *Europe and Its Others.* 2 vols. Colchester, England: University of Essex Press.

Barthes, Roland. 1967. *Writing Degree Zero.* Trans. A. Lavers and C. Smith. New York: Hill and Wang.

———. 1972. *Critical Essays.* Trans. R. Howard. Evanston, Ill.: Northwestern University Press.

———. 1975. *The Pleasure of the Text.* Trans. R. Miller. New York: Hill and Wang.

———. 1981. *Camera Lucida: Reflections on Photography.* Trans. Richard Howard. New York: Hill and Wang.

———. 1987. *Criticism and Truth.* Trans. and ed. Katrine Pilcher Kenneman. Minneapolis: University of Minnesota Press.

Baudrillard, Jean. 1981. *For a Critique of the Political Economy of the Sign.* Trans. Charles Levin. St. Louis: Telos Press.

Belsey, Catherine. 1980. *Critical Practice.* London and New York: Methuen.

———. 1985. *The Subject of Tragedy: Identity and Difference in Renaissance Drama.* London and New York: Methuen.

Benhabib, Seyla. 1984. "Epistemologies of Postmodernism: A Rejoinder to Jean-François Lyotard." *New German Critique* 33 (Fall): 103–26.

———. 1986. *Critique, Norm, Utopia: A Study of the Foundations of Critical Theory.* New York: Columbia University Press.

———, and Drucilla Cornell, eds. 1988. *Feminism as Critique: On the Politics of Gender.* Feminist Perspectives, ed. Michelle Stanworth. Minneapolis: University of Minnesota Press.

Benhabib, Seyla, Wolfgang Bon, and John McCole, eds. 1993. *On Max Horkheimer: New Perspectives.* Cambridge, Mass., and London: The MIT Press.

Benjamin, Andrew, ed. 1989a. *The Lyotard Reader.* Oxford and Cambridge, Mass.: Basil Blackwell.

———, ed. 1989b. *The Problems of Modernity: Adorno and Benjamin.* Warwick Studies in Philosophy and Literature, ed. Andrew Benjamin. London and New York: Routledge.

Benjamin, Walter. 1968. *Illuminations.* Trans. Harry Zohn. Ed. Hannah Arendt. New York: Schocken Books.

Bennington, Geoff, and Robert Young. 1991. "Introduction: Posing the Question." *Poststructuralism and the Question of History.* Ed. Derek Attridge, Geoff Bennington, and Robert Young. Cambridge: Cambridge University Press. 1–15.

Benston, Kimberly W. 1990. "I yam what I yam: The Topos of Un(naming) in Afro-American Literature." *Black Literature and Literary Theory.* Ed. Henry Louis Gates. New York and London: Routledge. 151–72.

Berger, John. 1972. *Ways of Seeing.* Harmondsworth, Middlesex, England: Penguin Books.

Bernheimer, Charles, and Claire Kahane, eds. 1985. *In Dora's Case: Freud—Hysteria—Feminism.* Gender and Culture, ed. Carolyn G. Heilbrun and Nancy K. Miller. New York: Columbia University Press.

Bernstein, Jay. 1991. "Art against Enlightenment: Adorno's Critique of Habermas." In *The Problems of Modernity: Adorno and Benjamin,* ed. Andrew Benjamin. London and New York. Routledge. 49–67.

Bhabha, Homi K. 1983a. "Difference, Discrimination, and the Discourse of Colonialism." In *The Politics of Theory: Proceedings of the Essex Conference on the Sociology of Literature, July 1982,* ed. Francis Barker et al. Colchester, England: University of Essex Press. 194–212.

———. 1983b. "The Other Question—The Stereotype and Colonial Discourse." *Screen* 24, no. 6: 18–36.

———. 1984a. "Of Mimicry and Man: The Ambivalence of Colonial Discourse." *October* 28: 125–33.

———. 1984b. "Representation and the Colonial Text: A Critical Exploration of Some Forms of Mimeticism." In *The Theory of Reading,* ed. Frank Gloversmith. Brighton: Harvester Press. 93–122.

———. 1985a. "Signs Taken for Wonders: Questions of Ambivalence and Authority under a Tree outside Delhi, May 1817." *Critical Inquiry* 12, no. 1 (Fall): 144–65.

———. 1985b. "Sly Civility." *October* 34 (Fall): 71–80.

———. 1986. "The Other Question: Difference, Discrimination, and the Discourse of Colonialism." In *Literature, Politics, and Theory,* ed. Francis Barker et al. London: Methuen. 148–72.

———. 1990. "DissemiNation: Time, Narrative, and the Margins of the Modern Nation." In *Nation and Narration,* ed. Homi K. Bhabha. London and New York: Routledge. 291–323.

———. 1994. *The Location of Culture.* London and New York: Routledge.

Blanchot, Maurice. 1987. "Michel Foucault as I Imagine Him." In *Foucault/Blanchot,* trans. Jeffrey Mehlman. New York: Zone Books. 63–109.

Bloom, Harold. 1973. *The Anxiety of Influence: A Theory of Poetry.* New York: Oxford University Press.

———, ed. 1979. *Deconstruction and Criticism.* New York: Seabury Press.

Bottomore, Tom. 1984. *The Frankfurt School.* Chichester, England: E. Horwood.

Bourdieu, Pierre. 1983. "The Philosophical Institution." *Philosophy in France Today.* Ed. Alan Montefiore. Cambridge: Cambridge University Press. 1–8.

Bové, Paul. 1986. *Intellectuals in America: A Genealogy of Critical Humanism.* New York: Columbia University Press.

Bradley, J. 1975. Review of *Negative Dialectics,* by T. W. Adorno. *Philosophical Quarterly* 25, no. 101 (October): 368–70.

Brenkman, John. 1987. *Culture and Domination.* Ithaca, N.Y., and London: Cornell University Press.

Brosio, Richard. 1980. *The Frankfurt School: An Analysis of the Contradictions and Crisis of Liberal Capitalist Societies.* Ball State Monograph 29. Muncie, Ind.: Ball State University Press.

Bruce, S. 1984. Review of *Against Epistemology,* by T. W. Adorno. *British Journal of Sociology* 35 (June): 297–98.

Buck-Morss, Susan. 1977. *The Origin of Negative Dialectics: Theodor W. Adorno, Walter Benjamin, and the Frankfurt Institute.* New York: The Free Press.

Butler, Judith. 1990. *Gender Trouble: Feminism and the Subversion of Identity.* New York and London: Routledge.

Caton, Hiram. 1974. Review of *Dialectic of Enlightenment,* by T. W. Adorno and Max Horkheimer. *American Political Science Review* 68 (September): 1308.

Chatterjee, Partha. 1993a. *Nationalist Thought and the Colonial World: A Derivative Discourse.* Minneapolis: University of Minnesota Press.

———. 1993b. *The Nation and Its Fragments: Colonial and Postcolonial Histories.* Princeton: Princeton University Press.

Cixous, Hélène. 1976. "The Laugh of the Medusa." Trans. K. Cohen and P. Cohen. *Signs* 1, no. 4 (Summer): 875–95.

———, and Verena Andermatt Conley. 1984 "voice i." Trans. Betsy Wing. *Boundary 2* 12, no. 2 (Winter): 9–39, 41–48.

———, and Catherine Clément. 1988. *The Newly Born Woman.* Trans. B. Wing. Minneapolis: University of Minnesota Press.

Clifford, James. 1983. "On Ethnographic Authority." *Representations* 1, no. 2 (Spring): 118–47.

———. 1988. *The Predicament of Culture: Twentieth Century Ethnography, Literature, and Art.* Cambridge, Mass. and London: Harvard University Press.

———, and George E. Marcus, eds. 1986. *Writing Culture: The Poetics and Politics of Ethnography.* Berkeley and Los Angeles: University of California Press.

Conley, Verena Andermatt. 1984. "Approaches." *Boundary 2* 12, no. 2 (Winter): 1–7.

———, and Jacques Derrida. 1984. "voice ii." *Boundary 2* 12, no. 2 (Winter): 68–93.

———, and William V. Spanos, eds. 1984. "On Feminine Writing: A Boundary 2 Symposium." *Boundary 2* 12, no. 2 (Winter).

Connerton, Paul. 1980. *The Tragedy of Enlightenment: An Essay on the Frankfurt School.* Cambridge: Cambridge University Press.

Conrad, Joseph. [1902] 1983. *Heart of Darkness.* Harmondsworth, Middlesex, England: Penguin Books.

Coward, Rosalind, and John Ellis. 1977. *Language and Materialism: Developments in Semiology and the Theory of the Subject.* London: Routledge and Kegan Paul.

Dallmayr, Fred. 1981. *Beyond Dogma and Despair: Toward a Critical Phenomenology of Politics.* Notre Dame, Ind.: University of Notre Dame Press.

Daly, Mary. 1978. *Gyn/Ecology: The Metaethics of Radical Feminism.* Boston: Beacon Press.

D'Amico, Robert. 1978. Review of *Discipline and Punish, Language, Counter-Memory, Practice,* and *The History of Sexuality,* by Michel Foucault, and *Oublier Foucault,* by Jean Baudrillard. *Telos* 36 (Summer): 169–83.

Davies, Miranda, ed. 1983. *Third World—Second Sex.* London: Zed.

Davis, Angela. 1983. *Women, Race, and Class.* New York: Vintage Books.

Davis, Robert Con, and Ronald Schleifer, eds. 1985. *Rhetoric and Form: Deconstruction at Yale.* Norman: University of Oklahoma Press.

De Beauvoir, Simone. [1952] 1971. *The Second Sex.* New York: Bantam Books.

Decker, Jeffrey Louis. 1990–91. "Terrorism (Un)veiled: Frantz Fanon and the Women of Algiers." *Cultural Critique* 17 (Winter): 177–95.

de Lauretis, Teresa. 1984. *Alice Doesn't: Feminism, Semiotics, Cinema.* Bloomington: Indiana University Press.

———, ed. 1986. *Feminist Studies / Critical Studies.* Bloomington: Indiana University Press.

———. 1987. *Technologies of Gender: Essays on Theory, Film, and Fiction.* Theories of Representation and Difference, ed. Teresa de Lauretis. Bloomington: Indiana University Press.

———, and Stephen Heath, eds. 1980. *The Cinematic Apparatus.* New York: St. Martin's Press.

Deleuze, Gilles, and Félix Guattari. 1977. *Anti-Oedipus: Capitalism and Schizophrenia.* Trans. Robert Hurley et al. New York: Viking Press.

de Man, Paul. 1979. *Allegories of Reading: Figural Language in Rousseau, Nietzsche, Rilke, and Proust.* New Haven and London: Yale University Press.

———. 1983. *Blindness and Insight: Essays in the Rhetoric of Contemporary Criticism.* 2d ed. Theory and History of Literature 7. Minneapolis: University of Minnesota Press.

———. 1986. *The Resistance to Theory.* Theory and History of Literature 33. Minneapolis: University of Minnesota Press.

Derrida, Jacques. 1972a. "Choreographics." *Diacritics* 12 (Summer): 66–76.

———. 1972b. *Marges de la philosophie*. Paris: Éditions de Minuit.

———. 1973. *Speech and Phenomena and Other Essays on Husserl's Theory of Signs*. Trans. David B. Allison. Evanston, Ill.: Northwestern University Press.

———. 1976. *Of Grammatology*. Trans. Gayatri Chakravorty Spivak. Baltimore and London: The Johns Hopkins University Press.

———. 1978. *Writing and Difference*. Trans. Alan Bass. Chicago: University of Chicago Press.

———. 1979. *Spurs: Nietzsche's Styles / Éperons: Les styles de Nietzsche*. Trans. Barbara Harlow. Chicago: University of Chicago Press.

———. 1981a. *Dissemination*. Trans. Barbara Johnson. Chicago: University of Chicago Press.

———. 1981b. *Margins of Philosophy*. Trans. Alan Bass. Chicago: University of Chicago Press.

———, and Verena Andermatt Conley. 1984. "voice ii." *Boundary 2* 12, no. 2 (Winter): 68–93.

———. 1985a. *The Ear of the Other: Otobiography, Transference, Translation*. Trans. Avital Ronell and Peggy Kamuf. Ed. Christie McDonald. New York: Schocken Books.

———. 1985b. "Racism's Last Word." *Critical Inquiry* 12, no. 1 (Fall): 191–99.

Dews, Peter. 1987. *Logics of Disintegration: Post-Structuralist Thought and the Claims of Critical Theory*. London: Verso.

———. 1991. "Adorno, Post-structuralism and the Critique of Identity." In *The Problems of Modernity: Adorno and Benjamin,* ed. Andrew Benjamin. London and New York: Routledge. 1–23.

Doane, Mary Ann, Patricia Mellencamp, and Linda Williams, eds. 1984. *Re-Vision: Essays in Feminist Film Criticism*. The American Film Institute Monograph Series, no. 3. Frederick, Md.: University Publications of America.

Dollimore, Jonathan. 1986. "The Dominant and the Deviant: A Violent Dialectic." *Critical Quarterly* 28, nos. 1–2 (Spring/Summer): 179–91.

Donaldson, Laura E. 1988. "The Miranda Complex: Colonialism and the Question of Feminist Reading." *Diacritics* 18, no. 3: 65–77.

Dubiel, Helmut. 1985. *Theory and Politics: Studies in the Development of Critical Theory*. Trans. Benjamin Gregg. Cambridge: MIT Press.

Dupre, L. 1974. Review of *Negative Dialectics*, by T. W. Adorno. *Journal of the History of Ideas* 35 (October): 703–14.

Eagleton, Terry. 1976a. *Criticism and Ideology: A Study in Marxist Literary Theory*. London: New Left Books, and Atlantic Highlands, N.J.: Humanities Press.

———. 1976b. *Marxism and Literary Criticism*. Berkeley and Los Angeles: University of California Press.

———. 1981. *Walter Benjamin; or, Towards a Revolutionary Criticism*. London: New Left Books.

———. 1985a. *Literary Theory: An Introduction*. Minneapolis: University of Minnesota Press.

———. 1985b. "Marxism, Structuralism, and Post-Structuralism." *Diacritics* 15 (Winter): 3–12.

———. 1990a. *The Ideology of the Aesthetic*. Oxford and Cambridge, Mass.: Basil Blackwell.

———. 1990b. *The Significance of Theory*. Oxford: Basil Blackwell.

———, Fredric Jameson, and Edward Said. 1990. *Nationalism, Colonialism, and Literature*. Minneapolis: University of Minnesota Press.

Edie, James. 1984. Review of *Against Epistemology*, by T. W. Adorno. *Husserl Studies* 1, no. 3: 315–20.

Eisenstein, Hestor, and Alice Jardine, eds. 1980. *The Future of Difference*. Boston: G. K. Hall.

Elliott, Gregory. 1988. *Althusser: The Detour of Theory*. London: Verso.

Etienne, Mona, and Eleanor Leacock, eds. 1980. *Woman and Colonization: Anthropological Perspectives*. New York: Praeger.

Fabian, Johannes. 1983. *Time and the Other: How Anthropology Makes Its Object*. New York: Columbia University Press.

Fanon, Frantz. 1965. *Studies in a Dying Colonialism*. Trans. Haakon Chevalier. New York: Monthly Review Press.

———. 1967a. *Black Skin, White Masks*. Trans. Charles Lam Markmann. New York: Grove Press.

———. 1967b. *Toward the African Revolution: Political Essays*. Trans. Haakon Chevalier. New York and London: Monthly Review Press.

———. 1968. *The Wretched of the Earth*. Trans. Constance Farrington. New York: Grove Press.

Feenberg, Andrew. 1981. *Lukács, Marx, and the Sources of Critical Theory*. Totowa, N. J.: Rowman and Littlefield.

Fekete, John. 1977. *The Critical Twilight: Explorations in the Ideology of Anglo-American Literary Theory from Eliot to McLuhan*. London: Routledge and Kegan Paul.

———. 1978. "Benjamin's Ambivalence." *Telos* 35 (Spring): 193–99.

Felman, Shoshana. 1983. *The Literary Speech-Act: Don Juan with J. L. Austin, or Seduction in Two Languages*. Trans. Catherine Porter. Ithaca, N.Y., and London: Cornell University Press.

———, ed. 1982. *Literature and Psychoanalysis: The Question of Reading, Otherwise*. Baltimore and London: The Johns Hopkins University Press.

Findlay, L. M. 1988. "Otherwise Engaged: Postmodernism and the Resistance to History." *English Studies in Canada* 14, no. 4 (December): 383–99.

Fitzgerald, Urzel. 1988. Review of *In Other Worlds*, by Gayatri Spivak. *Ariel* 19, no. 4 (October): 101–7.

Foley, Barbara. 1985. "The Politics of Deconstruction." In *Rhetoric and Form: Deconstruction at Yale*, ed. Robert Con Davis and Ronald Schleifer. Norman: University of Oklahoma Press. 113–35.

Forster, E. M. 1924. *A Passage to India*. London: Edward Arnold.

———. 1971. *E. M. Forster: Albergo Empedocle and Other Writings*. Ed. George H. Thomson. New York: Liveright.

Foster, Hal, ed. 1983. *The Anti-Aesthetic: Essays on Postmodern Culture*. Seattle: Bay Press.

Foucault, Michel. 1972. *The Archaeology of Knowledge and the Discourse on Language*. Trans. A. M. Sheridan Smith. New York: Pantheon Books.

———. 1973a. *Madness and Civilization: A History of Insanity in the Age of Reason*. Trans. Richard Howard. New York: Vintage Books.

———. 1973b. *The Order of Things: An Archaeology of the Human Sciences*. Ed. R. D. Laing. New York: Vintage Books.

———. 1977a. *Language, Counter-Memory, Practice: Selected Essays and Interviews*. Trans. Donald F. Bouchard and Sherry Simon. Ithaca, N.Y.: Cornell University Press.

———. 1977b. "Nietzsche, Genealogy, History." *The Foucault Reader*. Ed. Paul Rabinow. New York: Pantheon Books, 1984. 76–101.

———. 1979. "What Is an Author?" *The Foucault Reader*. Ed. Paul Rabinow. New York: Pantheon Books, 1984. 101–21.

———. 1980. *Power/Knowledge: Selected Interviews and Other Writings, 1972–1977*. Trans. Colin Gordon et al. Ed. Colin Gordon. Brighton, Sussex, England: The Harvester Press.

———. 1982. "The Subject and Power." Trans. (in part) Leslie Sawyer. *Critical Inquiry* 8, no. 4 (Summer): 777–97.

———. 1984a. *The Foucault Reader*. Ed. Paul Rabinow. Trans. Catherine Porter. New York: Pantheon Books.

———. 1984b. "What Is Enlightenment?" *The Foucault Reader*. Ed. Paul Rabinow. New York: Pantheon Books, 1984. 32–51.

———. 1986. *The History of Sexuality*. Vol. 2, *The Use of Pleasure*. Trans. Robert Hurley. New York: Vintage Books.

———. 1987. "Maurice Blanchot: The Thought from Outside." In *Foucault/Blanchot*. Trans. Brian Massumi. New York: Zone Books. 9–58.

———. [1980] 1988. *The History of Sexuality*. Vol. 1, *An Introduction*. Trans. Robert Hurley. New York: Vintage Books.

———. 1991. *Remarks on Marx: Conversations with Duccio Trombadori*. Trans. R. James Goldstein and James Cascaito. New York: Columbia University/Semiotext(e).

Fraser, Nancy. 1984. "The French Derrideans: Politicizing Deconstruction or Deconstructing the Political?" *New German Critique* 33 (Fall): 127–55.

Freud, Sigmund. 1953–74. *The Standard Edition of the Complete Psychological Works of Sigmund Freud*. Trans. James Strachey et al. Ed. James Strachey. 24 vols. London: The Hogarth Press.

Friedman, George. 1981. *The Political Philosophy of the Frankfurt School*. Ithaca, N.Y., and London: Cornell University Press.

Frow, John. 1986. *Marxism and Literary History*. Oxford: Basil Blackwell.

Gallagher, Catherine. 1985. "Politics, the Profession, and the Critic." *Diacritics* 15, no. 2 (Summer): 37–43.

Gallop, Jane. 1982. *The Daughter's Seduction: Feminism and Psychoanalysis*. Ithaca, N.Y.: Cornell University Press.

———. 1985. *Reading Lacan*. Ithaca, N.Y. and London: Cornell University Press.

Gates, Henry Louis, ed. 1984. *Black Literature and Literary Theory*. New York and London: Routledge.

———, ed. 1985–86. "Race, Writing, Difference." *Critical Inquiry* 12, no. 1 (Autumn 1985): 1–20; and 13, no. 1 (Autumn 1986): 197–200, 203–10.

Gay, Peter. 1966. *The Rise of Modern Paganism*. Vol. 1 of *The Enlightenment: An Interpretation*. New York: Alfred A. Knopf.

———. 1968. *Weimar Culture: The Outsider as Insider*. London: Secker and Warburg.

———. 1970. *The Science of Freedom*. Vol. 2 of *The Enlightenment: An Interpretation*. London: Weidenfeld and Nicholson.

Geuss, Raymond. 1975. Review of *Negative Dialectics*, by T. W. Adorno. *The Journal of Philosophy* 72, no. 2 (27 March): 167–75.

Gilbert, Sandra, and Susan Gubar. 1979. *The Madwoman in the Attic: The Woman Writer and the Nineteenth-Century Literary Imagination*. New Haven and London: Yale University Press.

Godzich, Wlad. 1983. "Introduction: Caution! Reader at Work!" In Paul de Man, *Blindness and Insight: Essays in the Rhetoric of Contemporary Criticism*. 2d ed. Minneapolis: University of Minnesota Press. xv–xxx.

Graff, Gerald. 1979. *Literature against Itself*. Chicago: University of Chicago Press.

———. 1989. *Professing Literature: An Institutional History*. Chicago: University of Chicago Press.

Greene, Gayle, and Coppelia Kahn, eds. 1985. *Making a Difference: Feminist Literary Criticism*. London and New York: Methuen.

Griffin, Robert J., Daniel Boyarin, Jonathan Boyarin, and Edward Said. 1989. "An Exchange on Edward Said and Difference." *Critical Inquiry* 15 (Spring): 611–47.

Guha, Ranajit, ed. 1982. *Writings on South Asian History and Society*. New York and Delhi: Oxford University Press.

———. 1985. "Nationalism Reduced to 'Official Nationalism.'" *ASAA Review* 9, no. 1 (July): 103–8.

Habermas, Jürgen. 1982. "The Entwinement of Myth and Enlightenment." *New German Critique* 26 (Spring/Summer): 13–30.

———. 1983. "Theodor Adorno: The Primal History of Subjectivity—Self-Affirmation Gone Wild." In *Philosophical-Political Profiles,* trans. Frederick G. Lawrence. London and Cambridge, Mass.: MIT Press. 99–109.

———. 1984. "The French Path to Postmodernity: Bataille between Eroticism and General Economics." Trans. Frederick Lawrence. *New German Critique* 33 (Fall): 79–103.

———. 1987. *The Philosophical Discourse of Modernity: Twelve Lectures.* Trans. Frederick G. Lawrence. Cambridge: MIT Press.

Hartman, Geoffrey, ed. 1978. *Psychoanalysis and the Question of the Text.* Selected Papers from the English Institute, 1976–77. Baltimore and London: The Johns Hopkins University Press.

Harvey, Irene. 1986. *Derrida and the Economy of Différance.* Studies in Phenomenology and Existential Philosophy, ed. James M. Edie. Bloomington: Indiana University Press.

Held, David. 1980. *Introduction to Critical Theory: Horkheimer to Habermas.* Berkeley and Los Angeles: University of California Press.

Henriques, Julian, Wendy Holloway, Cathy Urwin, Couze Venn, and Valerie Walkerdine. 1984. *Changing the Subject: Psychology, Social Regulation and Subjectivity.* London and New York: Methuen.

Hobson, Marian. 1991. "History Traces." *Post-structuralism and the Question of History.* Ed. Derek Attridge, Geoff Bennington, and Robert Young. Cambridge: Cambridge University Press. 101–16.

Holdheim, Wolfgang. 1984. *The Hermeneutic Mode: Essays on Time in Literature and Literary Theory.* Ithaca, N.Y., and London: Cornell University Press.

Holub, R. 1983. Review of *Prisms,* by T. W. Adorno. *German Quarterly* 56 (March): 285.

Horkheimer, Max. 1947. *Eclipse of Reason.* New York: Oxford University Press.

———. 1972. *Critical Theory: Selected Essays.* Trans. Matthew J. O'Connell et al. New York: Continuum.

Hullot-Kentor, Bob. 1984a. "Introduction to Adorno's 'Idea of Natural History.'" *Telos* 60 (Summer): 97–110.

———. 1984b. "Title Essay." *New German Critique* 32 (Spring/Summer): 141–50.

Hutcheon, Linda. 1986–87. "The Politics of Postmodernism: Parody and History." *Cultural Critique* 5 (Winter): 179–207.

———. 1987. "Beginning to Theorize Postmodernism." *Textual Practice* 1, no. 1: 10–32.

———. 1988a. *A Poetics of Postmodernism: History, Theory, Fiction.* London and New York: Routledge.

———. 1988b. "The Postmodern Problematizing of History." *English Studies in Canada* 14, no. 4: 365–82.

———. 1989. *The Politics of Postmodernism.* New Accents, ed. Terence Hawkes. London and New York: Routledge.

Huyssen, Andreas. 1975. "Introduction to Adorno." *New German Critique* 6 (Fall): 3–12.

———. 1984. "Mapping the Postmodern." *New German Critique* 33 (Fall): 5–53.

Irigaray, Luce. 1985a. *Speculum of the Other Woman.* Trans. Gillian C. Gill. Ithaca, N.Y.: Cornell University Press.

———. 1985b. *This Sex Which Is Not One.* Trans. Catherine Porter with Carolyn Burke. Ithaca, N.Y.: Cornell University Press.

Jacobus, Mary. 1986. *Reading Woman: Essays in Feminist Criticism.* Gender and Culture, ed. Carolyn G. Heilbrun and Nancy K. Miller. New York: Columbia University Press.

Jameson, Fredric. 1971. *Marxism and Form: Twentieth-Century Dialectical Theories of Literature.* Princeton: Princeton University Press.

———. 1972. *The Prison-House of Language: A Critical Account of Structuralism and Russian Formalism*. Princeton: Princeton University Press.

———. 1981. *The Political Unconscious: Narrative as a Socially Symbolic Act*. Ithaca, N.Y.: Cornell University Press.

———. 1986. "Third-World Literature in the Era of Multinational Capitalism." *Social Text* 15 (Fall): 65–89.

———. 1988. *The Ideologies of Theory: Essays 1971–86*. 2 vols. Theory and History of Literature 48 and 49. Minneapolis: University of Minnesota Press.

———. 1990. *Late Marxism: Adorno; or, The Persistence of the Dialectic*. London and New York: Verso.

JanMohamed, Abdul R. 1983. *Manichean Aesthetics: The Politics of Literature in Colonial Africa*. Amherst: University of Massachusetts Press.

———. 1985. "The Economy of Manichean Allegory: The Function of Racial Difference in Colonialist Literature." *Critical Inquiry* 12, no. 1 (Autumn): 59–87.

———, and David Lloyd, eds. 1987. "The Nature and Context of Minority Discourse." *Cultural Critique* 6–7 (Spring/Fall).

Jardine, Alice A. 1985. *Gynesis: Configurations of Woman and Modernity*. Ithaca, N.Y., and London: Cornell University Press.

———, and Paul Smith, eds. 1987. *Men in Feminism*. New York: Methuen.

Jay, Martin. 1973. *The Dialectical Imagination: A History of the Frankfurt School and the Institute of Social Research, 1923–50*. Toronto and Boston: Little, Brown.

———. 1984a. *Adorno*. Fontana Modern Masters, ed. Frank Kermode. London: Fontana.

———. 1984b. *Marxism and Totality: The Adventures of a Concept from Lukács to Habermas*. Berkeley and Los Angeles: University of California Press.

———. 1986. *Permanent Exiles: Essays on the Intellectual Migration from Germany to America*. New York: Columbia University Press.

———. 1988. *Fin-de-Siècle Socialism and Other Essays*. New York and London: Routledge.

Jayawardena, Kumari. 1986. *Feminism and Nationalism in the Third World*. London: Zed.

Johnson, Barbara. 1980. *The Critical Difference: Essays in the Contemporary Rhetoric of Reading*. Baltimore: The Johns Hopkins University Press.

———. 1987. *A World of Difference*. Baltimore: The Johns Hopkins University Press.

Kellner, Douglas. 1974. Review of *The Jargon of Authenticity*, by T. W. Adorno. *Telos* 19 (Spring): 184–92.

———. 1975. "The Frankfurt School Revisited: A Critique of Martin Jay's *The Dialectical Imagination*." *New German Critique* 4 (Winter): 131–52.

Kermode, Frank. 1967. *The Sense of an Ending: Studies in the Theory of Fiction*. London and New York: Oxford University Press.

Kim, Sang-ki. 1975. Review of *Drei Studien zu Hegel*, by T. W. Adorno. *New German Critique* 4 (Winter): 168–78.

Koelb, C. 1982–83. Review of *Prisms*, by T. W. Adorno. *Modern Fiction Studies* 28, no. 4 (Winter 1982–83): 694.

Kofman, Sarah. 1985. *The Enigma of Woman: Woman in Freud's Writings*. Trans. Catherine Porter. Ithaca, N.Y., and London: Cornell University Press.

Kolakowski, Leszek. 1978. *The Breakdown*. Vol. 3 of *Main Currents of Marxism: Its Origin, Growth and Dissolution*. Trans. P. S. Falla. Oxford: Clarendon Press.

Kristeva, Julia. 1980. *Desire in Language: A Semiotic Approach to Literature and Art*. Trans. Thomas Gora et al. Ed. Leon S. Roudiez. New York: Columbia University Press.

Krupnick, Mark, ed. 1983. *Displacement: Derrida and After*. Bloomington: Indiana University Press.

Lacan, Jacques. 1977. *Écrits: A Selection*. Trans. Alan Sheridan. New York and London: W. W. Norton.

———. 1978. *The Four Fundamental Concepts of Psychoanalysis*. Trans. Alan Sheridan. Ed. Jacques Alain-Miller. New York: W. W. Norton.

———. 1982. *Feminine Sexuality*. Trans. Jacqueline Rose. Ed. Juliet Mitchell and Jacqueline Rose. New York: W. W. Norton.

LaCapra, Dominick. 1985. *History and Criticism*. Ithaca, N.Y.: Cornell University Press.

Laplanche, Jean. 1976. *Life and Death in Psychoanalysis*. Trans. Jeffrey Mehlman. Baltimore and London: The Johns Hopkins University Press.

Lazarus, Neil. 1986. "Modernism and Modernity: T. W. Adorno and Contemporary White South African Literature." *Cultural Critique* 5 (Winter): 131–64.

———. 1990. *Resistance in Postcolonial African Fiction*. New Haven and London: Yale University Press.

———. 1990. "Imperialism, Cultural Theory, and Radical Intellectualism Today: A Critical Assessment." *Rethinking Marxism* 3, no. 4 (Fall–Winter): 156–64.

Lentricchia, Frank. 1980. *After the New Criticism*. Chicago: University of Chicago Press.

———. 1983. *Criticism and Social Change*. Chicago: University of Chicago Press.

Levin, Thomas. 1985. "Nationalities of Language: Adorno's '*Fremdworter*': An Introduction to 'On the Question: What is German?'" *New German Critique* 12, no. 3 (Fall): 111–19.

Lévi-Strauss, Claude. 1966. *The Savage Mind*. The Nature of Human Society, ed. Julian Pitt-Rivers and Ernest Gellner. Chicago: University of Chicago Press.

———. 1967. *The Scope of Anthropology*. Trans. Sherry Ortner Paul and Robert A. Paul. London: Jonathan Cape.

———. 1969. *The Raw and the Cooked: Introduction to a Science of Mythology: I.* Trans. John and Doreen Weightman. New York and Evanston, Ill.: Harper and Row.

Lewis, Thomas E. 1985. "Reference and Dissemination: Althusser after Derrida." *Diacritics* 15 (Winter): 37–55.

Lichtheim, George. 1971. *From Marx to Hegel*. New York: Herder and Herder.

Louden, B., and D. Trickett. 1979. Review of *Minima Moralia,* by T. W. Adorno. *Ethics* 89 (July): 415.

Lukács, G. 1962. *The Historical Novel*. Trans. Hannah and Stanley Mitchell. London: Merlin.

———. 1971. *History and Class Consciousness: Studies in Marxist Dialectics*. Trans. Rodney Livingstone. London: Merlin.

Lyotard, Jean-François. 1984. *The Postmodern Condition: A Report on Knowledge*. Trans. Geoff Bennington and Brian Massumi. Minneapolis: University of Minnesota Press.

MacCormack, Carol, and Marilyn Strathern, eds. 1980. *Nature, Culture, and Gender*. New York: Cambridge University Press.

Macherey, Pierre. 1978. *A Theory of Literary Production*. Trans. Geoffrey Wall. London: Routledge and Kegan Paul.

MacIntyre, Alasdair. 1973. "The Pessimists of the Left" (Review of *Dialectic of Enlightenment,* by T. W. Adorno and Max Horkheimer). *New Statesman* 86 (19 October): 567.

Marcus, George E., and Michael M. J. Fisher, eds. 1986. *Anthropology as Cultural Critique: An Experimental Movement in the Human Sciences*. Chicago: University of Chicago Press.

Marcuse, Herbert. 1990. "A Note on Dialectic." In *The Essential Frankfurt School Reader*. Ed. Andrew Arato and Eike Gebhardt. New York: Continuum. 444–52.

Marks, Elaine. 1984. "voice iv: Feminisms Wake." *Boundary 2* 12, no. 2 (Winter): 99–110.

———, and Isabelle de Courtivron, eds. 1980. *New French Feminisms: An Anthology*. Amherst: University of Massachusetts Press.

Marx, Karl. n.d. *The Eighteenth Brumaire of Louis Bonaparte*. New York: International Publishers.

———. n.d. "The German Ideology I." In *The Marx-Engels Reader,* 2d ed., ed. Robert C. Tucker. New York and London: W. W. Norton. 146–203.

Mayo, Bruce. 1974. "Introduction to Adorno's 'Lyric Poetry and Society.'" *Telos* 20 (Summer): 52–55.

McGraw, Betty. 1984. "Splitting Subject / Splitting Seduction." *Boundary 2* 12, no. 2 (Winter): 143–53.

Mehlman, Jeffrey. 1977. *Revolution and Repetition: Marx/Hugo/Balzac.* Berkeley and Los Angeles: University of California Press.

Memmi, Albert. 1965. *The Colonizer and the Colonized.* Trans. Howard Greenfield. New York: Orion Press.

Michie, Helena. 1986. "Mother, Sister, Other: The 'Other Woman' in Feminist Theory." *Literature and Psychology* 32, no. 4: 1–10.

Miller, Nancy K., ed. 1986. *The Poetics of Gender.* Gender and Culture, eds. Carolyn G. Heilbrun and Nancy K. Miller. New York: Columbia University Press.

Millett, Kate. 1970. *Sexual Politics.* New York: Avon Books.

Mills, Patricia J. 1987. *Woman, Nature, Psyche.* New Haven and London: Yale University Press.

Mitchell, Juliet. 1974. *Psychoanalysis and Feminism: Freud, Reich, Laing, and Women.* New York: Vintage Books.

Mohanty, S. P., ed. 1985 "Marx after Derrida." *Diacritics* 15 (Winter).

Moi, Toril. 1985. *Sexual/Textual Politics: Feminist Literary Theory.* London and New York: Methuen.

———, ed. 1986. *The Kristeva Reader.* New York: Columbia University Press.

———, ed. 1987. *French Feminist Thought: A Reader.* Oxford: Basil Blackwell.

Monod, Jacques. 1970. *Le hasard et la nécessité: Essai sur la philosophie naturelle de la biologie moderne.* Paris: Editions du Seuil. Published in English as *Chance and Necessity: An Essay on the Natural Philosophy of Modern Biology,* trans. Austryn Wainhouse. New York: Knopf, 1971.

Mowitt, John. 1988. "Foreword." In Paul Smith, *Discerning the Subject.* Theory and History of Literature 55. Minneapolis: University of Minnesota Press. ix–xxiii.

Mukherjee, Arun P. 1988. *Towards an Aesthetic of Opposition: Essays on Literature Criticism and Cultural Imperialism.* Toronto: Williams Wallace.

———. 1991. "The Exclusions of Postcolonial Theory and Mulk Raj Anand's *Untouchable:* A Case Study." *Ariel* 22, no. 3 (July): 27–51.

Mulhern, Francis. 1979. *The Moment of Scrutiny.* London: New Left Books.

Murphy, John. 1977. Review of *The Jargon of Authenticity,* by T. W. Adorno. *Studies in Soviet Thought* 17 (October): 267–72.

———. 1986. Review of *Against Epistemology,* by T. W. Adorno. *Social Science Journal* 23 (January): 118.

Nägele, Rainer. 1982–83. "The Scene of the Other: Theodor W. Adorno's Negative Dialectic in the Context of Poststructuralism." *Boundary 2* 11, nos. 1–2 (Fall/Winter): 59–80.

Nandy, Ashis. 1983. *The Intimate Enemy: Loss and Recovery of Self under Colonialism.* Delhi: Oxford University Press.

Nelson, Cary, and Lawrence Grossberg, eds. 1988. *Marxism and the Interpretation of Culture.* Urbana and Chicago: University of Illinois Press.

Newman, Karen. 1990. "Directing Traffic: Subjects, Objects, and the Politics of Exchange." *Differences* 2, no. 2: 41–54.

Newton, Judith, and Deborah Rosenfeldt, eds. 1985. *Feminist Criticism and Social Change: Sex, Class and Race in Literature and Culture.* New York and London: Methuen.

Ngugi wa Thiong'O. 1972. *Homecoming: Essays on African and Caribbean Literature, Culture, and Politics.* London: Heinemann.

———. 1986. *Decolonising the Mind: The Politics of Language in African Literature.* London: James Currey.

Niranjana, Tejaswani. 1992. *Siting Translation: History, Post-structuralism, and the Colonial Context.* Berkeley: University of California Press.

Nordquist, Joan, compiler. 1988. *Theodore [sic] Adorno: A Bibliography.* Social Theory: A Bibliographic Series, no. 10. Santa Cruz, Calif.: Reference and Research Services.

O'Brien, Conor Cruise, Edward Said, and John Lukacs. 1986. "The Intellectual in the Post-Colonial World: Response and Discussion." *Salmagundi* 70–71 (Spring-Summer): 65–81.

O'Neill, John, ed. 1976. *On Critical Theory.* New York: Seabury Press.

Ortner, Sherry B. 1984. "Theory in Anthropology since the Sixties." *Comparative Studies in Society and History* 26 (January): 126–66.

Osborne, Peter. 1991. "Adorno and the Metaphysics of Modernism: The Problem of a 'Postmodern' Art." In *The Problems of Modernity: Adorno and Benjamin,* ed. Andrew Benjamin. London and New York: Routledge. 23–49.

Parker, Andrew. 1985. "Futures for Marxism: An Appreciation of Althusser." *Diacritics* 15 (Winter): 57–71.

Parry, Benita. 1987. "Problems in Current Theories of Colonial Discourse." *Oxford Literary Review* 9, nos. 1–2: 27–58.

Pearson, Geoffrey. 1974. Review of *Dialectic of Enlightenment,* by T. W. Adorno and Max Horkheimer. *British Journal of Sociology* 25: 111–13.

Porter, Dennis. 1983. "*Orientalism* and Its Problems." In *The Politics of Theory: Proceedings of the Essex Conference on the Sociology of Literature, July 1982,* ed. Francis Barker et al. Colchester, England: University of Essex Press. 179–94.

Przybylowicz, Donna. 1989–90. "Toward a Feminist Cultural Criticism: Hegemony and Modes of Social Division." *Cultural Critique* 13–14 (Fall and Winter): 259–301.

———, Nancy Hartsock, and Pamela McCallum, eds. 1989–90. "The Construction of Gender and Modes of Social Division." *Cultural Critique* 13–14 (Fall and Winter).

Public Culture: Society for Transnational Cultural Studies. 1993. Vol. 6, no. 1 (Fall).

Quinton, Anthony. 1974. "Critical Theory: On 'The Frankfurt School.'" *Encounter* (October): 43–53.

Rabinow, Paul, ed. 1984. *The Foucault Reader.* New York: Pantheon Books.

Radhakrishnan, R. 1983. "The Post-Modern Event and the End of Logocentrism." *Boundary 2* 12, no. 1 (Fall): 33–60.

———. 1987. "Ethnic Identity and Post-Structuralist Différance." *Cultural Critique* 7 (Fall): 199–220.

———. 1990. "The Changing Subject and the Politics of Theory." *Differences* 2, no. 2: 126–52.

Raulet, Gérard. 1984. "From Modernity as One-Way Street to Postmodernity as Dead End." *New German Critique* 33 (Fall): 155–78.

Ray, Larry. 1987. Review of *Prisms,* by T. W. Adorno. *International Studies in Philosophy* 19, no. 1: 60–61.

Rich, Adrienne. 1979. *On Lies, Secrets, and Silence.* New York: W. W. Norton.

Ricks, Christopher, and Leonard Michaels, eds. 1990. *The State of the Language.* London and Boston: Faber and Faber.

Ricoeur, Paul. 1976. *Interpretation Theory: Discourse and the Surplus of Meaning.* Fort Worth, Tex.: Texas Christian University Press.

———. 1981. *Hermeneutics and the Human Sciences: Essays on Language, Action, and Interpretation.* Trans. and ed. John B. Thompson. Cambridge: Cambridge University Press.

———. 1984. *Time and Narrative.* Vol. 1. Trans. Kathleen McLaughlin and David Pellauer. Chicago and London: University of Chicago Press.

Ridless, Robin. 1984. *Ideology and Art: Theories of Mass Culture from Walter Benjamin to Umberto Eco.* New York: P. Lang.

Robbins, Bruce, ed. 1990. *Intellectuals: Aesthetics, Politics, Academics.* Cultural Politics 2. Minneapolis: University of Minnesota Press.

Robinson, Sally. 1989–90. "Deconstructive Discourse and Sexual Politics: The 'Feminine' and/in Masculine Self-Representation." *Cultural Critique* 13 (Fall–Winter): 203–27.

Roderick, Rick. 1986. *Habermas and the Foundations of Critical Theory.* Basingstoke: Macmillan Education.

Rosaldo, Renato. 1989. "Imperialist Nostalgia." *Representations* 26 (Spring): 107–23.

Rose, Gillian. 1976. Review of *Negative Dialectics,* by T. W. Adorno. *American Political Science Review* 70 (June): 598–99.

———. 1978. *The Melancholy Science: An Introduction to the Thought of Theodor W. Adorno.* London: Macmillan.

———. 1986. *Sexuality in the Field of Vision.* London: Verso.

Russ, Joanna. 1983. *How to Suppress Women's Writing.* Austin: University of Texas Press.

Ryan, Michael. 1982. *Marxism and Deconstruction: A Critical Articulation.* Baltimore and London: The Johns Hopkins University Press.

———. 1989. *Working Hypotheses for a Post-Revolutionary Society.* London and Hampshire: Macmillan.

Said, Edward W. 1979. *Orientalism.* New York: Vintage Books.

———. 1983. *The World, the Text, and the Critic.* Cambridge: Harvard University Press.

———. 1984. "Permission to Narrate." *London Review of Books* 16 (29 February): 13–17.

———. 1985a. *Beginnings: Intention and Method.* New York: Columbia University Press.

———. 1985b. "An Ideology of Difference." *Critical Inquiry* 12, no. 1 (Fall): 38–58.

———. 1985c. "Orientalism Reconsidered." *Cultural Critique* 1 (Fall): 89–107; also in *Europe and Its Others,* ed. Francis Barker et al. (Colchester, England: University of Essex Press, 1985), 1:14–27.

———. 1986. "Intellectuals in the Post-Colonial World." *Salmagundi* 70–71 (Spring/Summer): 44–64.

———. 1986. *After the Last Sky.* New York: Pantheon.

———. 1988. "Identity, Negation, and Violence." *New Left Review* 171 (September–October): 46–60.

———. 1989. "Representing the Colonized: Anthropology's Interlocutors." *Critical Inquiry* 15, no. 2 (Winter): 205–25.

———. 1991. *Musical Elaborations.* New York: Columbia University Press.

———. 1992. *The Question of Palestine.* New York: Vintage Books.

———. 1993. *Culture and Imperialism.* New York: Knopf.

———, and Christopher Hitchens, eds. 1989. *Blaming the Victims: Spurious Scholarship and the Palestinian Question.* London and New York: Verso.

Salusinszky, Imre. 1987. *Criticism in Society: Interviews with Jacques Derrida, Northrop Frye, Harold Bloom, Geoffrey Hartman, Frank Kermode, Edward Said, Barbara Johnson, Frank Lentricchia, and J. Hillis Miller.* New York and London: Methuen.

Sangari, Kumkum. 1987. "The Politics of the Possible." *Cultural Critique* 7 (Fall): 157–86.

Schrag, Calvin. 1984. Review of *Against Epistemology,* by T. W. Adorno. *Quarterly Journal of Speech* 70 (February): 98–100.

Schroyer, Trent. 1973. *The Critique of Domination: The Origins and Development of Critical Theory.* New York: G. Braziller.

Sen, Amartya. 1990. "More than 100 Million Women Are Missing." *The New York Review of Books,* 20 December, 61–66.

Sharpe, Jenny. 1993. *Allegories of Empire: The Figure of Woman in the Colonial Text*. Minneapolis: University of Minnesota Press.

Shell, Marc. 1978. *The Economy of Literature*. Baltimore and London: The Johns Hopkins University Press.

Showalter, Elaine. 1977. *A Literature of Their Own: British Women Novelists from Brontë to Lessing*. Princeton: Princeton University Press.

————. 1985. *The New Feminist Criticism: Essays on Women, Literature, and Theory*. New York: Pantheon Books.

————, ed. 1989. *Speaking of Gender*. New York: Routledge.

Silverman, Kaja. 1983. *The Subject of Semiotics*. New York and Oxford: Oxford University Press.

————. 1988. *The Acoustic Mirror: The Female Voice in Psychoanalysis and Cinema*. Theories of Representation and Difference, ed. Teresa de Lauretis. Bloomington and Indianapolis: Indiana University Press.

Slater, Phil. 1977. *Origin and Significance of the Frankfurt School: A Marxist Perspective*. London: Routledge and Kegan Paul.

Smith, Paul. 1988. *Discerning the Subject*. Theory and History of Literature 55. Minneapolis: University of Minnesota Press.

Snow, Benjamin [pseudonym for Susan Buck-Morss]. 1977. "Introduction to Adorno's 'The Actuality of Philosophy.' " *Telos* 31 (Spring): 113–19.

Soyinka, Wole. 1976. *Myth, Literature, and the African World*. Cambridge: Cambridge University Press.

Spelman, Elizabeth V. 1988. *Inessential Woman: Problems of Exclusion in Feminist Thought*. Boston: Beacon Press.

Spivak, Gayatri Chakravorty. 1983. "Displacement and the Discourse of Woman." In *Displacement: Derrida and After*, ed. Mark Krupnick. Bloomington: Indiana University Press. 169–95.

————. 1985a. "The Rani of Sirmur." In *Europe and Its Others*, ed. Francis Barker et al. Colchester: University of Essex Press. 1:128–50.

————. 1985b. "Three Women's Texts and a Critique of Imperialism." *Critical Inquiry* 12, no. 1 (Fall): 243–61.

————. 1986. "Imperialism and Sexual Difference." *Oxford Literary Review* 8, nos. 1–2: 225–40.

————. 1987. *In Other Worlds: Essays in Cultural Politics*. London: Methuen.

————. 1988. "Can the Subaltern Speak?" In *Marxism and the Interpretation of Culture*. Ed. Cary Nelson and Lawrence Grossberg. Urbana and Chicago: University of Illinois Press. 271–313.

————. 1989. "Woman in Difference: Mahasweta Devi's 'Douloti the Bountiful.' " *Cultural Critique* 13–14 (Fall/Winter): 105–28.

————. 1990a. "Gayatri Spivak on the Politics of the Postcolonial Subject: An Interview." With Howard Winant. *Socialist Review* 3: 81–97.

————. 1990b. *The Post-Colonial Critic: Interviews, Strategies, Dialogues*. Ed. Sarah Harasym. New York and London: Routledge.

————. 1991. "Theory in the Margin: Coetzee's Foe Reading Defoe's Crusoe/Roxana." In *Consequences of Theory: Selected Papers from the English Institute, 1987–88* (vol. 14), ed. Jonathan Arac and Barbara Johnson. Baltimore and London: The Johns Hopkins University Press. 154–81.

————. 1992. "Gendering in Contemporary Colonization." Paper presented at a conference, "Gender and Colonialism," University College, Galway, Ireland, 23 May.

————. 1993. *Outside in the Teaching Machine*. New York and London: Routledge.

Sprinker, Michael, ed. 1992. *Edward Said: A Critical Reader.* Oxford and Cambridge: Basil Blackwell.

Stimpson, Catharine R. 1984. *Where the Meanings Are: Feminism and Cultural Spaces.* New York and London: Routledge.

Suleiman, Susan, ed. 1986. *The Female Body in Western Culture: Contemporary Perspectives.* Cambridge: Harvard University Press.

Suleri, Sara. 1992. *The Rhetoric of English India.* Chicago and London: University of Chicago Press.

Tar, Zoltan. 1977. *The Frankfurt School: The Critical Theories of Max Horkheimer and Theodor W. Adorno.* New York: Wiley.

Thompson, E. P. 1978. *The Poverty of Theory and Other Essays.* New York: Monthly Review Press.

Thompson, John B. 1984. *Studies in the Theory of Ideology.* Berkeley and Los Angeles: University of California Press.

Todd, Janet. 1988. *Feminist Literary History.* New York: Routledge.

Todorov, Tzvetan, ed. 1982. *French Literary Theory Today: A Reader.* Cambridge and New York: Cambridge University Press.

———. 1987. *Literature and Its Theorists: A Personal View of Twentieth-Century Criticism.* Trans. Catherine Porter. Ithaca, N.Y.: Cornell University Press.

Tool, M. 1980. Review of *Minima Moralia,* by T. W. Adorno. *Journal of Economic Issues* 14, no. 1 (March): 236–38.

Trinh, Minh-ha T. 1989. *Woman, Native, Other: Writing Postcoloniality and Feminism.* Bloomington and Indianapolis: Indiana University Press.

———, ed. 1986–87. "She, the Inappropriate/d Other. *Discourse* 8 (Winter).

Tucker, Robert C., ed. 1978. *The Marx-Engels Reader.* 2d ed. New York and London: W. W. Norton.

Turner, Bryan S. *Marx and the End of Orientalism.* Controversies in Sociology, no. 7, ed. Tom Bottomore and M. J. Mulkay. London: George Allen and Unwin.

Viswanathan, Gauri. 1987. "The Beginnings of English Literary Study in British India." *Oxford Literary Review* 9, nos. 1 and 2: 2–26.

———. 1989. *Masks of Conquest: Literary Study and British Rule in India.* New York: Columbia University Press.

Walcott, Derek. 1975. "What the Twilight Says." *Dream on Monkey Mountain and Other Plays.* New York: Farrar, Straus and Giroux. 3–40.

———. 1978. "The Muse of History." In *Critics on Caribbean Literature: Readings in Literary Criticism,* ed. Edward Baugh. New York: St. Martin's Press. 38–43.

———. 1979. *The Star-Apple Kingdom.* New York: Farrar, Straus and Giroux.

———. 1981. *Derek Walcott: Selected Poetry.* Ed. Wayne Brown. London: Heinemann.

Watson, G. 1987. *Dilemmas and Contradictions in Social Theory.* Lanham, Md.: University Press of America.

Weber, S. 1985. "Ambivalence, the Humanities, and the Study of Literature." *Diacritics* 15 (Summer): 11–25.

———. 1987. *Institution and Interpretation.* Theory and History of Literature 31. Minneapolis: University of Minnesota Press.

Weedon, Chris. 1987. *Feminist Practice and Poststructuralist Theory.* Oxford: Basil Blackwell.

Williams, Raymond. 1960. *Culture and Society, 1780–1950.* Garden City, N.Y.: Doubleday.

———. 1973. *The Country and the City.* London: The Hogarth Press.

———. 1976. *Keywords: A Vocabulary of Culture and Society.* London: Fontana.

———. 1977. *Marxism and Literature.* Oxford: Oxford University Press.

———. 1980. *Problems in Materialism and Culture: Selected Essays.* London: New Left Books.

Wilson, H. 1987. Review of *Against Epistemology*, by T. W. Adorno. *History of European Ideas* 8, no. 2: 245–46.

Wollen, P. 1967. Review of *Prisms*, by T. W. Adorno. *New Statesman* 74 (1 December): 770.

Young, Robert. 1990. *White Mythologies: Writing History and the West*. London and New York: Routledge.

Zinner, Jacqueline. 1978. Review of *La volonté de savoir*, by Michel Foucault. *Telos* 36 (Summer): 215–25.

Zohn, Harry. 1973. "Presentation of Adorno-Benjamin." *New Left Review* 81 (September–October): 46–53.

Zuidervaart, Lambert. 1984. Review of *Against Epistemology*, by T. W. Adorno. *Canadian Philosophical Review* 4 (April): 49–52.

Index

Asha Varadharajan is an assistant professor in postcolonial literatures and theory in the Department of English at the University of Minnesota. Her work has focused on romanticism, critical theory, and the relations between feminism and postcolonialism.